DATE			

Donald C. Medeiros is an assistant professor of psychology and the author of many articles and professional books.

Barbara J. Porter is a school counselor and teacher.

I. David Welch is a professor of psychology and the author of many articles and professional books.

Donald C. Medeiros
Barbara J. Porter
I. David Welch

Children Under
STRESS

How to Help With
the Everyday Stresses of Childhood

A SPECTRUM BOOK

Prentice-Hall, Inc., Englewood Cliffs, New Jersey 07632

Library of Congress Cataloging in Publication Data

Medeiros, Donald C.
   Children under stress.

   "A Spectrum Book."
   Bibliography: p.
   Includes index.
   1. Stress in children.   I. Porter, Barbara J.
II. Welch, I. David (Ira David), date.
III. Title.
BF723.S75M43   1983   155.4'18   82-20446
ISBN 0-13-132522-1
ISBN 0-13-132514-0 (pbk.)

$$BF$$
$$723$$
$$.S75$$
$$M43$$
$$1983$$

1   2   3   4   5   6   7   8   9   10

ISBN 0-13-132522-1

ISBN 0-13-132514-0 {PBK.}

Editorial/production supervision: Marlys Lehmann
Cover design: Hal Siegel
Manufacturing buyers: Christine Johnston and Doreen Cavallo

This book is available at a special discount when ordered in
bulk quantities. Contact Prentice-Hall, Inc., General
Publishing Division, Special Sales, Englewood Cliffs, N.J. 07632.

Prentice-Hall International, Inc., *London*
Prentice-Hall of Australia Pty. Limited, *Sydney*
Prentice-Hall Canada Inc., *Toronto*
Prentice-Hall of India Private Limited, *New Delhi*
Prentice-Hall of Japan, Inc., *Tokyo*
Prentice-Hall of Southeast Asia Pte. Ltd., *Singapore*
Whitehall Books Limited, *Wellington, New Zealand*
Editora Prentice-Hall do Brasil Ltda., *Rio de Janeiro*

SSH
R

Contents

Preface

Perhaps no other topic has received as much recent attention in psychology as stress. Numerous books, hundreds of articles, and thousands of workshops have been devoted to explaining stress, pointing out its negative effects, and offering suggestions for reducing its impact. The parallel rise in interest on the part of the medical profession attests to the prominent and dangerous role stress can play in physical illness. Research has linked stress to many illnesses and diseases, including heart problems, elevated blood pressure, ulcers, and even cancer. In the minds of many, stress is the number one killer of modern life. With all that has been said and written, it is clear that no one is free from stress; to a greater or lesser degree it is a part of everyone's daily life. It simply can't be totally avoided.

Amidst all the research, books, articles, and workshops on stress, children seem to have been forgotten. Stress has been treated as an adult problem, as if children were immune from its effects. Nothing could be further from the truth. The idea that childhood is a time of carefreeness, happiness, and pleasure is simply not accurate. Normal, healthy children, just like adults, can encounter stressful situations almost daily. Because adults don't see through the eyes of children, events such as school, athletics, or illness aren't thought to be very demanding. And yet research clearly shows these and other events can be sources of great stress.

The harmful effects of stress on children are only beginning to become apparent. The dramatic increase in child suicide, drug abuse, and violence are only a few of the signs of the stress with which children must deal. They are, admittedly, the most dramatic manifestations of stress, but we see them as the tip of the iceberg. Just as most of an iceberg lies below the water, undetected, so too can stress. If parents don't notice dramatic signs, such as drug abuse or suicide attempts, they often believe everything is fine. This can be a dangerous attitude for at least two reasons. First, the effects of stress are cumulative. "Little," seemingly minor problems can build up over time and have profound effects on physical and mental health. Second, children may lack the intellectual skills necessary to determine what is causing stress or what to do about it. They may lack the power and ability to make any changes in a stressful situation. Thus, the danger exists that they will begin early to develop less effective ways of dealing with stress, ways that carry over and develop into noneffective adult patterns. The large number of adults who have problems dealing with stress strongly suggests that effective coping strategies were not developed when they were children.

We believe that it is imperative for parents to learn about potential sources of stress that occur in the daily lives of children. Furthermore, parents must become familiar with the symptoms of stress and help their children learn how to deal effectively with stressful situations. To this end we offer the following chapters. We have tried to point out the major stresses that occur in children's lives. We offer simple, concrete suggestions to parents for reducing stress and teaching effective stress-reduction strategies to their children.

Parents are obviously not the only adults who have significant influence over the lives of children. Thus, we have included recent research findings and suggestions which should prove helpful for professionals in their dealings with children. For teachers we have suggestions which, if used, can reduce the stress children encounter at school and at the same time reduce much of the teachers' own stress. Counselors and psychotherapists will also find useful information in the various chapters. Many of our suggestions may be employed directly by counselors or used as suggestions for parents to follow at home. Physicians, nurses, and other medical professionals should find the chapter on hospitalization helpful in dealing with the stress inevitably associated with having to undergo surgery or other treatments in a hospital setting. The final chapter, Calming Techniques for Children, should prove invaluable for any professional involved in working with children.

It is our belief that parents and others who read this book will be able to help children cope with the stress they inevitably encounter in their lives. We further believe that this book will help children develop effective stress reduction strategies they can carry with them into adulthood. The result, we hope, will be adults who are able to recognize stress in their lives and in the lives of children and are able to deal with it in a healthy, productive manner.

Acknowledgments

Dorothy Lee, who hurried through snowstorms, late hours, a broken leg, and last-minute changes to type this manuscript--we gratefully acknowledge your time and effort.

We also appreciate the following persons and publishers for permission to use their works: Geraldine Carro and the *Ladies' Home Journal* for permission to quote from her article; Stacia Robbins and *Senior Scholastic* for use of statistical information; Judith Viorst and *Redbook* for permission to use quotations; Nancy Lewis and *Children Today* for the use of children's poetry; Gloria McLendon and *Death Education* for permission to use a dramatic play; Delphie Fredlund and *Journal of School Health* for permission to use her article on stages of understanding of death and dying among children; Doris Lund and *Parents* for permission to use quotations from her article; Bridget Moore and *Reader's Digest* for permission to quote from her sensitive article dealing with the death of a parent; and *Journal of Divorce* for permission to use a dramatic play. We extend our special thanks to our colleagues Debra Carver, Mark Disorbio, and Clydette Stulp for contributing their section on calming techniques for children.

To Mom and Pop—your common sense made my
growing up easy.

DMC

To Ron and Lori, who welcomed me into their family and
taught me the meaning of love.

BJP

To David and Daniel, two boys facing the stresses of
childhood right now, and who remind me daily of the
obligations and joys of being a dad.

IDW

1

Children Under
STRESS

Bobby is ten years old. He is the older of two children in a middle-class family. His background is typical. He has friends, does reasonably well in school, likes sports but isn't really good at them, and has no serious behavior problems.

Lately, however, he has been listless, sleeping late, avoiding school, fighting with his friends, hostile toward his teachers and other adults. He has been falling further and further behind in his schoolwork. When questioned about school, he says it is too hard and he can't do the work anymore.

Bobby's behavior exhibits a pattern of a child under stress. Let's take a moment to look at Bobby's life. His family has just moved to a new city where his father took another job. Bobby had to leave all his old friends behind and begin the process of making new friends in a new city and at a new school. He is having trouble making new friends because he

1

makes friends slowly. He is not very good at sports, so he is unable to use athletic skill as a magnet to draw others to him. In fact, although he likes sports, he is actually rather clumsy and is often the last one chosen on the playground for games. Since his father has taken the new job, arguments between his parents have increased, and the likelihood is that they will separate and divorce. In his new school his teacher thinks he is a slow learner and has placed him in the slow group.

One doesn't have to be a psychologist to know that Bobby has problems. It takes only a bit more information to know that Bobby is a child under stress and that his behaviors are signs of that stress. It would be difficult to point to a single situation in Bobby's life and say it was the cause of his problems. Each one by itself probably wouldn't cause any significant changes in his behavior. But together they add up to a cumulative effect that has altered Bobby's behavior in noticeable and negative ways. It is a pattern that is becoming more evident for a growing number of children in the United States and other technological nations of the world. The idyllic world of childhood is under attack by the stresses of modern life, and children are ill prepared to cope with them.

What Is Stress?

Stress is a curious phenomenon, and the concept is actually relatively simple. Stress is a reaction to an event. The reaction we are speaking of is the generalized response of the body to demands placed on it, whether they are pleasant or unpleasant (Selye 1977). The body seems to have a general way of reacting whether an event is a failed exam, a birthday party, being spanked by a parent, or bringing home an excellent report card. This definition is easy to write on a piece of paper and to the point; the problem comes when the definition is applied to a child's life. At this point it becomes more complicated. In the short definition given above, there are two components of stress mentioned: an event and the body's reaction to the event. Actually, there is a third component, the child's perception of the event, its meaning to the child. Each of these three components can be analyzed separately.

The Event

Most people probably assume that identifying stressful events would be easy. Simply look for the bad things that are happening in a child's life and the events that are causing stress will be identified. Wrong! The reason it is difficult to pinpoint stress in a child's life is because some of the events that almost everyone thinks of as positive can also be stressful.

POSITIVE Some examples of events that most people would think are positive are birthday parties, getting a good grade on a test, making an athletic team, receiving a surprise present, going on a vacation, getting a puppy, making a new friend, or being selected as citizen of the week at school. All these events would be judged to be positive by most people. Yet all of them can and have been sources of stress for children.

NEGATIVE Some examples of events that most people would think of as negative are the death of a pet, the death of a relative (especially a parent or a sibling), divorce, separation, desertion by a parent or a friend, failing a test, not making an athletic team, insults from friends, moving to a new neighborhood, not getting a special present, breaking a glass at dinner, being caught stealing, being threatened by a bigger child, losing lunch money, or not having homework done for class. All these events would likely be rated as negative by most people and have been sources of stress for many children. It is possible, however, that any of these could be viewed by an individual child as positive.

NEUTRAL Although neutral events are probably rare in children's lives, there are events that most people would think of as neutral, neither positive nor negative. Some of these might be the arrival of the evening paper, daylight savings time, morning milk delivery, a telephone ringing, or mail delivery. Again, most people would probably see these as neutral although they may well be a source of stress for children.

Perception

We have discussed events that commonly occur in the lives of children and suggested that most people would probably agree whether they were positive, negative, or neutral. And yet events which most people think of as positive or neutral can be sources of stress. Events which are commonly thought of as negative, and should lend to stress, often don't. Why is this? Human beings, including children, have the capacity to interpret the events in their lives. They have the ability to attach meanings such as good, bad, great, terrible, and so on to events that occur in their lives. The interpretation a child makes of an event makes perfect sense to the child, even though it may make little or no sense to someone observing the child. For some reason, known only to the child, a seemingly happy event might be the source of stress. Or an event thought by most to be very negative might be viewed by the child as positive. Thus, it is most important to view events from the point of view of the child who is experiencing an event, not from the point of view of a capable, more experienced and sophisticated adult.

For example, a child might try out for a Little League baseball team and not be selected. Many would view this event as negative and a possible source of stress. However, it is also quite possible that the child might view being cut as a positive event. If the child's father was interested in the child playing and pushed hard for it, and if the child was afraid of being hit with a ball, not making the team might be positive to the child, a source of relief. The pressure of pleasing Dad may be gone, as well as the fear of being hurt. The negative event becomes positive due to the child's perceptions; there is little, if any, stress. However, if the child badly wanted to play ball, the same event might be interpreted as negative by the child and be a source of considerable stress. The fact of the matter is that it is the child's interpretation of events that determines stress rather than the events themselves.

Reaction to the Perception of an Event

Hans Selye has been called the "father of stress" in light of his pioneering work in stress research. He discovered that the body makes pretty much the same response to any demands placed upon it. Thus, there are similar bodily reactions to unpleasant events such as not making an athletic team and pleasant events such as making an athletic team. The first event may lead to a condition of negative stress known as *distress*, while the second may lead to a condition known as positive stress or *eustress*. The experience of distress and eustress are quite different, but the body's reactions are quite similar. What is important is that for reasons still unknown, positive events lead to far less stress than negative events. Even though the bodily reactions are similar, the effects are very different!

How Is Stress Different for Children?

While the stressors in the lives of children are not much different from the stressors adults face in their lives, and the responses bear a great deal of similarity, the major difference lies in children's lack of ability to understand stress and their inability to do anything about it should they understand it. Children live in a world controlled by adults. Many of the stressors that confront children are created by adults. Consider, for example, the problem of the breakdown of the family. Children are helpless to do anything about the problems that confront their parents and are powerless to prevent the separation of a family. Often, the only choice they have is which parent to live with. They can't opt for both. The choice itself is stressing because it means the selection of one parent over another when both are loved and needed. It is absolutely true that children are often not able to control the events in their lives. It is further true that children are often not able to understand the events of their lives because developmentally they are not sophisticated enough to understand the complex events that are causing them problems.

Childhood is a long time of life. It is a time when children continue their growth and development in many areas of their lives. They grow physically, which everyone can see. They also grow intellectually and emotionally, which is harder to see and to grasp. Children are most like adults emotionally. They can feel the same psychological pains that adults feel. What they lack is the intellectual ability to understand why the pain is there and how to control it. They are more vulnerable because they have not developed the cognitive skills necessary to understand what is happening to them and why. That is a terrible disadvantage when what is necessary to conquer stress is to gain control over one's own life.

Let us provide some examples. To persons who believe that human beings grow and develop, as the authors do, it is a fact that children are not little adults. They are children, and children are different from adults. One of their differences is in the way they think. Children's language and thought are different from adults'. For example, from the time language develops at about age two until about age six or seven, children's language is literal. This means they believe language is real and people mean what they say. If adults say they have frogs in their throats, then children are likely to look in their mouths to see the frogs. That is cute. The literalness of children is what accounts for much of the romanticism we have about childhood. It is also a source of much confusion for children. Consider some of these problems. If someone described death to a child as going to sleep, and the child is a literal thinker, then is it any wonder such a child is afraid to go to sleep at night? If someone says death is like going on a long trip, is it any wonder the child cries when mother tells the child she is going on a trip?

Children have a good deal of trouble with concepts such as causality and time. These are not easy concepts for anyone, but are especially hard for children. If causality is difficult to grasp, then the relationships necessary to understand and to control stress may be beyond children. If time is a concept that doesn't develop until eight, nine, or ten, then trying to reduce stress by telling the child the future will be better is probably not helpful.

How is stress different for children? Behaviorally, it is not much different from the stress responses of adults. Psychologically, it is very different. It is in this area of understanding that children need the most help and patience from adults.

Stress Is Cumulative

When children were studied with just one stressor in their lives they did not appear any different from children with no presumed stress in their lives (Rutter 1979). However, when the stressors increased to two, then the risk of stress increased four times. What that means is stress is cumulative and, in fact, it was more than additive. The way some people describe this relationship is that the increases are geometric rather than arithmetic. The effects are greater than the sum of each stress considered singly. This research indicates children with more than one stressor in their lives stand a much greater chance of psychological problems than children with one or no stressors. The figures look like this: If a child has zero or one stressor in his or her life, then the chance of psychological problems is about 1 percent. If a child has two stressors, then the chance of psychological problems increases to 5 percent. If a child has four stressors in his or her life, then the chances of psychological problems increases to 20 percent. One conclusion from this research is whatever can be done to alleviate stress in children should be done, even if only one of several stress factors can be eliminated. Even partial help is very important.

What Causes Stress for Children?

The causes of stress in children are both predictable and surprising. It takes little involvement with children to know that they are troubled with problems at home, in school, in sports, and with a variety of health-related issues (injury, illness, visits to doctor and dentist). This book deals specifi-

cally with a number of these in later chapters. In this section we will
discuss the stressors for children briefly.

The Family

Perhaps the major stress for children in America today is the breakdown
of the family. The chances of a marriage being successful are steadily
diminishing. Much of the research dealing with the effects of divorce on
children suggests that the younger the child the greater the effect (Eisen
1979; Gardner 1977). Divorce is difficult for everyone involved, but it
is becoming clear that it is most difficult for children.

In those families that do not dissolve there is often tension. Some
studies have indicated that the long-term discord in a household characterized by tension and violence takes a greater toll on children than those
households in which a divorce occurs (Gardner 1977). With children
exposed to divorce and ongoing tension, the predictions for their own
future successful marriages are not good.

There are at least five different impacts on children as a result of
marital breakdown. First, children are denied security and stability.
Second, children are often pressured to take sides with one parent against
another. Third, the positive image of both parents may be diminished and
distorted. Fourth, the children may have to witness physical violence
between parents. Fifth, the children find themselves deprived of one
parent through no fault of their own.

One final problem of families that causes stress is children may be
rejected by their parents or be subjected to harsh physical punishment.
Some of the punishment of American children is so harsh it is clearly
abusive and even deadly for too many children. It may be the harsh treatment of children in the United States has persisted so late into the twentieth century because of three prevalent beliefs. First, biological parents
are solely responsible for rearing children in our society. Second, children
are still considered property by many in our culture. Third, there exists
widespread belief in the acceptability of physical punishment as a method
of discipline in America. In a recent report, 80 percent of American
families believed in corporal punishment. Of that 80 percent, 60 percent
practiced it once a week! Even high school youngsters continue to receive
whippings as a method of punishment. In the same report, fully 46 percent
of the college freshmen polled indicated that they had been hit at least
once in their senior year of high school. This constant fear of being physi-

cally attacked by a parent is a major stressor for children (Gilmartin 1979).

School

The lack of the ability to read is a major stressor, and it has been tied to a host of other school problems. It has even been discovered that many discipline problems in school have been caused because a child lacked a specific academic skill. Rather than taking the time to discover what the missing skill was, it was easier to see the problem as one of discipline. Often, that specific lack was the ability to read.

The problem of math anxiety has received widespread publicity in America. It is another area in which an apparent cultural pattern, one that discriminates against females, is causing stress for children.

School also is the place where test anxiety is learned and must be conquered by children. Finally, the entire problem of school phobia is caused by an environment in which children are exposed to a number of stressors and few efforts are made at relieving that stress.

It is entirely possible that some schools actively prevent the cognitive growth of some students. (It is a lack of attention by the school staff to the kind of environment that has been established for students.) Where the environment results in rigidity, stereotyping, and concreteness of thought, then early stresses can become habits and follow a child into adulthood. However, in a school that fosters flexibility of thought, openness, and adaptability, children gradually gain the ability to think with more complexity; then, the understanding and control necessary to guide their own personal lives will develop. Schools that are sensitive and concerned can develop more than the basic skills. They can help children to move toward the skills and knowledge necessary to gain control over their own lives.

Gender

One of the discoveries of research into child stress is that boys react more negatively to stress than girls. While the research is not in total agreement, it seems clear at this point that males are at slightly more risk than females. This is perhaps a manifestation of our culture, in which, traditionally, males have carried the assumption of greater responsibility than have females. It is hoped that the women's liberation movement will carry with it the liberation of males from unnecessary and irrational stressors.

Socioeconomic Level

Since the children of poverty live in disadvantaged circumstances, their lives are filled with a variety of events which children of the privileged do not have to face. If the reports of cumulative stress are accurate, children of lower socioeconomic status are at much greater risk than middle and upper economic class children. It is certainly one of the undesirable inheritances of the unhappy, lower socioeconomic family that children from these homes tend to marry early, have children early, marry someone from a similar socioeconomic background, and suffer rates of divorce, psychological and parenting problems that far exceed those of more privileged middle and upper economic families.

Uncertainty

This is an era of rapid social change in America. Adults are having a difficult time coping with this changing society. (The reactions to rapid social change have ranged from a deep involvement with change to denial and total withdrawal.) Adults' responses have ranged from becoming reactionaries fighting for a return to a time that they believe is better to revolutionaries committed to the total destruction of our present way of life to make way for what they perceive as a better, more acceptable governmental structure. Most of us fall between these two extremes, trying to keep up with an obviously changing social structure. Our children are heirs to overpopulation, pollution, urban blight, a struggling economic system, and unsettled racial and religious wars across the planet. The fears of adults are felt by children as they witness many of these problems every day on television. The uncertainty of the future in a nuclear age is something with which many of us have grown into adulthood. Each passing year, rather than giving hope, seems to bring us nearer to a nuclear holocaust. As more and more nations come to have a nuclear capability, the chances of a nuclear war increase. It is not so much that children can make such an analysis themselves, but that they live in a nation in which adults feel these fears and the national leaders use such fears to promote political ends. The destruction of humankind is big news. If one has children, they are exposed to the same news events as adults. One of the authors sometimes watches Saturday morning television with his children (for scholarly research purposes only). During these Saturday morning cartoons (which themselves are reasonably violent!) there are periodic newsbreaks. The topics of a few of these have been the development of the B-1 bomber, the MX missile system, the war in Iran, the assassination attempts on President Reagan and the Pope, and the deaths of Anwar Sadat and John Lennon. Children are informed of the tragedies of this world.

Sometimes the persons to whom they turn for comfort have little background for effective support. Perhaps the most often used method of calming our children is a reassurance that things will turn out all right. Yet any reference to a future event is lost on young children. Sometimes we even lie to comfort them. There isn't anything particularly wrong with telling lies to comfort children. Sometimes a lie that reassures, comforts, and protects from truly dangerous (life-threatening) information is justified and humane. Most of the time, however, research suggests honesty is the best policy (Katz 1979). Lillian Katz indicates a number of lies we tell our children, resulting in the situation that children cannot even trust their parents to tell them the truth in an uncertain world. Among the lies and half-truths Katz points out is the teasing lie. We tell our children that melon seeds will grow in their stomachs or there is a boogeyman in the basement. Adults know these are jokes, but children often believe them. A second kind of lie is the threatening lie. We try to control our children's behavior with lies that threaten abandonment (children will be given to the gypsies if they don't act right). A third kind of lie is a lie of manipulation. We try to bribe our children with myths like Santa Claus, as we tell them what will and will not gain Santa's approval. Last, there is the white lie. We tell lies to protect our children's self-esteem. We do it because we underestimate the ability of our children to deal with problems in their lives. We underestimate them in the present and, as a result, handicap them in the future. The result of all such lies is to undermine the credibility of parents. While children need the support and advice of their parents, they may have been revealed as untrustworthy. Can a more stressful discovery be made in a time of uncertainty?

A Test

Here is a twenty-item test[1] to see if you actually know what is on children's minds and to determine whether what you believe stresses kids is what they believe is stressing them. Rank the following items from 1 through 20, with 1 being most stressful and 20 being least stressful. Rate them as though you were a child.

☐ Wetting your pants in class
☐ Having an operation
☐ Giving a report in class
☐ Having a scary dream
☐ Being sent to the principal's office
☐ Going blind
☐ Moving to a new school
☐ Going to the dentist
☐ Being made fun of in class
☐ Acquiring a baby sibling
☐ Being suspected of lying
☐ Being held back a year in school
☐ Not getting 100 on a test
☐ Getting lost
☐ Receiving a bad report card
☐ Losing in a game
☐ Hearing parents quarrel
☐ Being caught stealing
☐ Losing a parent
☐ Being picked last for a team

Place your rating in the box beside each event. The answers the children gave follow. Compare them and see how close you came. If you are like most parents, you will be surprised by the results. It is possible this exercise can cause us as parents to listen more closely to our children.

Kid's responses:

1. Losing a parent
2. Going blind
3. Being held back a year in school

4. Wetting your pants in school
5. Hearing parents quarrel
6. Being caught stealing
7. Being suspected of lying
8. Receiving a bad report card
9. Being sent to the principal's office
10. Having an operation
11. Getting lost
12. Being made fun of in class
13. Moving to a new school
14. Having a scary dream
15. Not getting 100 on a test
16. Being picked last for a team
17. Losing in a game
18. Going to the dentist
19. Giving a report in class
20. Acquiring a baby sibling

How Do Children Respond to Stress?

We previously mentioned that events, if perceived by a child in certain ways, can lead to a bodily reaction known as stress. However, it isn't always easy to observe what is going on in a child's heart or blood vessels. How can parents, then, know if their children are experiencing stress? Fortunately, there are more visible behavioral signs which suggest the presence of undue amounts of stress. Parents, once they are aware of these signs, can watch for stress and take action before it gets too serious. The following are some signs that may suggest the presence of stress.[2]

General Irritability

If the child begins to exhibit either unusual aggressiveness or unusual laziness, it may suggest the presence of stress. All children are irritable from time to time, which might be associated with tiredness or hunger. What is meant here is any unusual departure from regular behavior.

Pounding of the Heart

If the child complains of a pounding heart, this may indicate increased blood pressure. Have the blood pressure checked and begin to introduce exercises to decrease blood pressure. This may be done through medication, but biofeedback is also recommended.

Accident-proneness

Look for any general increase in clumsiness and in accidents. This is an area in which the relationship has been drawn so frequently that it is a good, quick indicator of stress. A series of accidents rather than a single accident would be a good indicator.

Anxiety

Anxiety signals that something is going on in the life of a child. Anxiety is a feeling that something is going to happen, but it is not tied to any specific event, action, or situation. The child won't know exactly what he or she is afraid of, and adults' questions don't help determine the source of the fear.

Trembling; Nervous Tics

Children may develop physical symptoms that show up as twitches or nervous jumps. These are sure signs of stress.

Easily Startled

Some children have a nervous temperament. This symptom is not good if it signals a change in behavior. If a child was not particularly nervous and now is, then look for some stressor in the child's life.

Stuttering

If a child begins to stutter or have some other speech difficulty, then look for stressors in the child's life.

Grinding the Teeth

Children might show their stress while asleep by grinding their teeth. Children might complain of jaw soreness if they are grinding their teeth.

Insomnia

If a child begins to act keyed up and then has trouble falling asleep and staying asleep, take some time to see if the causes of stress can be identified.

Bed-Wetting

Bed-wetting, especially among older children, is almost always a sign of stress. Another sign of stress is the frequent need to urinate.

Indigestion

Stress is often manifested in stomach upset. A sudden change in appetite can also serve as a sign of stress.

Nightmares

Stress can cause a child to have nightmares.

Alcohol or Drug Use

The use of alcohol and drugs has increased among young children. It is possible that a child could abuse alcohol in the same way some adults do, using it to enable him or her to relax and forget problems.

Specific behavioral responses to stress are varied and many. For example, children might begin to show increased hostility to other children and adults; they may begin to destroy personal belongings or the property of others. The child may appear sad, miserable, depressed, and tearful. Comments or jokes that are ordinarily and previously acceptable might bring tears and oversensitivity. The child might withdraw from the company of others. The child might begin to act helpless and unable to do things for himself or herself.

In general, watch for any marked changes in the usual behavioral patterns of a child. Three dimensions of behavior may be especially significant: 1) If the child is unwilling to try, it can be a sign the world is becoming too threatening for the child. 2) If the child withdraws, it may be a sign that the child sees no point to involving him or herself in the activities of home, school, or friends. The world could be seen as useless.

3) Finally, if the child begins to say that things are hopeless, it suggests that the events of the child's life are defeating him or her and the child is beginning to feel helpless and powerless. These three dimensions, while broad, encompass a great deal of behavior. They will be discussed more fully in the next section of this chapter.

How Can Stress Be Relieved for Children?

It has been known for some time high levels of stress can make a person more susceptible to physical illness. The higher the level of stress, so too the greater the chance of becoming physically ill. However, Suzanne Kobasa and Salvatore Maddi, two psychologists, discovered not all persons who experience "stressful" events became ill or showed signs of stress (Pines 1980). These people seemed to have an immunity to stress. Upon studying stress-resistant people, the psychologists discovered a set of attitudes which these people possessed. These attitudes, taken together, were named the hardiness factor. They allowed the stress-resistant people to view stressful events in positive ways, which in effect made the event less negative and less stressful. A situation of positive stress was created.

What are the attitudes which seemed to make some persons immune to the effects of stress? The three attitudes are challenge, commitment, and control.

Challenge

This refers to a person being open to change. People with this attitude seem to welcome change and novelty. They try to avoid boredom and a repetitious life-style. People with this attitude can transform an ordinarily stressful event into a challenge to be met with excitement and enjoyment. People without this attitude tend to avoid new and challenging experiences. They prefer the safety of the familiar and the known. When a novel or demanding situation occurs, people such as this feel threatened and experience more stress. As an example, consider a person who has been fired. This event can be seen as a disaster, a reason to be depressed and worried about the future. A person with the attitude of challenge can see this same event quite differently. Being fired can be seen as an opportunity to move to a new, exciting place, to learn a new skill or trade, to improve one's life. The second person will likely experience much less threat and stress.

Commitment

This refers to a feeling of involvement in what a person is doing and with people. The opposite would be simply putting in time or going through the motions with no sense of involvement. People who have the attitude of commitment believe what they are doing is important and meaningful. When some drastic change occurs, such as the loss of a loved one, being deeply committed to one's career and one's family can provide a continuing source of satisfaction to help offset the stress associated with the change.

Control

This refers to how much persons believe they can direct their own lives. Persons with strong attitudes of control believe they can, by their own effort, make an impact, cause something desirable to happen for themselves. Persons with weaker attitudes of control might believe nothing they can do will improve things. Control of their lives resides outside of themselves, probably in the hands of more powerful people who are directing things. When confronted by a potentially stressful situation, such as not receiving a needed raise, such persons would likely believe they had to accept such a decision. They would experience the situation as threatening and stressful. Persons who believe they had control over their lives would likely devise some plan of action to meet this threat, such as talking to the boss, looking for another position, or deciding what else could be done at work to earn the raise. Such a person would probably experience less stress.

Earlier in this chapter we discussed the crucial role played by children's perceptions of events. Whether an event is interpreted as positive, negative, or neutral can influence whether or not stess is experienced. The three attitudes of challenge, commitment, and control can all affect a person's perceptions. A person with a strong hardiness factor will be less likely to perceive common events as stressful and therefore will minimize the damaging effects of stress. It seems certain that such attitudes are learned, probably from childhood. Thus, our approach to relieving stress in children will center around developing high levels of the attitudes of challenge, commitment, and control. Our general suggestions in this chapter and our specific ones in subsequent chapters are all designed to help instill these three attitudes. The best medicine is preventive, and that is the thrust of our recommendations. However, for children already under stress these suggestions should also provide some immediate relief.

Challenge

In order to help develop the attitude of challenge, we offer the following suggestions.

Encourage children to engage in as many different types of activities as possible The goal here is to develop an attitude that welcomes change and novelty. If children like sports, encourage them to participate in a wide variety of sports. If they like artistic activities, encourage them to become involved in a variety of media of expression. If a child enjoys athletic activities, also encourage some participation in creative and other non-athletic activities, for example.

Praise more than one area. Don't praise attempts in sports only. Look for success in school, with friends and siblings, and in chores around the house. Look for successes in physical, intellectual, social, and emotional areas; praise each one equally, if possible. In this way, children can develop into well-rounded individuals who are not trapped into success in only one aspect of life.

Arrange a child's environment so novelty and new experiences are commonplace. Simple ways to do this might include taking children shopping so they can see different people and different situations, taking children on walks to different neighborhoods or different parks, going on bus rides with children to new parts of town, allowing children to participate in groups such as scouting, junior achievement, etc. At home, encourage children to redecorate their room, rearrange furniture, plan varied menus, do different chores from time to time, or do anything that might add novelty and variety to their daily lives. Going to museums, concerts of varying kinds, and arts-and-crafts exhibits is another way to build novelty into a child's life.

Control

In order to help develop the attitude of control, we offer the following general suggestions:

Don't insist on perfection. Accept the performance of your child for what it is: the performance of a child. Don't compare children within the family or to adult performances. If a child does something that could be done better, accept what was done and look for improvement so that the child knows performance will be rewarded.

Praise your children for trying. If children know that parents appreciate an attempt as much as a success, the chances are good that many more attempts and many more successes will result.

Help your children succeed. This is most easily done by presenting children with chores, tasks, or problems that don't require more skill than the child has. If something is beyond your child's ability, divide it into smaller parts that can be more easily accomplished. Pitch in and help, if possible. By successfully accomplishing tasks, children develop self-confidence and learn they can control what happens. Praise your children for what they do accomplish. Many believe that children need to experience failure in order to learn to deal with a tough, cruel world. In fact, failure is not good preparation for learning to create success. Success does that. It teaches the child he/she is powerful enough to attack a task again with a better chance of success. Failure prepares one to fail again. It teaches that failure is all we can do. Teach children they are competent and they will strive for success all the rest of their lives.

Whenever possible, allow your children to have some choice about what rewards and punishments they will receive. If a task has been completed and a reward is due, let the child express what he/she thinks the job was worth. Afterward, discuss the connection between what the child did and what the consequences were (rewards or punishments). This will help develop the idea that the child has control over his/her destiny.

When problems arise in a child's life, such as an argument with a brother, sister, or friend, let the child try to work out a solution. Afterward, discuss with the child how he/she handled the potential stressor. Praise the child for handling a stressful situation. Let him/her know that when difficulties arise he/she is quite able to handle them.

Commitment

In order to help develop the attitude of commitment, we offer the following general suggestions:

Pay attention to the good things. Without being naive, try to teach children there is much of life that is enjoyable and meaningful. It is perhaps an unfortunate characteristic of too many of us that we spend so much time complaining about the bad things that we pay no attention to the good things.

Create a support system for children. Family members who support one another have the greatest chance to resist negative stress and live exciting, happy lives. A recent study provides useful suggestions for developing the kind of family that provides support for all its members (Milofsky 1981):

- Spend time together. Plan time for all members of the family to be together. If families spend time together they can build up a reservoir of good feelings to help them past the bad times.
- Spend time talking to children. Families that share their feelings have developed the skills to help them talk with one another during stressful times.
- Appreciate one another. Families that celebrate the achievements of all the family members create a climate of warmth, support, and involvement.
- Deal with crises positively. As a family, strive to see the positive aspects of any crises and then band together as a family to meet those crises.

Other General Suggestions

Learn to relax. It is important to strive for success. It is also important that your physical and psychological health not be sacrificed to success. If parents can learn to relax, they can then teach their children to relax. There are specific activities in the back of this book for parents and children to do together to learn to relax.

Teach children not to put off painful decisions. What is important is for the child to learn that stress can build up over time. If a painful task is completed quickly, the chances of stress building up are reduced.

Use your child's own past experience to help relieve stress. For example, if a child is afraid to go to the dentist, remind the child of how he/she was able to make it the last time. Or if a child is anxious about a coming performance in a play or show, recall the last success the child had in a play and remind the child of it. Try to remember adult experience doesn't have much meaning for children, but their own personal experiences are most meaningful.

Conclusion

This chapter has dealt with the problem of stress in children. While the concept has a seemingly simple definition (stress is a reaction to an event) it becomes complex when we realize the real determination of stress is due to the interpretation of the individual. What makes it hard for the rest of us is the difficulty of getting inside the minds of others to discover how they see the world. Children do not have the intellectual sophistication to understand the relationships of their perceptions and stress, but adults do; therefore, it is up to the important adults in the lives of children to help kids deal with stresses in their own lives.

Is Stress Just a Fad?

In the early 1900s the top ten killers of humankind in the United States were all infectious diseases. In the 1980s it is estimated that the top ten killers of humankind are all stress-related diseases. The medical profession, changed economic conditions, and child protection laws have all worked to reduce substantially our risk from infectious diseases. Now, the problem confronting medicine and our population is how to bring stress under control. This is even more pressing for children, since they usually lack the sophistication necessary to understand stress and its effects on them.

Is the interest in stress just a fad? A fad is by definition an event or interest of short duration. It comes quickly and leaves quickly. There are many in our society who would maintain that stress is merely a fad. They may be partly right. Stress is a buzzword right now, a subject of discussion almost everywhere. It is on the minds of many in our society; numerous people are writing about it and conducting stress-management workshops. Beyond this, however, the fact is while the buzzword may drop from use, the conditions that created the need for the word are not likely to disappear. The condition of our world does not promise to get any less stressful. Rather, the indications are that our world is going to become even more complex than it is right now. The conditions that lead to stress are not likely to disappear. Thus, it becomes even more important for us to learn to deal with stress, since it will be with us in the future.

What adds to this problem is our relative lack of knowledge about children and about stress. The work of Freud in the early 1900s and that of Erikson and Piaget later in the twentieth century made the study of childhood popular. The study of stress is only about forty years old. The result is that we know far too little about the causes and effects of stress in childhood.

Childhood was once, even in the United States of the recent past, a relatively protected stage of life. That is no longer true. Children now are participants in world events through the media of mass public education and the probing eye of television. The disasters, terrors, and fears of the whole world are now visited upon children. Their privacy, play, fantasy, and dreams are all invaded by current events. They live in a nuclear age which is broadcast daily to them. If their parents fear the destruction of society, those fears are reinforced by the daily disasters reported in the television news.

Some argue that stress is a reality for adults, but that we need not concern ourselves with the effects of stress on children because they are so resilient. They may be exposed to stress, but they bounce back so quickly it has no real effect on them. Others might argue that we don't know the long-range effects of stress on children and shouldn't do anything until we have more information. Whatever the outcome of these arguments between psychologists and other theorists, the fact remains that our world is already extremely complex and stressful and is likely to become more so. A conservative estimate of the percentage of children negatively affected by stress in their lives is placed at 20 percent. In fact, all children are exposed to many potential stressors in their daily lives. With the increase in the number of children in the world, the number of children directly affected by stress could increase dramatically.

What can we conclude from this discussion? First, while stress as a "hot topic" may be a fad, the conditions that led to its becoming so topical are not likely to disappear. They may get worse. Second, there seems to be a tendency on the part of some to assume that children need not be protected from stress. There may be a tendency to ignore the stressors affecting children. Third, it is clear that stress has a cumulative effect, and the children who are most at risk are the ones who often receive the least attention. This is especially true in a welfare society, where individuals assume the government will take care of the poor. Even if social disadvantage is not considered, there is an increasing breakdown of the family unit, with problems of desertion, separation, divorce and its resultant single-parent families, decreasing income, school and behavioral problems. These mounting stressors promise an increasing number of problems for children. Even if stress is a fad, which we believe it is not, then there are serious problems which must be dealt with even during the time of the fad. Only in this way can we increase the likelihood of our children reaching adulthood intact.

Notes

1. Carro, Geraldine. "What Worries Kids Most?" *Ladies Home Journal.* June 1980, p. 126. © 1980 LHJ Publishing, Inc. Reprinted with permission of the author and Ladies' Home Journal.

2. Selye, Hans. "How to Master Stress." *Parents.* Nov. 1977, 25, pp. 34-35.

2

STRESS
in the Home

*It is customary, but I think
it is a mistake, to speak
of happy childhood. Children,
however, are often over-anxious and acutely sensitive . . .
but children are at the mercy
of those around them.*

Sir John Lubbock, Baron Avebury
(1834-1913)

The family is dead. One doesn't have to read very much to come across such a sentiment in newspapers and magazines. Generally, the reports on the American family are pessimistic. The picture is not pretty.

In the 1970s, divorce reached an all-time high. The United States has the highest divorce rate in the world. Two young people marrying for the first time in recent years had only a fifty-fifty chance of having a success-ful marriage. That's right, 50 percent of all recent marriages are ending in divorce. Most end within the first two years, with the greatest percentage of divorces taking place within two to five years of marriage. Teenage marriages are four times more likely to end in divorce than those occurring later.

In this era of pro-family pressures from religious conservatives, it is frightening to realize that the kind of family they are talking about represents a minority of the living arrangements for American families. We need to understand the changes that are taking place in American life in order to deal with these pressing social problems. The traditional nuclear family represents fewer than 50 percent of households (Robbins 1981). The greatest increase has come in households headed by females. This group makes up 25 percent of U.S. households. In fact, one out of every six children in the United States will spend at least two years living in a single-parent family.

Finally, in spite of the fact both males and females say they have the same goals for marriage—affection, respect, communication, and fulfill-ment—it seems clear that for many in our society those desires are not met. Finally, violence has become one of our major social problems. Spousal violence and child abuse are being reported in record numbers, and many experts believe the reported cases are far outnumbered by the unreported incidences (Spanier 1981).

This is a dismal picture indeed, one that is largely true. However, the conclusion that the family is dead is largely false. Despite the alarming statistics and the well-documented family turmoil, there remains wide-spread commitment to the concept of marriage and to family life. Interest in families and the problems of family life has never been higher. There are more than a dozen professional journals devoted to marriage and family concerns; in recent years, despite current setbacks, federal grants to study the family have steadily increased.

It is perhaps ironic, in the face of all the evidence suggesting marriage and families are in trouble, that marriages are on the increase in the United States. While many delayed their marriage in the early seven-ties, beginning in about 1976 and continuing into the present marriages have increased every year (Spanier 1981). Eventually, many choose marriage in the United States. In another positive sign, the median age of marriage is creeping up, with males waiting until about twenty-four years of age and females until about twenty-two years of age. Statistically, this signals a hopeful decline in divorce. Further, despite popular wisdom to the contrary, teenage marriages in the United States are on the decline.

Even those persons who decide to end their marriages tend to re-marry later (Spanier 1981). Fully 25 percent of divorced persons remarry within the first year; 50 percent remarry within three years. Eventually, four out of five divorced persons remarry. While these persons may be making statements regarding their previous marriage, it should be clear they are not making a decision to reject marriage itself. Many experts would argue that marriage and family concerns are stronger now than they have ever been in United States history. We are faced with a paradox. Both divorce and marriage are more popular than they have ever been.

Finally, in spite of the widely reported disasters in family living, children report the family is a good, happy place to be. Fully nine out of ten children report they find the family to be a cohesive, supportive place to live.[1]

Table 1 reveals some telling changes in family life in the United States.

TABLE 1. Changes in U.S. Family Makeup[2]

	1970	1980	Percentage Change	
Marriages performed	2,159,000	2,317,000	up	7.3
Divorces granted	708,000	1,170,000	up	65.3
Married couples	44,728,000	47,662,000	up	6.6
Unmarried couples	523,000	1,346,000	up	157.4
Persons living alone	10,851,000	17,202,000	up	58.5
Children living with two parents	58,926,000	48,295,000	down	18.0
Children living with one parent	8,230,000	11,528,000	up	40.1
Average size of household	3.3	2.8	down	15.2
Families with both husband and wife working	20,327,000	24,253,000	up	19.3

What becomes apparent from an analysis of this chart is that adults have found ways of handling their problems with changing marriage and family patterns. They have been able to seek out new patterns of living together and of achieving economic security. It appears to be children who have had to carry the brunt of the negative impact of the changing U.S. family makeup. Although divorces are up, so are marriages and unmarried couples living together; there is also an increase in the number of households in which both parents work. It is in the category of children living with parents that we see the most dramatic change. The number of children living with both parents is dramatically down, and the number of children living with one parent is dramatically up. Adults are dealing with their concerns, but unfortunately children appear to be suffering the consequences.

Overall, children report the home as a happy place to be, but they also report a number of fears.[3] For example, eight out of ten children indicate they are worried about their families. That figure increases to nearly 100 percent when the mother in the family reports that the marriage is in trouble. Children are beset by a number of fears that can be aggravated by family concerns. When asked, more than six out of ten children between the ages of seven and eleven report they are afraid someone will break into their house and hurt them. Of the 2200 children interviewed, 25 percent said they were afraid they might be "hurt" when they left the house. And in all types of neighborhoods more than 50 percent of the children said they think their neighborhood was not a very good place to grow up.

We are left with a bewildering set of facts and figures. On the one hand, it is widely reported that marriage and family life are in trouble in the United States. On the other, there are good indications those fears are the results of misinterpretations of the information. In one breath children report the family is a good place to be, and in the next they report a host of fears generated by deteriorating family relationships. What the authors of this book conclude is that the family is in turmoil but that this turmoil does not signal any departure from a desire to find a marriage and family relationship that is affectionate, respectful, fulfilling, and characterized by open and frank communication. In the adult struggle to find such fulfilling relationships, it appears children are being exposed to a number of pressures that are creating problems for them in their daily lives. What are some of these pressures?

Stress in the Home

Eleven Beliefs that Create Stress for Children

1. We don't have to do anything special for our children in a crisis because children will get over it as they grow up. The entire point of this book is that children are not prepared to cope on their own with the predictable crises of their lives. Part of the responsibility of being a parent is to arrange situations in children's lives so they are able to meet crises with a reasonable chance of coping successfully with them. This doesn't mean an over-protective parent is any better than a neglecting parent. It does mean, however, that parents who believe children are unharmed by crises and will simply bounce back in time seriously misunderstand children. In the situations of death, divorce, hospitalization, and other crises in children's lives it is a sensitive and communicative parent who can help children cope with both mild and serious pressures in their lives.

2. *If children are happy, then they won't cry or be angry.* As unusual as it may seem to many of us, there are adults who believe crying or anger in a child somehow means they are failures as parents. In order to prevent these kinds of behaviors, they will go to any length to pacify, please, or punish children when they cry or express anger. What is false about this belief is that the behavior it expects is unhuman. All of us express emotions. Some of us cry. Some of us might hit walls (crying is better). Some of us take cold showers or run, but all of us do something with our emotions. Parents who deny this to their children have expectations that are impossible to meet. Children in those homes are under incredible pressure to be something impossible. A more truthful statement would be that children who do not cry or express anger are probably unhappy. They certainly are not learning to use the full range of human emotions.

3. *It's not fair for us to impose our values on our children.* Parents who believe this statement in an exaggerated form leave their children in a moral vacuum. The children are left in the world without any clear guidelines for right and wrong to challenge. Notice we said "to challenge." It is not necessary for children to absolutely believe what their parents believe, but it is necessary that they be told and that they observe their parents' value systems in operation. It is in the testing, challenging, agreeing, and disagreeing with parental values that children move toward an eventual firm value system of their own. Confronted with parents who refuse to make stands on moral issues, children may come to believe nothing matters.

Children need firm, clear guidelines as a starting place to begin to explore their world. Children who do not have such guidelines face the danger of being overwhelmed by the world or possibly developing an aggressive stance toward the world as a defense against the uncertainty created by their uninvolved parents. Children have a right to know and challenge the beliefs of their parents.

4. We can't say "no" to our children without losing their love. Actually, it is more likely that parents who don't say "no" to their children lose their respect and perhaps even their love. Parents who won't say "no" to their children have given up their responsibility as parents and abandoned their children to a world without reason. Such children have lost the opportunity in the home to learn to live in a society in which cooperation is the rule. Such parents have simply given up their responsibility to the social institutions such as schools, churches, or jails to do the job they failed to do.

5. If I make a promise, then I must keep it. What makes this a dangerous belief is that it seems so right. Who among us would advocate breaking promises to children, or to anyone else, for that matter? Isn't it important for children to learn that adults are trustworthy and can be counted upon to keep their word? Yes, it is. It is also important for children to learn that sometimes in life things happen that prevent even their parents from keeping a promise. It is important to learn that even if a person promised, events can occur that prevent the adult from keeping the promise. What is more important is to share with children one's own disappointment at not being able to keep a promise, rather than guiltily overlooking other obligations or pressing concerns that have made keeping the promise impossible. Let us give an example. What reasonable adult would feel guilty about having to attend the funeral of a close friend on the day he or she promised to take the children to the amusement park? Events occur that prevent any of us from sometimes keeping promises to one another. It is from the experience of disappointment and responsibility that children can learn more about life than from a guilt-ridden adult who can't responsibly explain obligations.

6. All we have to do is listen to our children and they will tell us how to raise them. Some adults have such a romantic notion of childhood that they would allow children to follow their every impulse without adult supervision or intervention. What they have not learned, apparently, is that children's ambitions, desires, and goals often far exceed their skills. Children are inexperienced human beings who positively need the help and guidance of adults. They may not profit much from criticism, but they surely can profit from guidance in which adults offer them the benefit of their experience and help children clarify and understand their ambitions, goals, and desires. Children need us. Without adults, chances are the world would overwhelm them. What research into this issue has revealed, in spite of all the material one might read about "superkids," is if children are asked to accept too much responsibility too soon, the chances are they will end up as less competent adults. However, with children who are allowed time to grow up slowly, with adult guidance, the chances are good they will develop more and more competence to become self-confident and strong adults.

7. *If we're not our children's friends, then we aren't good parents.* One thing we can learn is that children are dependent on adults. It is gradual growth in decision making, accepting responsibility, and eventual financial independence from the family that makes being a parent different from being a friend. It is possible to make friends with our children—but probably not while they are children. After they have established an identity of their own and have been away from home for a few years, then it might be discovered that aside from, apart from, and different from the parent-child relationship, a new relationship can develop—one of friendship. Friendship is a relationship of mutual dependence—interdependence. A family is a relationship in which some of the participants are dependent on others. It is the job of parents to provide for their children. It is not appropriate for adults to enter into parenthood recognizing they have made a decision to accept dependents and then try to pretend that their children are not dependent on them.

Parents and friends are different. It is entirely possible to be good parents without ever having the kind of relationship that characterizes friendship with our children.

8. *There is nothing more important to us than our children.* There is nothing more guilt-producing in a child than a parent who goes around saying such things. It is probably a good deal more healthy, psychologically, for adults to understand the part children play in their lives and to also recognize they have a life outside parenthood. It is also probably true that the degree of satisfaction one has outside parenthood can contribute significantly to one's happiness as a parent. The belief above is virtually guaranteed to produce sad parents and resentful children.

9. *There is no way our children can repay us for the sacrifices we have made for them.* Absolutely right! There is no way for the children of parents who believe this ever to be grateful enough to please their parents.

So, what we have is a family in which the parents are resentful and the children are ungrateful. It is almost as if the parents had children so that the children could thank them. It is a bit of a cliché, but who asked them to have children? Children actually didn't ask to be born. They don't owe a debt of gratitude to their parents. Parents decide to accept the responsibility of raising children. Any thanks they get for doing that is gravy. Grateful children are a blessing, but they aren't a necessity. If we expect our children to be grateful for the sacrifices we make for them, then we actually have set up the conditions for an angry severing of family ties. Remember, it is the adults in this situation who are creating all the problems.

10. We're going to give our children everything we didn't have in life. Here is a foolproof strategy to produce lazy, weak, and insecure children. Give them everything they want and don't let them ever have to strive for anything. Don't let them have to struggle for something important in their lives. Don't let them want for anything and they will learn the importance of nothing. Children are like adults in at least this way—they prize more the things they have had to work for or the things they have received unexpectedly from people they really like. Plenty doesn't breed selfishness, but it probably does breed lack of appreciation. If we allow our children to work for their own goals, then they are more likely to grow up appreciating both their gains and us.

11. Our children are going to be all the things we never could be. It is not infrequent to see parents trying to live a life they could not have for any number of reasons through their children. Because it is so does not make it any more acceptable. It doesn't take a psychologist to know that a child who isn't allowed to move toward establishing a personal identity separate from his or her parents is, later on, an adult who is in trouble. Most of us resent "stage-door" mothers who force their personal ambitions on their children. It is no less reprehensible to be an "operating room" father or a "courtroom" uncle.

Family Communication

Perhaps no other area of family life can affect stress in children (as well as other family members) for good or bad as the area of communication. If family communication is good, parents can pick up the signs of stress in children and talk about it before it results in some crisis. If family communication is bad, not only will parents be insensitive to potential crises, but the poor communication will contribute to problems in the family. Poor communication is not only a problem itself, but is also the cause of a number of other problems.

Discipline

One of the most important areas of family life for children is the discipline their parents use to guide and direct their development. While children wouldn't use the language in the sentence above, they would share the sentiment. Children really do care about how they are treated. Discipline is often practiced to extremes in U.S. households. We seem caught between too much and too little. We seem to pass from one discipline fad to another, in which experts recommend either little discipline or strict discipline. If parents are permissive, they are making a statement to their children that they don't care—they don't care how their children act. They don't care who they are. The children are left without clear values of right or wrong.

When parents do punish their children, the tendency seems to be to overdo it. For example, in one study, more than one third of U.S. parents reported they punish their children more than they deserve.[4] More than one half admitted they are inconsistent in their punishment (in all fairness to everyone, who isn't?). Children reported the same sort of feelings. Over one third of the children interviewed felt they were punished when they didn't deserve it and their parents were unfair. Almost 30 percent of the children felt they were hit unnecessarily by their parents.

There are important issues here. First, let us say the important issue is not whether the statistics above are accurate. Rather, the important issue is that parents and children report as they do. It is important to understand they believe what they are saying. In that sense, what we are talking about is a problem of communication. It is a problem of communication when a child reports his or her parents to be unfair. Something has not been explained or received or both. Children will live better in a family, and with less stress, when they know the things they do not understand are going to be explained to them; they should also know that the events of the family are their business too. When they are a part of the family decision-making process, the chances (we are talking about a guarantee) are that better discipline will be less of a stress for children and parents.

Bickering

When family communication is poor, the chances are no family discussion will be productive but will, rather, end up in name-calling, yelling, and anger. In U.S. families, we can almost predict that this way of interacting will be the norm. One reason is few families have any practice at any other way of communication or, for that matter, any practice at family communication at all. Research reveals that the average U.S. family spends only about *thirty minutes a week* in any serious family discussion.[5] Further, two out of three parents report they have difficulty talking to their children about sensitive topics such as drugs, sex, death, money, or problems in the family. Good heavens! What's left to talk about? The weather and the ball game?

It is the very lack of discussion in families that causes bickering. If people in the family know they are not going to have any honest opportunity to discuss meaningful problems in frank and open ways, then it isn't surprising they resort to trickery, baiting, and insults to try to have other family members guess they have some unresolved issue that needs help. The most often reported causes for family fights are problems with other members of the family, relatives, and money. Two of the topics mentioned as the most avoided in two out of three homes are family problems and money. It should come as no surprise to any of us that the solution to ending bickering in families is to talk to one another more often, without blaming, making judgments, or insulting one another. Good communication means family members know they can talk in their families and be heard.

Siblings

Often the family members who cause each other the most grief are siblings. We seem to have an assumption that brothers and sisters ought naturally to love one another, and so we spend little time on activities aimed at building a positive relationship between children. If the children fight, we punish them. There does not seem to be a point where we teach them. Most parents know that firstborn children tend to make poor siblings. They have been "king of the hill" or "queen of the mountain" for some time, and they are reluctant to share the unqualified attention they have been receiving with some newcomer. They are, in a word, jealous. Sometimes they may not be jealous, in which case they are, in a word, guilty. They might be saying sentences to themselves like "Is there something the matter with me that my parents want another baby?" It is certainly true when a new baby enters a home there is less attention for everyone. Babies are attention magnets; they draw all eyes and attention to themselves. An older child will be left out unless parents make special arrangements to compensate.

Even if parents have made special arrangements, the likelihood is that conflicts between the firstborn and the parents are going to increase. The child will be more demanding, try to take back what was once an unquestioned position in the family.

The plain simple truth of the matter is that children bicker and argue with one another. Siblings are not immune from these struggles (how well parents know!). The problem in many homes is parents who don't accept even the natural quarreling that goes on between siblings and who fail to provide opportunities for genuine affection to develop between brothers and sisters.

Money

Money is a source of stress for children in two ways. First, if the family is having money problems, then the stresses between husband and wife over finances spill over to the children. Second, money is a stressor for children because they need money to buy things just like everyone else. The temptations to buy things are broadcast daily from television. Television preaches materialism. Further, since children have a limited understanding of money and a limited awareness of how adults get money, they often don't understand why they can't have everything they see on TV. "Just write a check, Dad." "We can use the credit card." It is difficult for adults to deal with children who do not understand money. It is difficult for children to deal with adults who do not understand that children observe the steady flow of cash around the house and simply want their share.

We have already said money is a sensitive topic, and many parents in our society don't like to talk about it. Money is a sign of approval. It is a symbol of love. It is a source of power. For all of those reasons, the way money is handled in a family can be a real indicator of stress for children.

Privacy

Children are people. People like privacy from time to time. Nearly every person in a family is given rights to privacy except children. Remember the days when our own parents would come into our room unannounced and say something like, "I came to check up on you. There wasn't any noise, so I know you must be doing something wrong." That they were often right isn't the point. The point is that children seldom get to go anywhere, do anything, or see anybody without being questioned about it by their parents. Sometimes it is a sign of love. Sometimes it is idle curiosity. Sometimes it is pure meddling. If we could learn to restrict our questions to those times when it is a sign of love, lack of privacy would not be the stressor it is now for children.

It isn't too much to ask for children to have a little time to themselves. It is possible they need to think over the problems they see in their own lives just the way many adults do. It is also possible, given a little to themselves, that children could solve some of their own problems and have the chance to grow into stronger, more competent adults.

Quality of Parent-Child Relationship

If things are not going well in the home, it is not unusual for parent-child relationships to be both cause and symptom. Strife between children and parents can cause a number of other problems in families. It is also possible that other problems in the family (money, communication) contribute to the deterioration of the parent-child relationship.

Generally, parent-child relationships can deteriorate because parents are just too busy with their own lives to give any quality time to their children. Children then might become discipline problems just to get their parents' attention. Being punished is better than being ignored. The parent-child relationship can suffer because of a parent who is physically present but psychologically absent. This is the kind of a parent the child knows only from the back of a newspaper, a disembodied voice saying, "Be quiet, kids. I'm trying to read the newspaper" (translation—I don't want to be involved with you). These parents are not punitive toward their children—they just don't interact with them at all. The children don't have a relationship with these parents. You can't have a relationship with a dishrag! Finally, there are guilty parents who, feeling obligated to do things with their children, engage in all kinds of artificial interactions children hate (the yearly camping trip). The substitute for genuine affection is a series of planned, highly structured activities that prevent any real contact between family members because it is hard to talk on a roller coaster between the cotton candy, hot dogs, and soda.

Any of these problems can exist in any family, although there are classes of families that are noted as having special problems with parent-child relationships. These are families in which both parents work outside the home and single-parent families.

Working Parents

Every mom isn't Supermom and every dad isn't liberated. For some families the challenges of mixing a career and raising children don't work out. In our society, where household chores have traditionally been seen as "woman's work," working wives have had to not only work outside the home but have also been expected to carry out the same duties as a woman who is not employed outside the home. They have to do their career job and take care of the house, too. In such families, it is not long before the hostility of such an arrangement will surface, producing stress for everyone in the family. The likelihood of both parents working has been steadily increasing over the years. For example, in 1960 only 19 percent of mothers with children under the age of eighteen were working outside the home. In 1970, 45 percent of mothers with children under the age of eighteen were working outside the home. Presently, over 52 percent of these mothers are employed outside the home (Van Horne 1978). This has been the source of criticism for many self-styled pro-family advocates who assume one cannot be a working mother and a good parent at the same time. Interestingly, this criticism is reserved for those working mothers who occupy relatively low-status positions. The criticism is much less harsh when the working mother holds a high-status job—say, a physician, college professor, or attorney. These women are criticized for an entire new range of prejudices—they are too much like men!

Whatever the case, there are serious issues raised by working parents. There are over four million children between the ages of six and thirteen who are called latchkey children.[6] These children as a group suffer greater potential for violence, accidents, and crime than children with parents at home. They are more likely to be the victim of gangs, sibling abuse, and sexual assault by strangers or even seemingly friendly neighbors. They are more likely to suffer an accident. It is not unusual for these children to be in the care of the "flickering blue babysitter," television. The possible outcomes for latchkey children are those that are possible for any group of children. They can thrive and be superkids. They can muddle through somehow or cope. They can be at risk. Or they can be harmed. This is the actual issue. It is not whether parents both work or not. It is the quality of the care the parents provide for their children that is most crucial. In fact, many families in which both parents work are doing a fine job of raising their children. If we can believe the research, it appears that many working mothers are highly disciplined and responsible parents who take extra precautions to protect and care for their children. The research on this issue has revealed some interesting facts (Van Horne 1978). Children of working mothers are more likely to have eaten breakfast than children of mothers who do not work outside the home. They are likely to miss less school. It is also likely that the children of working mothers take pride in the jobs their parents do, especially if the mothers have any sort of high-status job ("My mother the banker!"). One way this is revealed is through other research which indicates that the children of welfare mothers do not do as well in school as children of mothers who work and that they tend to watch more television than any other group of children. Obviously, this has something to do with money, but it also has something to do with pride in family.

Single Parents

While it would be a joy to write that the children of single-parent families do as well as the children of two-parent families, the evidence doesn't suggest this conclusion (Leo 1982). Too often, the children of single-parent families are required to grow up too fast. That is, they are often required to care for themselves, make decisions that are too complicated, and involve themselves in adult concerns without preparation long before these demands are made on other children. Those parents who do not see the importance of childhood, or ignore it, condemn their children to the insecurities of growing up without the comforting presence of adults when children need them most—during the unpredictable crises of childhood.

Some single parents come to rely on their children as confidants and advisors (Leo 1982). These children are sometimes cast as "heads of families" as little boys ("You're the man of the house now") or to little girls as "Mommy's best friend." They have lost their right to childhood. Since they love their parents they try to live up to these unrealistic expectations. Doomed to failure, they suffer the increasing loss of self-esteem.

The children of single parents, as a group, achieve less in school, are absent from school more often, and have more discipline problems in school than children from two-parent families.

Finally, the likelihood of a single parent providing the same economic security as is found in a two-parent family is unrealistic. This is due to actual social inequities in our society. First, men are the heads of only about 20 percent of single-parent families. Females now are the heads of 25 percent of all families in the U.S. The sad fact is that females are less likely to make the same amount of money as males. It has been recently reported that equally educated and trained females will make 38 percent less than males doing the same job. The economic stresses of single parenting, especially for women, are great. These stresses do not spare the children in single-parent families.

Finally, the same criterion applies here as it does for working parents. What is at question is not the marital status of the parent but the quality of the parenting. Unfortunately, research reveals that single parents are not yet performing their task as well as either two-parent families in which the mother is at home or those in which both parents work.

Family Crisis

In general, a crisis is anything that upsets the routines of family life. One other way to look at crises is to understand that some routines of family life are themselves crises. What ordinarily happens in a crisis is that members of the family find themselves without adequate resources to handle some new or unexpected situation. For example, some of the chapters in this book deal with crises in the family (death, divorce, hospitalization). Other unexpected crises may include a parental illness (either physical or emotional), marital quarrels, the addition of a new family member (birth, adoption, live-ins), or a sudden change in career or life-style.

Moving

One of the sudden changes in the life of a family that can have an effect on children is moving. There seems to be a critical time when moving is most stressful for children, especially boys (Horn 1977). Psychologists call this the "vulnerable age." It is the years from six to about eleven. Children, more likely boys than girls for some unknown reason, react badly to having to move during this period of their lives. It has been demonstrated that a child who has made a good adjustment to school in previous years can suffer from moving and begin to do poorly in school. Some would say that the children will get over the stress of moving after a while; and some do. The point here is that some do not. Interest as well as ability is stunted. We don't know why. But some never recover what was a good start, and research has reported lasting changes in the child's ability to adapt.

This is a serious matter, because in the United States moving looks like the national pastime. For example, one out of every five U.S. families moves every year. The average U.S. family moves once every five years. That is a lot of moving around. This high mobility places stresses on everyone, but it seems especially important to children who are just beginning to get a sense that they have some control over their lives. A move can take all that security away.

Alcohol

The most serious continuing disruption of homes involves substance abuse, most commonly the misuse of alcohol. The problem discussed below could apply equally well to any drug that is abused by parents. However, the research into the effects on the children of alcoholics is most readily available. Perhaps the most serious effect of an alcoholic parent is that the children in the family perceive their family to be much less happy than the families of other children (Wilson and Orford 1980). They might see their family as "no family at all." These children are, in effect, growing up without the support of a family, even though both parents are present. Because of their shame, children try to protect themselves by keeping their parent's drinking a secret. They end up as social isolates without close friends. Their shame may not be justified, but their fear is. The children of alcoholics suffer from far more parental violence and personal threats than do children of nonalcoholic families. They involve themselves more in parental fighting, either trying to protect a parent or trying to protect themselves. If the description strikes the reader as unpleasant, it should. Alcoholism is unpleasant; its effects on families are devastating. It is a crisis in a family that can last for the entire childhood of some children. They have been denied most of the joys of this time of life not because of an accident or fate or an unpredictable crisis, but because one of their parents abused alcohol. The abuse of alcohol is doubly sad in a family for this reason: It can be controlled.

Family Violence

For the authors, this is the most difficult section to write. Children need the protection of the adults in their world. In this unique society, parents have a special obligation to their own children because so much of the obligation of child rearing—and consequently, so much power—is given to parents. When these adults fail in their obligation, children are left without defense. The laws of the United States are weak in protecting children. When the parents become the ones who represent the danger in the lives of children, then, sadly, it is often only an accidental discovery by some other caring adult that will intervene to save them. Then, for society to intervene, the danger must be life-threatening. For those children for whom the danger is real, but not life-threatening, the larger society is reluctant to intervene. What this means for many children in our society is that they spend their childhood in constant fear of injury. Injury, as we all know, doesn't always appear as bruises. Too often in violent families the injuries are emotional and follow the children into adulthood.

Why do we tolerate so much family violence in the United States? There are probably three main reasons. First, even this late into the twentieth century, children are often considered property. Second, in the U.S., parents are considered solely responsible for the upbringing of their children. Third, corporal punishment as a method of control and discipline is widely accepted and even approved of by U.S. families. In a recent survey, 80 percent of the families interviewed reported that they used corporal punishment in their homes. Of the 80 percent, 60 percent reported that they spanked their children at least once a week (Gilmartin 1979). Spanking is not abuse, but not infrequently physical abuse is the result of a parent accepting that hitting a child is proper discipline.

Child Abuse

Let us begin with some frightening facts. From one to six months of age, only Sudden Infant Death Syndrome (SIDS) accounts for more deaths than child abuse. Physical abuse is a greater killer of six- to twelve-month old infants than any malformation, cancer, or infectious disease. After one year of age, child abuse is second only to true accidents as a killer of infants. Most victims of child abuse are under the age of three years. Finally, 50 percent of all battered children who are returned to their homes after a reported abuse *die* of abuse or neglect.

Let us attend secondly to some misconceptions. First, many believe that child abuse is invariably a problem of the lower socioeconomic class. Second, many believe that child-abusing parents are abnormal, psychotic, criminals, or retarded. Third, many believe that child abuse is rare. All of these beliefs are false; each is dangerous in its own way. The first is dangerous because it fails to alert us to the fact that middle-class or upper-class abuse is hidden. Since these income groups do not have to resort to public care, their abuse is taken to private physicians, who may even be friends of the family. This reduces the number of child-abuse cases reported and protects the parents at the expense of the children. The second is dangerous because it presents the fiction that there is some clear difference between the abuser and the rest of us. We may even be led into the belief that child-abusing parents could be detected by their behavior outside of the home. When we discover that an acquaintance of ours is an abusing parent, we often say, "It just can't be true. He (or she) is so easy-going." Our doubts may prevent us from acting to protect the child. Finally, the third is dangerous because such a belief may prevent us from enacting the kind of legislation needed not only to protect the children identified as abused, but also begin to afford some protection to those who are not identified as children at risk.

Child abuse is not confined to children who are physically attacked by their parents. That is only one of several forms of abuse. Another category of abuse involves both physical and emotional neglect. Neglect is the failure of the parents to properly provide an atmosphere in which the child has reasonable safeguards for physical health, safety, and general well-being. Emotional abuse occurs in families where children are terrorized, berated, and rejected. Children raised in families where they are constantly threatened with being abandoned or given away, locked in dark rooms, or constantly being told they are stupid can be considered victims of emotional abuse. Finally, a far greater number of children than would be suspected are sexually exploited by their families.

Child abuse does not occur in a vacuum. There are predictable factors that are present in most instances in child abuse. First, it is not uncommon for parents to have a background of abuse themselves. Here it is important to recognize that we are discussing "victims of victims" when we discuss abused children. The parents are caught in a trap of lack of any role modeling which could have saved them from ultimately abusing their own children. The only world they may have ever known is a world of violence. Abusive parents see corporal punishment as an appropriate way of dealing with discipline problems, even with babies. Abusive parents also seem unable to challenge their parents' ideas of child rearing and, more importantly, they seem incapable of acting independently to break the cycle of violence.

Second, abused children are often seen as unlovable and disappoint-ing. It may be as small a thing as having a boy baby when the father wanted a girl baby. Because of that disappointment the child is more likely to be abused in the face of a number of other factors: The child may be sickly. The child could have colic. The child may be seen as ugly.

Third, some crisis triggers the abuse. Most people would think crisis would have to be something earthshaking to provoke the abuse of a child. However, if people believe that they are wrong. The two most frequently reported "crises" that trigger a reaction of abuse are (1) crying and (2) toilet-training accidents. It must be obvious that child abuse is not a rational act. It is not premeditated; it is usually followed by grief and guilt. As often as not, an abusive parent is an adult who has little information on what children are actually like. It is because of these unrealistic expecta-tions that they contribute one more factor to the dangerous climate they create for their children.

Fourth, abusive parents are often parents who are cut off from others. They have no "lifeline." They do not have lines of communications with friends, family, or even social agencies to whom they can reach out for aid. They are isolates. Interestingly, single parents as a group are rather less abusing than are two-parent families. In two-parent families, it is usually one parent who is the abuser and the other parent who acts as a silent partner. This is not to say that the one who is not an abuser does not know what is happening in the family. It just means they do not do any-thing to stop the abuse.

It is the last sentence in the paragraph above that is most disheart-ening in the whole matter of child abuse. Children are vulnerable. They need protection. The very ones who are most responsible for their protec-tion are often the ones from whom they need the most protection. Their parents have become dangerous to their very lives. Nothing can be more insidious than that.

Sexual Abuse

Sexual abuse is perhaps the most underreported crime in the United States. It is estimated that there are ten times as many cases of sexual abuse in the United States as are reported. Currently, reported cases are approaching 80,000 a year (Kanigher 1982). Some would even consider the figure of 800,000 cases a year to be conservative. Considering the nature of sexual abuse, is there any wonder that arriving at accurate figures is difficult?

Sexual abuse for children is defined as involving children in sexual activities that they cannot fully understand, to which they cannot give informed consent, and which violate our socially accepted family roles. It may include pedophilia (sexual preference for children), rape, and incest. All of these are truly sexual exploitations because they all involve children in situations in which they can in no sense accept or even understand the responsibility for their actions. Any indication by adults that they were seduced, invited, or had a child's consent for any sexual activity is impossible. A child cannot give consent for sexual behavior with adults. It is the adult's responsibility.

It is important to understand that children do not invent stories of sexual activity. This is especially true if the stories are very detailed. If this is the case, the child has been involved or at least been a witness to the sexual activity being described. The point is as children approach their parents with stories of sexual activity, they should be believed. This is true if the children approach a minister, teacher, physician, nurse, or any other adult who might have their confidence. They should be believed even if they are talking about their parents. The important consideration here is the detail with which the child tells the story.

Incest is a form of sexual abuse that seems to be on the increase in the United States. It may be the result of changing life-styles that involve greater incidence of divorce and remarriage where no blood relationship exists between members of newly created households. These households may involve contacts between stepchildren who are not related and are thrown together, often at times of sexual exploration.

Whatever the reasons, incest appears to be increasing in the United States. Father-daughter incest is by far the largest category of incest, accounting for 75 percent of all incest cases. Brother-sister, mother-son, and mother-daughter incest make up the other 25 percent.

Incest is usually not violent. Tragically, some of these father-daughter incestuous relationships have been "arranged" by the mother. While not always the case, the idea that the mother in the family does not know what is going on can usually be dismissed. She is often the silent but agreeing partner for any number of reasons (Browning and Boatman 1977), one of which may be to keep the marriage together either for financial or emotional reasons. Each member in the incestuous relationship plays a part that results in silence, to protect the entire family from shame and public humiliation. While every member of the family is ultimately injured by incest, it is the child who is robbed of appropriate sexual exploration, behavior, and emotional development. The children are caught in a conspiracy of silence in which any effort to seek help is as personally humiliating as it is freeing. The result is depression, isolation, shame, guilt, and an overall loss of self-esteem for the child involved. Incest victims are at a loss for protection. The ones who are supposed to protect them are the very ones who are hurting them. It is, however, encouraging that incest victims are likely to recover without lasting hurt if the incest is detected early and does not continue into adolescence. If this should be the case, however, the outcome can be much more serious. For some reasons which are not fully understood, girl victims seem to recover from an incestuous relationship far better than boys.

Finally, what is most important is that the children involved receive treatment. It is far more important for children to receive treatment than it is for the incestuous adult to be punished. While this is not an either/or situation, our laws have been written more to punish the adults than to treat the victim. This is a sore deficiency. It, unfortunately, follows the pattern in which the child finds him or herself. There is far more consideration given to the adults in incestuous families than there is to the children.

Suggestions for Reducing Stress in the Home

In the following section we will provide some suggestions that it is hoped will help reduce stress in the home. Some of the suggestions are more general than others. It would be desirable to provide concrete suggestions to help solve all the problems that parents face in their interactions with one another and with their children. While it is desirable, it is also unrealistic. Families are different. Therefore, the suggestions that follow are merely that. Each parent has to decide if what we recommend fits the particular family situation in which he or she lives. Try what seems helpful, maybe experiment with some of the other suggestions to see if they will work. They have worked for many families and therefore are recommended as possibilities for other parents too.

Characteristics of a Good Family

Much of what has come earlier in this chapter has focused on the negative. Stress is a problem in families. It is equally important to report that some families deal with their stress and are actually happy. That is a startling pronouncement when we are so overwhelmed by the reports of the break- down of the family. It is difficult to believe that there are families in the United States who are doing well. Nevertheless, a recently completed study of 350 families from all over the U.S. reveals that there are such families and that they have much in common. This is all the more startling because the families come from different age groups (from mid-twenties to couples in their sixties), from rural and urban communities, and from different ethnic backgrounds. While not claiming that all happy families are exactly alike, this study does seem to identify similarities that not only describe happy families, but provide suggestions that might help others move toward a more happy, productive family life. The National Study of Family Strengths was conducted by two faculty members of the Univer- sity of Nebraska, Nick Stinnett and John Defrain. The study, as reported in *Redbook*,[7] listed six characteristics that happy families shared in common.

First, happy families spend time together. This probably comes as a surprise to no one. One of the important implications of spending fun time together as a family seems to be that it works to build up a reservoir of goodwill which can help carry a family through some hard times. It helps to remember the family as a place of pleasant memories.

Second, happy families have established good communication patterns. Specifically, this means they have developed ways of dealing with their problems. It doesn't mean that these families don't fight or are free of problems. It means they have probably learned to fight fairly. Two of the rules of fighting fairly that can help all of us are: (1) Ownership. About the best way of defining ownership is to explain that it is the opposite of blaming. Sometimes it is as simple as starting sentences with the pronoun *I* instead of the pronoun *you*. Actually, there is more to it than that. It means accepting the responsibility of sharing one's feelings with another person and owning that we are the one who brought it up. We have the problem and want the other person to help us solve it. We accept the responsibility of bringing up the problem and accept the fact that we are the one who has a problem. Blaming tries to deny that we have a problem and claims it is the other person who has the problem. (2) Listening. This means hearing the other person so well that you could tell them what they meant, to their satisfaction, after they have finished talking. It doesn't mean rehearsing what we are going to say all the while the other person is talking.

Much of the research that has been done regarding communication aimed at helping other people suggests there must be three basic components if the communication is going to be successful. If we are going to be able to communicate effectively with another person, then we have to be able to *understand* what the other person is feeling and be able to *express* that understanding. We have to be *real*. We can't play a role with them or be phony about what we say. Parents sometimes end up playing parent with their children rather than being real people with them. The reason communication is interrupted when this happens is that it is very hard to have a true relationship with a role. Last, we need to have a *genuine concern* for communicating with the other person. If we are talking with another person because we have to, we are likely to be curt, sharp, and unhearing, since our primary motivation is to get away from the person as soon as we can. Communication works best in the presence of the factors discussed above. If we can understand and express our understanding, be authentic, and have a real concern for communicating with the other person, the chances are excellent that we will establish good communication patterns with the other person.

Third, happy families appreciate one another. More important, they show their appreciation for one another. When we appreciate someone, show that appreciation, and have it accepted by the other person, we are building a mutual support system, which is another strength to help to get us past the hard times families may experience. It is as important to accept a compliment as it is to give one. To deny the appreciation coming from someone teaches them not to compliment us. It also insults them. The result of an unaccepted compliment, especially across time, is to create rejection and anger. Rather than building mutual support, we would build mutual hostility. Accepting and giving compliments builds warmth and appreciation in the family.

Fourth, happy families are committed to the family group. This means that the family is the number one priority. If it comes to attending family night at school or a seminar in some work-related subject, parents would opt for family night. When it comes to a choice or what might be good for the family or what might be good for a career, the family gets the nod. It is not that there aren't other important things in the lives of the family members, but if those other things are causing family problems, the members would make room for family life and cross something else off the list. Often this means difficult decisions for families. These choices are tough. Happy families make the tough decision in favor of the family group.

Fifth, happy families deal with crises positively. As we said above, it is not that happy families do not have problems. When they do, however, they tend to try to solve them in the family group. They also tend to find something positive in the problems they have. For example, a family might find itself in a situation in which neither parent had a job. This is a source of tension in many families, and could be a time of recriminations and insults. It can also be a time when the husband and wife turn to each other for mutual support and understanding. If they find it, then the marriage is strengthened, and what is a stressful situation has become a positive one. These two characteristics (working out problems together and finding the positive aspects of the crises) help keep the members of the family committed to the family group.

Sixth, happy families share a common value system. For many families in the study, this took the form of a religious orientation. It is this common base of values that can provide a major source of strength for family members. It is equally possible that this common source of values can come from some other aspect of life, but the major commitment reported in the study was religious in nature.

Family Communications

There are problems in living together. It may be one of the flaws of our way of mating and marrying that not much is taught about what to do after we get married. Our knowledge of child rearing is often only what we experienced as children from our own parents. Talking together seems not to have been a concern of any formal system of instruction for the great majority of us. The suggestions in this section are concerned with the basic patterns of communication that have been found to be effective. They involve talking with children and adults. They discuss how to solve problems like children fighting, allowances, and husband-wife arguments. All are intended to help improve communication in the family.

Talking to Children

Here are seven "rules" for talking to children. In many of our families, parents make the assumption that all they have to do is tell the child what to do and if the child doesn't do it, they punish him or her. It is an assumption that, perhaps, causes more problems in family communication than any other. These "rules" challenge that assumption. They provide for the child to be actively involved in solving their own problems, with parents acting as guides rather than as "drill sergeants." If this way of talking to children challenges the way you were brought up or the way you are raising your children now, you might try it to see what differences in parent-child communication result.

1. Know when to talk to children and when not to. Children are not so different from adults that we can't use ourselves as a guide to know when it is a good time to talk about something and when it is not. Consider yourself. Do you like to talk about a problem when you are angry? Tired? Worried? Hungry? Busy? Probably not. Neither do children. Pick a time when the child is rested. One way to know is to ask the child if he or she wants to talk. If they say no, then ask when a good time will be. Be specific about setting a time to talk.

2. Don't forget to follow up on the time set to talk. If you have set a specific time to talk about something, don't forget it. Consider writing it down. Remind the child you have remembered and that it is time to talk.

3. Accept the fact that children's problems are as important to them as yours are to you. Think back to those times as a child when you tried to talk to an adult about a problem you had and all they said to you was "Wait until you grow up." Or perhaps they gave you a long lecture about how many problems they had. None of this was helpful. If you were lucky, some adult took you seriously and listened.

4. Listen. There is no substitute for listening to children if we want to know what is going on in their lives. If they have a problem, sometimes listening is all it takes to help them solve it. There is also a concept called *active listening*, in which what is being listened for is the underlying feeling the child is expressing. In this case, the purpose of listening is to help

47

the child clarify for himself or herself how he or she feels and what the actual problem is.

5. *Raise questions–suggest alternatives.* Children are inexperienced persons. Often they do not see that a decision they are making can have problems in the future. The future is tough for children. It is not uncommon for children to pick a solution and then not be able to understand there are other things they could do. They are stuck in their thinking; just by asking some leading questions or asking if there are other things which might be done, a parent can unstick them. Suggesting alternatives can help the child begin to create other alternatives independently. By raising questions and suggesting alternatives rather than giving answers, parents can teach their children that they can solve many problems for themselves.

6. *Encourage them to "keep trying."* Even when asking questions and suggesting alternatives hasn't worked to help a child find a solution, resist the temptation to give the child a solution. If the child can't come up with something, then encourage him or her to keep thinking and trying out different solutions until they find one that works. This suggestion and the one above can help develop the attitude of control which was mentioned in the initial chapter.

7. *Provide reassurance that you will be there when they need you.* In point 6, we are not trying to suggest you abandon the child. Encourage the child to keep trying; reassure them you are available to talk about the problem again if the child wants to. You are their support. They need your reassurance. Then they can move more confidently in the direction of solving more and more problems for themselves.

Talking to an Angry Child

Talking to an angry child can be a bit different from talking about other problems a child may encounter. Here are some suggestions that can defuse the anger and allow parents to move into the problem-solving steps discussed above.

Show interest. This means the parent should not ignore an angry child. Anger must be confronted. It does not go away. It is stored unless something is done about it. Often, showing interest can mean simply saying, "I know you are angry." This can provide an opportunity for the child to talk.

Allow the child to vent his/her anger. The only qualification on this is that they should not be allowed to hurt themselves or others.

Provide a physical outlet. Perhaps the best way to get anger out is to do something physical. Think about how many adults run, go for a walk, play racketball. It may even be possible to have a child hit a pillow or Bobo the Clown toy. Hitting something like a bed gets anger out and hurts neither the child nor anyone else.

Give the child in fantasy what he/she can't have in reality. This means that if the child is frustrated and angry because of something they can't have, then give it to them in fantasy. If the child is angry about you not being able to take them to a movie, then say, "I wish I could take you to a movie tonight." It is surprising how the simple recognition of their wish can defuse anger in children.

Bring some closure to the anger. After the steps above, say something positive, make a joke, give affection, or perhaps, at this point, provide an explanation. After saying you wish you could take the child to a movie and that has been accepted, then you might joke, "Besides, our fights are better than the ones in the movie anyway!" Or you can provide an explanation such as, "Now that your anger is over, I want to tell you why I can't take you to the movie tonight. I had to make an appointment with the furnace repair company for tonight. This is the only night they could come." At this point, both the parent and child are ready to seek some solutions to the problem that created the anger.

Handling Sibling Rivalry

This section may be a bit deceptive if anyone believes something can be done to prevent sibling rivalry. One of the authors went to considerable trouble to prepare the first child for the second. Both parents made a deal that when a lot of attention was being paid to the newborn, one of the parents would make certain the first child received some attention as well. When there were a number of visitors, the first child conducted tours. The first child had chores that were associated with helping to care for the newborn. All of this was meant to deal with the idea of subverting sibling rivalry—all to no avail! Siblings argue and fight with one another. That is the fact of the matter.

BE PREPARED As the story above indicates, siblings are going to squabble, argue, and fight with one another. Whatever precautions parents take to prevent it are probably wasted. This doesn't mean that since it is going to happen there is nothing to be done about sibling fighting. One of the things that can be done by parents is to accept that it is going to happen. Part of what parents do can prepare siblings to grow into adulthood still speaking to one another.

PRIVACY Privacy is important for all children, just as it is for adults. For siblings, it can be an especially important part of their growing up. Part of one's identity can be a private place that no one else violates without permission. For children, a quiet place where they can be alone provides the private time to think over the problems and issues of their own lives without fear of being disturbed. Here are some recommendations to help establish a private place for chidren:

Close off some private place for each child. If a home has enough space so each child can have a room, then at some point (when parents feel the child is old enough or the child requests it), move each child into a private room. If there is not enough space so that each child can have a room, then figure out a way to close off parts of a room that can be identified as each child's area.

- Put a name tag on the private place and allow the child to use it as he or she wishes. They may have their own things there and decorate as they wish.

- Make sure every person in the family knows the private place is private. Make a Do Not Disturb sign for every child and allow them to hang it out when they want. Then respect it. Remember, privacy is both physical and psychological.

- Finally, remember even knocks can be disruptive. Don't violate a child's privacy unless it is necessary. Think of this in the same way you think of your own privacy. What would be legitimate reasons for interrupting?

ESTABLISH A STRATEGY OF COMPLIMENTS BETWEEN SIBLINGS
Make sure siblings in the family take time occasionally to praise one another. This can be done formally at family meetings or informally in some
gimmick like a friendship tree or family appreciation box. A friendship
tree has branches where a note describing something good someone in the
family did for someone else can be hung. There can be the expectation
that at least one good thing per week should be done for each member of
the family. An appreciation box accomplishes the same purpose by having
family members drop a little note to each other once a week describing
something they appreciate about the family member. Such signs of
appreciation can go a long way toward building support between siblings.

ESTABLISH RULES ABOUT FIGHTING Make rules for the parents
concerning when they will intervene in sibling fighting. Make sure the
children know the rules. For example, one of the authors does not interfere in children's arguments as long as each child has a reasonable chance
of success. If one of the children in the argument is too big for the other
or too old, then it is unfair and the argument should be stopped. Other-
wise, it is important for the children to work it out for themselves.

Parents Fighting Around Children

One of the best ways of improving family communication is to improve
communication between the husband and wife. No one who has been
married for long maintains the myth that happily married people don't
fight and argue with one another. The difference is some people know how
to fight fairly and some don't. We have discussed fighting fairly above. Another aspect of fighting is that some parents know how to fight in the
presence of their children and others do not. Here are some suggestions for
adult fighting around children.

Don't hide fights from children. Children know when the atmosphere
around the house changes. Parents who try to hide their fights from children are kidding themselves if they think their children don't know that
there is tension between the parents. If parents fight fairly, they can provide a model for their children which helps them better understand the
world of adults. It should be clear that this book is concerned with open,
frank communication with children about the stresses of their lives. It is

a misguided desire to protect children from some harsh reality that creates a number of stresses discussed in this book. Children are members of a family. They have a right to know what is being fought over in the family.

Don't use the children as an excuse for a parental fight. Children don't cause their parents to fight. Adults fight for their own reasons. It is wrong to blame children or even to imply that they are the cause of adult disagreements.

Don't make children take sides in a parental argument. Children love, want, and need their parents. It is wrong for one parent to try to get at the spouse by using children. Children want to be aware of the reasons for the argument so they can still know they are going to be protected. Forcing them to take sides destroys at least a part of the protection they need. Allow children to be present, but do not force them to participate. Be frank and open. "Daddy and Mommy are having an argument. We will be done as soon as we work out our disagreement. You can stay and listen if you want, or we will let you know what we decide."

Don't make children a target of anger generated in a parental argument. Too often, parents end up punishing their children because they are still angry at their spouse. It is clear that this is wrong when we see it on paper, but when we are caught up in an argument and its aftermath, we may forget that our children did not cause the argument, should not be blamed, and should not be the target of misdirected anger.

Clear the air. After the argument is over, let everyone in the family know that it is over and a resolution has been found. Share the argument if you want, as well as the solution.

Allowance

Children need money. As they grow older they need more money. They need money for essentially the same reasons that adults need money. They need to buy stuff.

How should this allowance be given? Here are four don'ts.

1. Don't tie an allowance to chores around the house. Children are members of a family and should be expected to do family duties in the same way the mother and the father are expected to do family chores.

2. Don't tie an allowance to grades in school or to good behavior. Again, these are expected and should not be attached to any monetary reward. Don't bribe, reward, punish, or seek to control children through money.

3. Don't criticize the way children spend their allowance.

4. Don't give children money any time they ask for it. Children have enough trouble understanding money without the misconception that their parents have an endless supply and only have to write a check or use a credit card to buy anything they want. If parents do this, they deprive their children of any opportunity to learn to manage money. In fact, that is one good purpose of an allowance.

As we said above, children need money. They need it regardless of whether they get good grades, violate a family rule, or offend a parent. Here are some suggestions for giving children an allowance.

Do give an allowance. It is important for several reasons. Children need money. It provides a chance to learn to manage money. It provides the opportunity to make decisions. It gives the child a chance to practice responsibility.

Do give a fixed, regular sum. Do not vary the amount the child gets each week. This allows for planning and also allows the child to enter into discussions regarding amounts and needs.

Be aware of today's costs. Many parents give allowances based on the allowance they receive when they were a child. Those days are long gone. An allowance of one dollar a week for a 10-year-old won't even buy an ice cream cone for the child and a friend! Figure out what the child needs, what the allowance should cost, and then provide that amount (if possible within the budget of the family).

Do recognize that an allowance should not be expected to cover all a child's expenses. Be prepared to provide money for extra expenses. However, also be prepared to deny money if the child's allowance runs short for expected, planned expenses and the child has overspent his or her allowance. It is probably not reasonable to assume that the child could pay for his or her own vacation, school expenses, medical needs, food, and so forth. It is important, too, that there be times of family entertainment when the parents are treating.

Give the children opportunities to earn extra money. Children can learn responsibility from working to earn extra money for extra things they want for themselves. It might even be worthwhile to plan an allowance that fairly regularly falls short of covering the purchase of new toys, dates (yes, children nowadays still go on them!), skating, and the sort of entertainment that is important; this provides an opportunity for earning extra money.

Accept the fact that children will use their money foolishly. There is no getting around it. Children are inexperienced. They make mistakes. Sometimes their mistakes are positively foolish. But it is their money!

Provide guidance. This point is the saving one so far as the point just above is concerned. Children do a lot of dumb things. They spend their money in foolish ways. So how are they going to learn? Adults can teach them. For example, a parent can have children compare a product advertised on TV with the real thing in the store. Parents can take children shopping and have them compare prices and select the best buys of specific products in stores. A parent can go through a catalog with children and ask them to choose things they would buy if they had five dollars or twenty-five dollars. Finally, a parent could have a child plan a party, using a budget. The child could be given a budget of ten dollars and be asked to plan a lunch for five friends in which they had to eat, play games, and each receive a present to go home with. In these ways children can move toward understanding money, which is one of the best reasons for providing children with an allowance in the first place.

Suggestions for Reducing Stress in Nontraditional Families

The traditional family is considered to be an intact family with the father working, the mother at home, and children. While this type of family constitutes a minority of living arrangements in the United States, it is still spoken of as the "family." The families considered in this section do not fit this traditional description. These are families in which both parents work or single-parent families. These families face special problems; the suggestions here are meant to help these families ease the special stresses of their living arrangements.

Safety and Well-Being of Children

Since single parents who work and families in which both parents work will probably not be at home much of the time when their children are at home, special precautions need to be taken to insure their protection, safety, and well-being. Some of these are everyday concerns that the child will need to learn in order to help take care of himself or herself.

Teach survival skills. Children of working parents need to learn how to take care of themselves. They need to know how to cook for themselves, sew on buttons, organize their time, know where medical supplies are kept around the house, and a number of other things they will have to do independently. A part of the time spent between parent and child can be used to teach these necessary skills to children of working parents.

Emergencies. Children also need to learn how to identify and handle emergencies. Children who are at home while their parents are at work will need to know some basic skills of first aid. They need to know what to do for cuts and scrapes. They need to know emergency procedures in case of fire. They need to know what to do if they smell gas fumes. They need to know what to do if they come home and discover a burglary. In order to know these things, they must be taught by their parents.

Prepare a list of emergency telephone numbers. Children can be aided in handling emergencies if they know persons and/or places to call for specific emergencies. They need to know the telephone number of their parents' work place. They need to know hospital and physician telephone numbers. They need to know ambulance emergency numbers. They need to know the number of the fire department. They need to know the number of the police department. In some cities all of these agencies can be reached at a single number. In other places, each has a separate number. Consider running drills where children practice "responding" to various types of emergencies.

Finally, children need to know persons they can contact if they can't reach their parents. Such a friend or neighbor should be reasonably available much of the time so that the child does not feel as if there is no one he or she can reach in an emergency.

Suggestions for Children Alone After School

While emergencies do occur, they are not expected as daily routine. There are things that happen every day that require planning for working parents.

Strict agreed-upon rules of conduct. Working parents and their children need to establish agreed-upon routines so that both the parents and the children have as much security in their relationship as possible. Parents need to provide clear information about where they will be and how they can be reached if necessary. Children need to agree to follow a routine in coming home every day and checking in so parents know the children are safe and secure. There need to be established rules about having other children at the house after school and visiting other children after school. There needs to be a clearly understood policy regarding contact with other adults after school.

Check-in. One way to facilitate a feeling of security for both parents and children is to create a check-in procedure for after school. Part of the check-in procedure could be a phone call from the child to the parent(s) right after school. Another important way would be to have an adult in the community, neighborhood, or apartment building whom the child would visit every day after school or who would be willing to drop by the house to check on the child. Some communities have established what are called "block moms," who have been selected or who have volunteered to be available for all the children on the block in case of emergencies.

Structured time. Provide children with a set routine after school each day. Children could be expected to complete a select group of chores every day after school. They might be expected to do their homework, clean up their rooms, read, write letters, watch TV for thirty minutes, and begin preparations for dinner. The point of all of this is not to work the child to exhaustion, but to provide a routine each day that keeps the child occupied until parent arrives at home. One of the problems that the children of working parents face is loneliness. A daily routine can work toward reducing some of the loneliness.

Have snacks available. Before parents leave in the morning, they can prepare snacks for when the children come home in the afternoon. It wouldn't hurt to put a little note in the snack each day to welcome the child home or just to say hello.

Check into after-school programs. It is possible that the school system provides an after-school program for children of working parents. If so, this is a very good way for children to spend their time and to reduce the amount of time they are home alone. Some programs last long enough for parents to pick up their children after the program.

Check into community services. While schools may not provide after-school programs, some communities do. There might be churches that provide this service. It is possible that there is a community recreation center or Y that provides after-school care. It would then be possible to drop by the center to pick up the child and to play a game or two before heading home.

Surrogate parent. One last possibility to check into is that of a permanent afternoon substitute "parent"—perhaps a relative, but not necessarily. This person would provide afternoon care while parents work and could be included in a number of family get-togethers so that he or she is a regular part of the family. Their afternoon care then is not something special that is seen by the child as babysitting, but as a regular routine of family life.

All of these suggestions are aimed at creating a climate of security and protection for both parents and children. Working parents are a reality of life. If precautions like the ones described above are followed, there is no reason to assume any harm will come to children.

Children and the Work Place

For some reason we have not traditionally felt that children and work mix very well. However, it is increasingly common practice for parents to bring their children to work from time to time just so they will know what their parents do. If necessary, influence employers to set up a children's day when many employees bring their children to work.

For single parents, try to work out a flexible schedule so employers recognize that emergencies in the home (accidents, flu) may require you to be able to go home on short notice or miss a day from time to time. Many employers are sensitive to the special problems of single parenthood, since many employers are single parents.

Spending Time Together

Just because parents work does not mean they do not have opportunities to spend time—very often high-quality time—with their children.

Before work. While it is a bit of a hassle, it is possible to get up earlier than usual just to share breakfast together and to talk about the day. Take some time each morning to make plans for time that will be shared that evening or that weekend.

After work. It isn't always necessary to come home, get dinner ready, wash the dishes, clean up, and then have time for the children. Some days, push dinner back and spend time with children before dinner. Take time to play board games, draw and color, throw a football, or talk about school and work together.

Also, make sure children know you are available to talk any time you are home, even if it means putting off some chores or dinner after work. It might even be worthwhile to have a pre-established fifteen or twenty minutes after parents get home specifically designated as talking time.

Weekends. Make every Saturday morning a special breakfast time for the whole family. Parent(s) and kids all pitch in to make breakfast and sit down for a leisurely meal together to talk about what went on that week and what is going to happen that weekend. Spend time together grocery shopping and housecleaning. The weekend is a time to work and play together.

The stresses in some families are more than can be corrected by changing schedules and seeking out neighborhood friends. Their problems are deep-seated and long-lasting. They are the families in which the crisis is of substance abuse, violence, or sexual exploitation. These families cannot be helped by this book or suggestions from friends or relatives. These families require professional help. If you know of such a family or find yourself a member of one, follow the suggestions below to find a professional helper who will know how to begin the process of reducing the crisis.

1. Recognize that the family needs professional help.

2. Ask a friend, relative, physician, or member of the clergy to recommend someone. Word-of-mouth recommendations still seem to constitute the best way to find someone who will be able to help.

3. Who can help? There are many different types of therapists. For example, there are medical doctors called psychiatrists. Less than 25 percent of psychiatrists work with families. Psychologists usually have a doctorate degree (Ph.D., Ed.D., Psy.D., or others). Many hold a license from the state to practice. See if they do. Some people hold master's degrees and might be called counselors or family/ marriage counselors. Others hold degrees in social work. Many members of the clergy are trained counselors. All are qualified to help. Again, the best recommendation is someone who has benefited from a specific person's help.

4. Costs. Because of their level of training or size of their practice, many private therapists are expensive. However, it is possible to get help even if one does not have a great deal of money. Frequently, ministers do not charge for counseling. It is highly likely that there is a community health center in your city and/or county. These centers have highly trained counselors who are salaried and do not charge for therapy. The center charges according to the ability of a person to pay. The scale is reasonable and may not involve any charge at all. The personnel at a community center are as qualified as persons in private practice, and the help available in such centers is generally considered to be excellent.

Notes

1. Robbins, Stacia. "The American Family—How Is It Changing?" *Senior Scholastic.* February 20, 1981, 17. Reprinted by permission of Scholastic Inc. from *Senior Scholastic* Magazine (2/20/82). Copyright © 1982 by Scholastic Inc.

2. *Science News.* 1977. Vol III, pp. 214-215.

3. Ibid.

4. *Intellect.* November, 1977, pp. 177-179.

5. *U.S. News and World Report.* October 27, 1975, pp. 41-43.

6. *U. S. News and World Report.* September 14, 1981, pp. 42-43.

7. Milofsky, David. "What Makes a Good Family?" *Redbook.* August 1981, pp. 58, 60, 62.

3
STRESS
of Divorce

*As a child misses the unsaid goodnight
and falls asleep with heartache.* *

Robert Frost
(1875-1963)

Nine yellow candles glow on the chocolate birthday cake. "Hurry, Melanie! Close your eyes; make a wish," shouted her best friend.

As Melanie slowly inhaled, determined to have enough air to blow out every candle, she thought, "How easy this wish is to make. Please! Oh, please! Make my daddy come home to stay!"

Her friends cheered her heroic ability to extinguish each candle, but deep inside Melanie felt no laughter, no happiness. She knew her wish would never come true. Daddy was gone, and his absence hurt.

There will be more than one million Melanies feeling the pain from divorce this year. In the United States alone, the lives of twelve million children under the age of eighteen are touched by their parents' separation and divorce. The numbers are overwhelming. In any classroom, divorce will touch one of three lives before children leave high school.

More frightening is that the incidence of divorce is increasing. Chil-

*From "The Black Cottage" from *The Poetry of Robert Frost* edited by Edward Connery Lathem. Copyright 1930, 1939, © 1969 by Holt, Rinehart and Winston. Copyright © 1958 by Robert Frost. Copyright © 1967 by Lesley Frost Ballantine. Reprinted by permission of Holt Rinehart and Winston, Publishers and Jonathan Cape Limited.

61

dren, the quiet victims of divorce, are at risk in our society. Their sense of security is threatened, if not destroyed. The experience of divorce is only slightly less traumatic than the death of a parent. For most children, divorce hits without any warning. Children are powerless and vulnerable, feeling aftershocks months and years later. In a recent study, it was found that five years after their parents' divorce, 25 percent of the children studied were still unable to adjust and appeared depressed, lonely, and angry. Thirty percent of the children still felt the divorce had been a mistake (Wallerstein and Kelly 1980).

While the divorce experience is detrimental to children of all ages, elementary-school-age children are especially vulnerable. The primary responsibility for children of school age is to enrich their intellectual capabilities and to test their identity in social situations with their peers. Divorce changes that focus. Energies that should be directed toward school and establishing healthy peer relationships are redirected back to the home as worry and fear. Too many children suffer socially, academically, and emotionally from the psychologically crippling experience of divorce.

Divorcing Process

Divorce is not a single event. Parents and children are forced to live through a series of stages requiring major and continuing adjustments in their lives. The parent-child relationship is no longer secure and familiar. Radical changes are likely to take place at any time along the way. Even when parents separate and the arguing stops, children continue to describe divorce as painful. It is especially traumatic to those children who believed their homes were happy and secure.

The divorce process begins months and often years before adults seek a legal separation (Rubin and Price 1979). Some psychologists describe this as the period of emotional divorce. During this time adults, for the most part, stop communicating effectively with each other. As time passes the emotional distance widens, anger builds, and a once-happy marriage is in serious trouble. Too often when adults shut each other out of their lives, the children are shut out as well. A typical scene sees Dad come home from work, talk to no one through dinner, and leave the table to hide in the den behind a newspaper and in front of the TV. Dad may be home physically, but he no longer provides a nurturing role for his children. From the child's point of view, the parents are emotionally absent. They are, in fact, nonparents when it comes to providing emotional support, sharing together, and nurturance.

In some cases, when parents stop talking to each other, they turn to their children for emotional support. This may bring parent and child closer together and improve their relationship. Unfortunately, these children can be among the most seriously affected by divorce, especially if the warm, loving parent is taken away.

Many adults, finding themselves alone for the first time in years, are frightened and begin to depend on their children. These children may grow up too quickly and may assume the responsibility of the absent parent or may become Mom or Dad's confidant. These adultlike role assumptions place an enormous burden on the child (Leo 1982). Instead of the parent supporting the child, the process is reversed. If parents turn to their children when trouble begins, by the time the divorce decree is granted these children are not only overburdened with their own problems, but with many of the parents' problems as well.

The beginning of the divorce process is a crisis period filled with marital tension. Children, no matter how old they are, are not protected from this tension. Parents tend to involve their children in their arguments. They become pawns in the parents' blaming and/or hurting.

In a recent study of children whose parents divorced, 25 percent said they had witnessed their parents physically abusing one another frequently. Another 25 percent said they had seen at least one physically abusive act between their parents (Wallerstein and Kelly 1980). This exposure to physical violence was terrifying to many of those children. They felt completely powerless and were scared for their own safety as well as the safety of the people they deeply loved.

Inappropriately, parents going through divorce often blame their children for their problems. Because it is hard to accept responsibility for failure and problems, some children become "safe" scapegoats and find themselves dragged into their parents' problems. Some parents desperately need an audience to fight, so the only time they argue is when the child is present. Some children take advantage of parents fighting and play one parent against the other. This results in an escalation of the conflict. For some children, seeing their parents together fighting is better than seeing them apart. If they're together, maybe they will remain together. The temperamental child may evoke more anger and become the focus of parent hostilities. The only child is more susceptible to stress and receives the brunt of parental hostilities.

Children can be used as weapons during this initial stage of divorce. Some parents, suffering in their own personal grief and agony, desperately need an ally. They enlist the help of their children to gang up on the other parent. Probably one of the most destructive acts a parent can commit is to demand that the child choose sides. Children need to retain a good relationship with both parents, but that becomes impossible when they are forced to affirm their love and loyalty to one parent and not the other.

One of the authors had an experience with a fourth grade boy whose mother was forcing him to show his love for her by denouncing his father. Mother made him remove every picture of his dad from the walls of his room. The boy could no longer keep his baseball trophy in his room (Dad was his Little League coach). The boy talked of keeping his baseball cap inside his pillowcase and crying in his pillow every night because he missed his dad. The more demanding his mother became, the more upset he grew. He loved them both, and he wished his mother could accept that.

Not all children of divorce are exposed to physical violence or the torment of having to choose sides, but the stress they experience may be just as real. Some adults attempt to protect their children by remaining quiet and not discussing their marital problems with their children. Many reasons are given for such protective silence. Too many end up hurting the children. For example:

If I tell my children about my divorce, it will be harmful to them. First of all, the exact opposite of that belief is true. By not talking about the divorce, the child may feel more stress because the unknown is more stressful than the known. Children are very perceptive; they intuitively know when there is something wrong in the family. They see Mom in tears and hear arguments late at night. They notice Dad's frequent absence from the dinner table.

The following play was written by a third grade boy who, fortunately, was in a children's discussion group on separation and divorce. It provides an inside view of a child's knowledge of the emotions of divorce.

Divorce Play[1]

Narrator:	It took place in the kitchen when Mom dropped the eggs.
Mother:	I didn't mean to drop them.
Father:	Well, you did, didn't you?
Kids:	Stop fighting!

Father: Go in the other room, damn it! As I was saying, that is the second time you ruined them.

Mother: Then make them yourself.

Father: I might just do that.

(Curtain)

Narrator: It took place in the living room when Dad was watching TV and Mom wanted to watch something else.

Father: Who do you think you are, coming in here whenever your programs are on and changing the channel?

Mother: Well, it's my TV also, so get that straight.

Father: I know it's your TV also, but you always do this, whenever I'm watching TV. But this time I'm not going to let you, so get that straight!

Mother: I don't have that straight and who are you to tell me what to do? For all I care, you could leave.

Father: I might just do that.

(Curtain)

Narrator: The next day, they all wake up. But where in the world is Dad?

Kids: Where's Daddy? Maybe he's playing hide and seek.

Mother: Where the hell is he?

Kids: Mommy, don't curse.

Mother: Be quiet.

(Curtain)

Narrator: Two hours later, the phone rang.

Mother: Hello. So it's you. By the way, where the hell are you?

Father: I don't want to talk about it. All I have to say is for you to meet me at the Holiday Inn at 8 P.M.

Mother: You kids go play a game.

(Curtain)

Narrator: The next day they decided to tell the kids that they're getting a divorce.

Mother: Do you kids know what a divorce is?

Kids: No.

Mother: Well, I'm going to tell you. A divorce is when two people stop loving each other any more, but that doesn't mean they can't be friends.

(Curtain)

Narrator:	The next day Mother and Father met with their lawyers.
Mother's lawyer:	So you're getting a divorce? I never thought that it was going to happen between you two, and plus I knew you two for such a long time.
Mother:	We both understand that, but it just didn't work out.
Father's lawyer:	Do you know it's going to take a pretty long time before you really get to court?
Father:	I understand that, but it has to be done.
Father's lawyer:	We will try as fast as we can.

(Curtain)

Narrator:	One week later it was Tommy's birthday.
Tommy:	I'm sad.
Jane:	Why?
Tommy:	Because neither Daddy or Mommy will be here for my birthday.
Jane:	Don't worry, I'll find a way to get them both here.

(Curtain)

Narrator:	The next day it was his birthday and both his parents came.
Mother:	Here's your present. Happy birthday.
Father:	Happy birthday, Tommy.
Tommy (to Jane):	Mommy and Daddy might not get a divorce, because they look like they're becoming friends.
Jane:	Don't be silly.

(Curtain)

Narrator:	Eight months later they went to court.
Judge:	Hand me the papers.
Mother's lawyer:	Yes, Your Honor.
Judge:	As I understand it, your last name is Johnson. And have you decided who the kids are going to live with?
Father:	Yes, Your Honor. The kids will live with their mother.
Judge:	And have you decided on an alimony?
Father:	Yes, Your Honor, we have.
Judge:	And what is it?
Father:	Two hundred dollars every two weeks.

Judge: Do you object, Mrs. Johnson?
Mother: No, Your Honor.
Judge: I pronounce you divorced.

It's obvious that children are perceptive on many levels regarding the emotional climate of their families. The play indicates that the children feared being left alone and not cared for. These fears begin early and can become twisted and exacerbated by the parents believing that they are protecting their children with silence.

Divorce can't be discussed without blaming one parent or the other. Parents sometimes feel that if they tell their children about the impending divorce, the kids will blame one parent over the other.

Certainly that potential exists, but *how* the parents tell their children becomes the critical factor.

Parents shouldn't criticize each other in front of the children. This belief may have some positive aspects. The key is moderation. Certainly undue criticism is degrading, hostile, and tension producing. Since the child is a part of both Mom and Dad, something of the child is being destroyed by the constant degrading of one parent by the other.

Parents aren't perfect, and there is no need to pretend there aren't problems in the family. Frank and open discussion with the children will not be harmful. However, personal attacks meant to hurt will.

Parents can't break down and cry in front of children. This attitude denies the opportunity for both adults and children to express their fears. When the parent doesn't cry, the children lose the opportunity of seeing a role model that says feelings are natural. Fears are expected. Divorce hurts and it's okay to show it. At a time when a child needs to release emotions, receiving a message that says "Suppress those feelings" is dangerous.

Children begin the divorce process at a disadvantage. Parents who are frightened, confused, and in need of taking care of their own emotions find telling their children very difficult (Wallerstein 1980). When a group of divorced parents were asked how they told their children about divorce, most replied that they couldn't remember. Thinking back to that emotional period of their lives was confusing—a blur. Children need support right from the beginning, but rarely get it. For many, the problems multiply from not being told early enough. It seems clear that the manner in which children are told about their parents' divorce has an impact on how successful the divorce process will be for children.

Children's Initial Reactions to Being Told About Divorce

Most children sense changes in family relationships to a greater or lesser degree. They may feel their family has some problems, but they know all families have their ups and downs. Their home and parents represent their security, familiarity, the place to which they can always return. Home is a place of security. It has always been and always will be.

Then one day, without warning, a bomb explodes, shattering that stable security. For more than 80 percent of all children, divorce comes as a shock (Francke et al. 1980). No one has prepared them. Yesterday they were a family; today they're scared, uncertain, angry, sad, and missing a parent.

While it is not clear why some children respond to divorce more positively than others, early evidence indicates several factors influence that reaction. They include:

1. The manner in which the parents relate to each other.
2. The way they tell the children about divorce.
3. The child's developmental stage and age.
4. The child's personality and past experiences.
5. To some degree, the sex of the child.

All of these factors can play a part in how each child responds to divorce. While it is apparent that some children are only mildly affected by divorce, there is no way of predicting how an individual child will respond. Therefore, with the prognosis uncertain and the realization that divorce places children under emotional stress, it is imperative that adults use every means available to protect and insure the emotional well-being of children during this period of crisis.

There is an assumption in our society that suggests divorce is the "magic" key to happiness. One need only look at magazine racks in grocery stores to find titles such as *Creative Divorce* and *Divorce: Gateway to Self-Realization*. Adults are led to believe that ending a bad marriage is the first step to fulfilling every dream. Unfortunately, these books do little to prepare one for the emotional shock of divorce. Divorce is cruel. It hurts. It hurts everyone involved. One psychologist calls it "drastic surgery." No matter how "right" divorce may be for adults, when children are involved, the complications intensify. Children, who have little to say in the decision, often suffer the most.

The authors are not advocating "Stay together for the sake of the children." If anything, recent studies have shown that tension, hostility, and physical abuse in poor marriages can be just as harmful as divorce (Rubin and Price 1979). Neither the unhappy marriage nor a subsequent divorce are psychologically beneficial to children. Therefore, adults with children have the responsibility to use every means available to work through the problems in marriage. If, and only if, every opportunity to resolve conflict has been exhausted is divorce a viable option. Once that decision has been reached, then, "for the sake of the children," parents must focus their attention on the needs of their children.

Unfortunately, adults feeling lost, angry, and confused are barely able to keep their own emotional world together. As seen in such popular movies as *Kramer versus Kramer* and *Shoot the Moon*, children are not always the adults' primary concern. It is a well-documented fact that divorced or divorcing adults experience more health and emotional problems than married couples (Hetherington 1979). While dealing with their own emotional turmoil, many adults have little energy or thought to give to their children. What all this means is that often children face divorce alone and with little support from adults. If ever there is a time when children need support and understanding, it is during the crisis of divorce. Tragically, when Mom and Dad are needed most, they just aren't there. Children are frightened, lonely, and without support. The familiar ones they have grown to depend upon are slipping away.

Children of divorce are losers. They lose the availability and presence of one parent—most often Dad. Since divorce almost always creates a loss of income, Mom is forced to work outside the home. Thus, Mom is lost in the sense that she must work and be a single parent. In some families, siblings are split between parents. Aunts, uncles, grandparents, and friends may all leave. Because Mom can no longer afford the family home, it's sold. With the loss of the home, there is an accompanying move to a new address, causing loss of neighborhood, school, and friends. Time spent with parents is less frequent; and with one parent assuming the role of two, there is a loss in the amount of attention the parent can provide.

A happy, psychologically healthy, well-adjusted child most likely has a better chance of coming through the divorce process intact. It appears that difficult children, the temperamental ones, have a difficult time adjusting to change. This type of child seems to be an easy target for marital scapegoating. These children seem to exacerbate arguments and, in turn, are drawn into family hostilities. Thus, they become the focus for blame and therefore experience more stress.

Boys, it seems, also carry an added vulnerability to divorce (Lamb 1977; Hetherington 1979). There may be a number of reasons for this. First, boys react to losing a father as a role model more seriously than do girls. They no longer have a male to identify with; they feel abandoned. Boys are also more likely to be witnesses to more physical violence by their parents. "Boys are tough and can handle violence." This myth is both erroneous and detrimental to a boy's healthy emotional development. Also, boys are viewed more negatively by their mothers, teachers, and peers during and after divorce (Francke et al. 1980). Therefore, they have no safe adults to reach out to for nurturance and support. What this means is boys are more susceptible to greater stress than girls because they're exposed to more aggression and have fewer support systems available to them. There's a greater tendency in boys to describe their homes as unhappy. They act out in school and at home, disrupt routines, can't relate with friends very well, and show higher rates of behavioral disorders. Further, boys are more likely to act out their anger than girls, so they are more characterized as behavioral problems.

Children's reactions to divorce differ according to age (Rorlich et al. 1977). There are general emotional responses that most children display. Parents need to understand that their children are trying to cope with this new unsettling change in the best way they know how. The following responses are similar for many children.[2]

Denial

It's sometimes easier to ignore an event than to face the pain evoked by that event. Many children tell their parents, "Be quiet. Don't talk about it." This is a natural reaction. Children feel if it's not talked about, it will never happen. Verbalizing the pain and future uncertainty is just too painful.

Other children may respond quite casually, as seen by this short scenario.

Dad: I want you to understand, Son, why Daddy is moving out of the house.

Mother: This is a sad time, Jeff. Mommy and Daddy are getting a divorce.

Jeff: Okay. Can I have some money to go to the Dairy Queen?"

Parents in the midst of their own hurt and confusion may find this reaction hard to take. They may, mistakenly, believe their child doesn't love them or doesn't care what happens to his parents or, worse, is taking the news so well that no special precautions need to be taken. What children like Jeff are doing is covering up the anguish they feel by treating the divorce as something ordinary—not emotionally charged with pain.

A third way a child may use denial is by forgetting things. Susie, an eight-year-old, had always been conscientious. She enjoyed keeping her room organized, making her bed, arranging her clothes for school, and so forth. After her parents told her of their divorce, Susie began to forget things. Her shoes would be missing in the morning. She'd leave her lunch on the bus. She started to forget what assignments were due in school. Naturally, forgetting homework created more problems for her. It seemed her parents and her teacher were always angry with her. All Susie was doing by this sudden, but temporary, forgetfulness was attempting to focus on other parts of her life. By daydreaming, she could keep her mind away from facing the cruel reality of divorce.

Another denial behavior is to show a sense of relief. One child told his parents he thought a divorce was great; now Dad could have his own crash pad and he could throw newspapers everywhere and it would be fun to play with him. Adults may assume their child is insensitive, but in actuality, he's avoiding the pain of separation. He's not yet ready to face the reality of losing one parent.

Regressive Behavior

While preschool children may show more evidence of losing skills they had previously learned, all children may revert to a younger form of behavior. One of the authors had a third grade student begin "baby talk" when speaking in front of the class. Her parents had recently separated and she was coping by returning to a previous period of her world that was safe and secure. Another physical condition, enuresis (bed-wetting) is quite common among children of divorce. It is found twice as often than in intact families (Magrab 1978). Punishing this behavior is not helpful, but talking and having the child take care of his or her bedding and clothing are an act of responsibility that can begin the process of allowing the child to regain control of his or her bladder at night.

Guilt

One of the most common beliefs children have about their parents' divorce is that they somehow, some way, caused the breakup.

Kimberly was not too pleased over sharing her time, toys, and bedroom with her younger sister. Her younger sister was "a pain" (as most younger siblings are to big brothers and sisters). Her father scolded her concerning her selfishness and lack of cooperation after some ugly, sisterly fight.

When her parents informed her they were divorcing, she knew that it was all her fault. If only she had been nicer to her little sister, Daddy wouldn't be leaving.

Sometimes a child who feels responsible tries to be as good a son or daughter as possible. They believe their bad behavior caused the divorce, so if they're super good, they can reverse the decision. To parents this type of thinking sounds unreasonable, but to a child it is quite logical.

When guilt is allowed to grow, some children become depressed. They may withdraw from others for a while. They might stop playing with friends, preferring to stay alone in their rooms. Or they may stop eating and have little physical energy. All of these symptoms may be responses to guilt.

Anger

Anger may be one of the more difficult reactions for parents to tolerate. A once complacent, easygoing child overnight becomes the neighborhood bully. Doors are slammed, toys are broken, and parents often respond in kind, creating more family tension. These children are frustrated, saying, "Why me?" They want to hurt back, retaliate. They feel powerless to change what is happening to them, so they feel a need to strike back. This anger is directed at the parent the child perceives as causing the divorce. It becomes easier to blame and try to hurt the one responsible for causing so much grief. Angry children act out in school as well as at home. Parents need to be aware these aren't bad kids. They're children who have been hurt and are coping by expressing deep resentment over their unsettling circumstances.

Reconciliation Obsessions

Hardly a child of divorce doesn't entertain the thought of his or her parents reuniting. Some children never give up the wish for a magical "someday" waiting in the future when they will all be a family again. Children desperately plan ways to keep their parents together. They attempt to bargain. "If you and Daddy start together I promise I'll do all my homework, get all A's on my report card, and do all the dishes without being asked" or "If you don't have to stay together then I don't have to spend the summer at Uncle Lestor's."

When one of the authors was teaching school, a fifth grader asked to use the office phone. He called both his parents at their places of employment, leaving a message saying there was an emergency at school and they should come immediately. The parents arrived, only to find their child smiling and happy. When the child was asked what this was about, the response was, "I missed seeing you together. If you got together again you'd feel good like me and never leave each other."

For some children the desire truly is an obsession, and they will stop at nothing to bring about their wish. All too often, that wish is dashed when one of the parents remarries. This in turn brings about another form of stress—the end of the family dream.

Panic

The security of home and parents' love is taken for granted. Then, suddenly, those safe, familiar parts of a child's world are gone. The child experiences fear.

"If Mom can stop loving Dad, then maybe she will stop loving me." "Who will take care of me now that Dad won't live with us? He works to make the money for food, but now he's not here. How will I eat?"

No matter how unfounded or ridiculous these fears may seem to adults, they are real to children. They have worries and often no way to alleviate those worries.

Since age plays an important part in how a child responds, the following characteristics may reveal the differences between a first-grade child and junior-high youngster. These are general categories with over-lapping feelings and behaviors.

AGE THREE TO FIVE These children may regress in their behavior more than other children. They may begin to wet their beds, have problems eating, and be unable to sleep through the night. These children are dependent upon their parents' care. When they perceive that their security is leaving, they can feel threatened. One four-year-old took a green marking pen and wrote his name on his bedroom walls and furniture. He was frightened he would lose his possessions, just like he "lost" his dad.

Often these young children feel detached and lost. They're sad and angry and feel responsible for causing their parents' separation.

AGE FIVE TO SIX When a child enters school, there is pressure to conform to new social ways of behavior. Demands are made by teachers to perform intellectually. Peers have expectations to adopt new social norms. The child's most important focus is no longer the home, but the school. When divorce happens, the child's energy is split. For some children, school is all but forgotten as they place their attention and worry on Mom and Dad and home.

These youngsters are better able to understand why their family is changing. They may try to repair the split and wish it wasn't happening. This age child is usually able to express sadness over missing the absent parent, and this sadness doesn't leave when the child goes out to play with friends. These children are unable to successfully relieve their suffering. They also feel torn between their parents, and these divided loyalties cause them stress.

AGE SEVEN TO EIGHT The largest number of children affected by divorce falls into this age group. These children usually exhibit a pervasive sadness. They are completely aware of their pain, but lack the experience and coping skills to express their sadness. Finding relief from their emotions is hard.

Many of these children want their parents to remain together no matter how much they argue and fight. They hope for their family to be united at any price. Twenty-five percent of this age group felt that they had to choose sides between one parent and the other (Wallerstein and Kelly 1980).

Because of the importance of school and social pressures, these children are sensitive to the feelings and attitudes of their peers. Sometimes students can be cruel to one another. A second-grade class was having a tea for mothers. Erica's mother had left the family months ago, so she invited her dad for teatime. Since he was the only father at this social gathering, Erica's friends began to tease her about a "mother with a beard." The pain and embarrassment can be overwhelming for some children. Erica's school performance began a downward spiral that lasted for many weeks following that event.

AGE NINE TO TEN As children mature, they have a better understanding of time and reality. They have adequate skills to overcome their anger. These children feel a sense of shame about divorce (girls appear to be more sensitive to this than boys). To hide their embarrassment, many get involved with school activities to avoid the reality of divorce.

These children are torn, feeling they have to relate to one parent. If that need is strong, they usually ally with the custodial parent. Since intense anger is also characteristic of this age, it is usually directed at the parent perceived as having caused the divorce. They believe they just can't have a good relationship with both parents.

Often these children are depressed and lonely. Their schoolwork declines. They can't relate to their friends; they feel isolated. Friends are little comfort. Those students who do have friendships are children whose families are not as torn and broken by the divorce process.

ADOLESCENCE At this age, youngsters are in a process of seeking their independence from their families. Sometimes, when divorce comes at this age, it hurries this process. These children still feel lonely, angry, and a sense of loss, but they often cope by getting involved with school activities and staying away from their troubled home. They are better able to sort out responsibility and not choose sides and place blame. They can make separate decisions about their parents, for they view them as individual people rather than as the single unit, Parents.

The danger of divorce for this group is that it may force a young person to accept adult responsibility before he or she is ready.

Custody

Divorce hurts all children in some fashion, but those children involved in a custody battle are injured most of all. Custody is decided by the parents in 90 percent of divorce cases. But for the remaining group, custody determination becomes an area of stress for children. Just as the terminology of "custody battle" and "custody fight" implies, there is a winner and a loser. The winner takes possession of a child or children. This battle is often cruel, degrading, and vicious, for at the heart of its outcome is the adult's status of parenthood. In our society it's not fashionable to have your children taken away from you by the courts. There's always a suspicion surrounding your loss, suggesting that there was something wrong with you for not being awarded your child.

No matter how much a parent's ego is identified with winning or losing a custody fight, the children are the ones who suffer the most. They are trapped in the middle; and the longer the legal battle continues, the more anxiety children must face.

From the personal experience of one of the authors, the court system can drag on and on, focusing emotions to the point that people become bruised and scarred permanently. Because of a crowded court calendar, there was a nine-month waiting period before a custody hearing was to be held. An eight-year-old daughter in the temporary care of her mother was ambivalent about which parent she wanted to live with. As the months passed and bitterness grew between the parents, the child felt more compelled to align loyalties with her mother. As she watched her mother grow more depressed, she felt she had to remain with her to provide support. This child's belief—that her mother would die without her presence—continued to grow stronger until she couldn't see any other alternative. No longer did she have positive feelings about living with her father. She grew more and more frightened that she would be taken away from her mother. When the hearing finally took place, this child was hysterical. Although she expressed her only wish, that being to remain with her mother, the court awarded custody to the father. This child was devastated. For many months, living in her father's home, she had recurring nightmares and would awake screaming. She still believed her mother would die without her.

While this story may seem extreme, the anguish children experience when their parents go to court is enormous. The mere thought of choosing one parent over another is stress producing (Hetherington 1979). Children want to love both parents and be loved by each in return. The fear is that if they are forced to pick sides, the parent they didn't choose will be hurt, angry, or both, and will ultimately reject them.

There is a real danger parents face by placing the decision of custody in the hands of our court system. Often, judges are not in a good position to determine custody. They listen to a half day of testimony, during which each side tries to make the other side appear unfit. The result is that the judge bases his or her decision on small pieces of evidence, which often means that the child's best interest is not represented. Also, the circumstances at the time this decision is made, may change three to five years in the future (Henning and Oldham 1977). What may appear to be a workable, successful decision at the time of divorce may be completely inappropriate in the future.

Another stressful decision at the time of divorce is how much child support a noncustodial father is to pay. It is a fact that the family's standard of living decreases in a divorce. More often than not, there is not an adequate amount of money to provide the standard of living the family had become accustomed to. Major items such as dental care, new school clothes, or extras like money for camp are usually not included in child support. Often, the custodial parent (usually the mother) may use money issues as a weapon against the former spouse. If the father doesn't make child support payments, then the mother takes the attitude that Dad won't be allowed to visit his children. The reverse is also true. A father may withhold money to negotiate some special interest he may have. This practice seems prevalent. One study showed that only 47 percent of the time are child support payments made on a regular, timely schedule (Everly 1977). Once again, it's the child who ultimately suffers. Support payments mean little to children. All they can really see is that they're denied the opportunity to be with a parent whom they love, or that there is not enough money to go out to McDonald's or to buy that baseball mitt or pair of skates. Sometimes this power play between the adults works. Even though the custodial parent can file contempt charges in court, demanding payment, the process may take several months. Those weeks and months without money are painful. Some parents grow weary of the battle and avoid court. They give in, meeting the demands of the former spouse.

Joint Custody

There are both advantages and disadvantages to any custody arrangement. Any time a child is shuffled between two homes, two neighborhoods, two schools, and so forth there is bound to be some initial stress on parents and children. Separate homes are a financial burden. Seven-year-old Nancy was crying, sitting on the front steps of her school. When her teacher asked her to explain why she was crying, all Nancy could say was, "I don't know which one." Her parents had decided to share Nancy equally. They would pick her up from school on alternate days. This constant shifting and disruption of routine was obviously detrimental to her sense of security.

With values changing, there is a growing trend to share the legal responsibilities of raising children. Adults may be dissolving their marital relationship, but they still view themselves as parents. They want to continue their legal and moral roles as caretakers of their children. The assumption that men are not nurturing has been challenged and proven wrong. More women are pursuing careers and are not staying at home to be the primary care givers. Joint custody is an option that allows both parents to feel that they haven't lost their child; the children are fortunate to have the love, support, and guidance of both parents. When parents share child rearing it takes pressure off both adults and children.

Some argue that children in joint custody remain unsettled and that there is less consistency in a joint custody arrangement. Yet it would appear that if the adults are psychologically healthy enough to cooperate with each other over this type of arrangement, the children are the ultimate benefactors. It is important to remember that the success of any custody arrangement is directly related to how successfully the parents interact with each other. If they're willing to put their children's needs foremost, the arrangement can be successful.

Child Snatching

As unlikely as the figure sounds, over 25,000 children are kidnapped or hidden from their custodial parents each year (Francke et al. 1980). Perhaps our judicial system, in reflecting the value that "mother cares best," is at the root of child snatching: less than 1 percent of the children of divorce live with their fathers. Sometimes judges make inappropriate decisions by awarding mothers custody, and many men find that decision intolerable. The result of that frustration is the kidnapping of one's own child.

Parents who steal their children are constantly on the run. They don't enroll their children in school because they're never in town for any lengthy period of time. Most of these children, if not found within six months, may never be found for years.

Currently, stealing your child is a federal offense. On the state level, thirty-nine states have adopted the Uniform Child Custody Jurisdiction

Act, which essentially honors and enforces custody and visitation decisions made in another state. The remaining eleven states may have become a safe ground for kidnappers. There is debate as to whether child snatching should be considered a criminal act. Some fear that if child snatching is made a criminal offense, it may initiate a potentially more violent situation. Thus, children could be exposed to various forms of physical danger. It's frightening to imagine a police roadblock, with guns aimed at a battered station wagon hobbling down a country road. How tragic if any child should be injured or, worse yet, killed because of this offense.

It is hoped that parents won't continue to resort to such desperate acts to maintain their parental status. Clearly, steps need to be taken to protect the thousands of children who are taken from their homes every year.

Visitation

In every divorce involving children, whether custody is contested or not, a judge will always provide visitation for the noncustodial parent. The exception would be for extreme cases where the child would be harmed by such visitation. The oft-used term "reasonable visitation" is broad and allows for a wide variety of visiting patterns. There is no way to determine the visiting pattern of the noncustodial parent. Despite beliefs to the contrary, the love a parent feels toward children is not an indicator for determining how often the parent will visit. Some genuinely close, loving parent-child relationships before divorce produce erratic visitation patterns after divorce. On the other hand, some parents who are seemingly emotionally detached from their children before divorce respond with frequent visits after.

For the sake of clarity in the following discussion on visitation, the authors will refer to the father as the noncustodial parent, since most children of divorce live with their mothers.

The Custodial Parent

Although many women welcomed their former spouse's visits with their children, more than 60 percent of them were stressed by the visitation the year following divorce (Wallerstein and Kelly 1980). In another study, 20 percent of the women felt the visits were useless and directly attempted to sabotage them. When the mothers were encouraging, visitation was usually a positive experience. Surprisingly, fathers were not dissuaded from visiting merely because the custodial mother was unsupportive. Often, the more a mother would object, the more frequent the visitation became. While visitation itself may create a stressful event in the lives of parents and their children, mothers' attitudes had little affect on the frequency of visitation.

Noncustodial Parent (Father)

Most fathers become less available to their children after a divorce. The noncustodial parent awakens one day feeling both relief for being free from the daily responsibility of child rearing and sadness because he misses his children. He finds himself in a new role without clear boundaries for behavior or emotions (Wallerstein and Kelly 1980).

One father described his new role as that of a camp director ("Uncle Disneyland") planning one activity after another. These fathers are often frustrated. They aren't sure about what to do or where they should go with their children. Without Mom around to interpret the children's desires, Dad and children must find ways to communicate with each other.

When children of varying ages visit in groups, the noncustodial parent experiences maximum frustration. The chess game that would satisfy his eleven-year-old becomes the sandbox toy for his four-year-old. Since younger children with shorter attention spans and short-term activities require movement, variety, and short-term activities, all too often older children grow bored and restless. One father described a Sunday afternoon as the most chaotic six hours of life. He attempted to meet the needs of three children ages four, seven, and eleven. He failed miserably. They all left angry, unhappy, and complaining that they didn't wish to return for some time. The father felt impotent.

Noncustodial parents always feel the pressure of time. There's a pickup time, return time, and all the time in between. Visiting with each sibling individually cuts down on the circus of activities, but it also has the potential of evoking envy, jealousy, and a feeling of being cheated in the siblings left at home.

Two of the most influential emotions noncustodial fathers feel that affect their visitation are depression and guilt. Many men react with pain to seeing their children. The more they see their children, the more their depression grows. Being with them is a constant reminder of the failed marriage and how much they have lost. Since many men felt rejected by their spouses, they fear their children will reject them as well. Therefore, to avoid this pain, they begin to visit less often. Some stop visitation completely.

When father and child relationships are good previous to the divorce, many fathers feel guilty for leaving. Other men feel guilty for leaving their children in the care of a mother who is less stable or psychologically unfit to parent. This pervasive sense of guilt also leads to a decline in visitation. The behavior begins to reinforce more guilt, until visitations all but cease. It's understandable that fathers may not want to spend all of Christmas or summer vacation with their children. Rather than express that concern, it becomes easier to avoid the fears of rejection and not visit at all.

Children are the losers in this situation. They cannot comprehend the psychological reasons why Dad doesn't come around anymore. All they know is that he doesn't come very often, which is interpreted as a lack of care. These scars of rejection can lower self-esteem and stay with children for many years.

The visiting arrangements rarely please most children. The every-other-weekend routine is not satisfying because most children want to see their fathers more often. The younger the child, the greater the tendency for fathers to visit. The reason may be one of reinforcement. Fathers tend to visit more when children verbally express their enjoyment over being with them. Younger children are quite verbal, which may explain why parents see more of children between the ages of two and eight years.

Older children who are more challenging also express their feelings openly. As a group, nine- and ten-year-olds express their dissatisfaction loudest. This reinforces some avoidance behavior, which further increases the children's anger. Over 50 percent of the children in this age group experience erratic visitations by their fathers; 25 percent see their fathers less than once a month. These children are especially stressed. They are always uncertain about visiting arrangements.

Boys appear to suffer more from erratic visitation patterns than daughters because fathers tend to visit their sons either much more or much less than their daughters. Father-daughter relationships remain more stable because of a more consistent visitation pattern.

Children continue to be exposed to stress and anger when their parents interact at each visitation period. They also encounter stress, depending upon how each parent responds to visitation. One little boy told his friend he could always tell the day Daddy was coming to visit. His mom would go around the house banging things, slamming doors, and shouting "bad words" to herself.

Certainly not all visitations provoke such anxious behavior, but children are once again victims of divorce, encountering unneeded and unwanted stress in their lives because they wish to be with parents whom they love.

School

If children are feeling the pressures and conflicts accompanying their parents' divorce, school is one obvious place where stress will exhibit itself. Some educators believe that the school environment can direct attention away from painful thoughts and fears. While this may have some merit, not all children will function successfully in school when their personal world is crumbling around them.

Children are not about to broadcast to the world (or their teachers) that Mom and Dad are not living together any more. In the Wallerstein (1980) study, 50 percent of the children's teachers had no awareness of divorce in their students' families. Obviously, parents aren't telling and neither are the kids. Thus, teachers need to be sensitive to changes that children experience as a result of divorce. It is important to understand that not all children of divorce react negatively in school, so teachers need not expect problems from all divorced children. Remember, some kids sail through divorce with little psychological scarring. They aren't in the majority, unfortunately, but they are there. Many children can't cope with the intense emotional trauma at home. They are often agitated, tense, and hurting when they leave for school. It's not surprising to find students responding in the following manner inside the classroom[3]:

FORGETFULNESS A student could be daydreaming, trying to focus on pleasant experiences. The child may forget to finish some activity or may appear to have forgotten the rules to a game.

RESTLESSNESS Not being able to remain seated or interrupting the teacher may be signs of stress in a child who previously did not behave in such a manner.

EXCESSIVE TIREDNESS A child putting his or her head on a desk or requesting to stay inside and rest instead of playing with the other students at recess may indicate that he or she is emotionally torn and not sleeping at night.

MOODINESS Drastic changes in a child's emotions; for example, a student could be reading a story to the class and begin to cry without any apparent reasons.

WITHDRAWAL Fearing embarrassment and ridicule from teachers and peers, some students clam up, refusing to say anything to anyone. This child may refuse to be involved with classroom activities.

POOR ACADEMIC ACHIEVEMENT With the child's energies focused on problems at home, homework and completing assignments are no longer terribly important. Too many stresses at home—such as continual parental hostility, being left alone after school, or shuttling between two house-holds—can prevent children from concentrating on academic tasks.

ACTING OUT, DISRUPTIVE BEHAVIOR Sudden outbursts by a previously complacent student may be a warning sign that there is tension building at home.

PHYSICAL SYMPTOMS Headaches and stomachaches are not uncommon symptoms of children under stress. If there's no apparent organic reason for the physical ailment, more than likely it is psychologically caused.

NO REACTION Some children handle stress better than others. They maintain their daily routines and relationships without giving anyone a clue that anything out of the ordinary is happening in their world. You can't always tell how children are feeling inside by their outward behavior. Children who remain calm may be hurting deeply inside but are unable to express that hurt.

Remarriage/Stepfamilies

Although divorce is on the increase in this country, so is remarriage. Over 80 percent of all divorced adults remarry within three years of their divorce. Millions of children who hardly have enough time to grieve the loss of one parent and adjust to the changes of living in a single-parent home are once again thrown into another dangerously explosive emotional crisis.

How does marriage open the wounds barely healed from divorce? When a parent remarries, the doors are closed for good on the possibility of reuniting the previous family. One of the authors' stepdaughters said, "I always thought Mom and Dad would get back together, even the day before your wedding. On your wedding day, I was happy for you but sad for me. I'd never see my wish come true."

The feelings of loss are stirred again. Children begin to wonder, "Where do I belong in this new family? How do I fit in? What will happen to me now?" It wasn't that long ago they experienced the loss of one parent. Now there is this stranger, an intruder who is taking up all Mom's time. Thus, this fear is based on the belief that the custodial parent will be taken away as well. One child expressed a fear of loss this way:

"They don't want me around. I can tell they want to be alone together and I'm just in their way. So I go outside, but there's nothing to do. Having a new parent isn't such a neat thing."

Having to share a parent's love and attention can create jealousy, competition, and anger. Sometimes children feel shut out, which brings about more pain.

Children also begin to worry in a remarriage situation. They begin to feel conflicting loyalties between the stepparent and biological parent. If they allow themselves to love their new stepparent, does that mean they no longer love Daddy? "If Daddy finds out that I love my new step-father, will he be angry and stop loving me?" This feeling of betrayal to the biological parent motivates some children to reject the stepparent. To avoid this emotional conflict, it's easier to never love and care for the new stepparent. This response is often misunderstood by adults. They may try even harder to win the love of their stepchild. The harder the stepparent pushes, the more stressful the relationship may become.

Adults have a tendency to view this reconstituted family as one would a biological family. But remarriage creates a completely new social unit. Old patterns and expectations need to be replaced by new ones. Unfortunately, the only model of family is the biological one. Thus, parents and children are bound to be involved in conflicting periods of testing and adjustment.

In a biological family, parenting is taken for granted. Mom doesn't expect to hear, "Hey! You've done a good job mediating the fights between siblings." That doesn't seem to be the case in a stepfamily. Quite often, the new parent seeks reassurance and appreciation for successfully fulfilling the role of parent. But appreciation is rarely given.

Some stepparents resent a stepchild because the child symbolizes the previous marriage. If there is friction between the biological parent and the stepparent of the same sex it is more than likely caused by jealousy or competition. When adults feel threatened, they may place added demands on stepchildren. One remarried father who had custody announced to his children that they now had a new mother and therefore they should give all their love to their new mother and stop loving their biological mother. Forcing a child to renounce love for a parent is painful and cruel. Children, in time, can learn to love a mother, father, and a stepparent. Forcing and manipulating a child's emotions will only create resentment and anxiety.

A common mistake of stepparents is to try to overwhelm the "new" child with kindness. To compensate for some imagined insecurities, stepparents try to become "superparents." This is one of the quickest ways to create distance between stepparent and child. This often results in the stepparent simply wearing himself/herself out, as well. Children cannot be forced to care. They need time to adjust.

Quite often stepchildren and stepparents, trying to establish their position in the new family, find themselves fighting and arguing with one another. The source of the anger is not always understood. For example, children who haven't seen their natural father for many weeks are angry and resentful. The stepfather becomes the target for that disappointment and hostility. Children and adults may unconsciously displace their emotions by transferring their feelings from the source (biological father) to the stepparent. The stepparent may feel unjustly accused and may retaliate in kind.

It is not easy to assume responsibilities for your emotions. One little girl told her father that her new stepmother hated her and wanted her to move out of the house. In reality, those feelings were exactly how the child felt about the stepmother. It was easier to project those negative emotions onto the stepmother than to assume the responsibility of owning up to her own feelings.

All stepfamilies experience change, uncertainty, and intense internal and external conflicts. This doesn't mean remarriage should be avoided. What is suggested is that adults need to be sensitive to children's needs. Remarriage can bring back all the anguish from divorce which places children at risk. At the same time, a new family can provide stability and broaden children's support base. New adults, siblings, and grandparents can also play a supportive and nurturing role in children's lives. Given enough time and adult understanding, a new family can bring joy, security, and love to children who have been starved for those feelings for a long time.

The following suggestions are offered to parents and teachers with the hope that the stresses from divorce in the lives of children can be reduced. Divorce will always create tension and uncertainty for children, but adults, by means of patience, understanding, and support, can help children through the rough spots.

How to Tell Children About Divorce

Both parents should talk to the children—and together. This reduces the tendency to blame the other parent. Children feel more secure.

Parents should physically hold the children. Children fear abandonment. Feeling the warmth of their parent's touch can reassure them.

Tell them one or two weeks before one parent moves out of the home. To tell the children too soon is to foster reconciliation fantasies. The longer the parent remains, the more the child believes the event will never happen. Telling the child a few days before does not allow enough time to adjust.

Parents should plan to discuss the subject during a period of calm, not after an argument. The creation of undue stress is minimized when both parents are rational and sympathetic to their child's needs.

Parents should allow sufficient time for the discussion. Don't be in a hurry. Children have many questions and fears and need to feel their parents are there for them.

Begin with honesty, explaining the reasons for divorce appropriate to the age of the child. You might begin by saying "Maybe you've seen that Mom and Dad haven't been too happy with each other for some time." You don't have to elaborate the minute details that children won't understand. For example, one parent said they were getting divorced because of financial problems. The child responded with, "You don't have to pay me any allowance. I'll do my jobs for nothing. Now you don't have to get a divorce."

Listen to the children to gain an understanding of what they are experiencing. One mother was delighted when her child asked if she would remarry. Mother asked, "Would you like to see that happen?"

Child: "That would be great!"

(Pause—mother feeling relief)

"Hope you marry Daddy."

Parents need not fear openly expressing their emotions. Don't be afraid to cry. Tears are an expression of love. When adults cry in front of children they're giving their children permission to cry as well.

Let children express anger and resentment. This reaction is normal; children should not be punished for it.

Establish an atmosphere where children are free to ask questions. Many children will ask the same questions over and over again. Be patient and always answer each question. This reassures the children of their parents' availability. Never dismiss children's questions or thoughts as unimportant.

Be consistent and firm about the decision to separate. Help children understand and accept the fact that nothing they did caused the decision and that Mom and Dad are firm about the decision. Respond with sympathy, but insist the separation will happen.

Explain what life may be like in the future as best you can. If you know you're going to sell your home, share that information. By supplying details of common everyday experiences, children can feel a sense of stability about their future.

What All Divorcing Parents Must Tell Their Children

Children are not responsible for the divorce. In no way did they cause it and there is no way they can prevent it from occurring.

Although Mom and Dad may be divorcing one another, they are not divorcing their children. They will always have their parents.

Assure children that although parents are living apart, the children will not be abandoned. They will always be cared for.

Parents will never stop loving their children. They may not be able to live with each other, but their love for their children will always be there.

Tell children the empty, sad, and frightening feelings are normal and okay to have. They won't last forever and in time will go away. Talking about those feelings helps.

Children need to know they don't have to choose sides. They can continue to love both parents.

Recommendations for Schools to Help Children Cope with Divorce

Robert Allers offers several suggestions for helping schools learn to help children cope with the stresses of divorce. We recommend his helpful article in the November-December 1980 issue of *Today's Education.*[4]

Hold class discussion. Such class discussions need not be held only when some child in class is in the middle of a divorce. They may be held as a regular part of the school curriculum. In this way, children can learn what other children in class think and can express their own feelings to their classmates. It is probably best to let parents know that a controversial topic is planned for discussion.

Take time to learn more about divorce. In this way, teachers can prevent themselves from making assumptions that are no longer accurate, especially concerning the composition of families and the behavior of children during and after a divorce.

Identify problems. If the teacher is informed concerning divorce, then he or she can be on the lookout for signs of stress in children.

Encourage special programs. It is possible for school psychologists, school social workers or counselors to conduct special groups for the children of divorce. In this way, these children can have a support group, guided by trained adults, of children in similar circumstances.

Keep literature available. There are several good books to help children understand divorce and their feelings. Two suggestions are Judy Blume's

It's Not the End of the World and P. Mann's *My Dad Lives in a Downtown Hotel.*

Talk to the child individually. Private talks allow children to express their feelings, and the teacher may gain insights into the private feelings of the child that can help the child cope with divorce.

In these private talks, the teacher can provide support, give understanding, and show interest and concern for the child. The child is able to learn that he or she is not completely abandoned and that the teacher is willing to take the time to listen to the child.

Recommendations for Visitation

Children need love, protection, and security from both their parents. The absence of the noncustodial parent's presence in a child's life is detrimental to a child's self-esteem. A general rule could be stated that regular, dependable visitation patterns will help children cope with the stresses of divorce.

Suggestions for Soothing the Trauma of Visitation

Take children to father's new residence. Young children especially need to be reassured that Dad will be okay. Show them the refrigerator and bed so they will know Dad won't die of starvation and that he has a place to sleep.

Don't force visitations. Circumstances change. If there's a baseball game scheduled the weekend your son is supposed to visit, don't demand he miss the game. Let him decide which he would rather do. Support that decision.

Be sure children have their own bed and a private space to keep their belongings. They need to feel they belong during visitation.

Be cautious of separate visits for siblings. While this may seem reasonable when there is a range of ages in one family, some siblings may feel they aren't receiving fair and equal time. This doesn't mean that separate visits cannot work. It just suggests they need to be thought through so all children feel they aren't being cheated.

Be thoughtful, considerate, and consistent when dealing with children's feelings. Call if you may be late. Set up another time if you can't make a particular date. Recognize that the visiting pattern you establish directly affects a child's sense of well-being.

Custody Suggestions

Try to arrive at the decision of custody without having to rely upon the court system to make that determination. The legal process is often impersonal and painful; it is not always in the best interest of the child.

If a judicial custody decision is required, have an independent attorney represent the interest of the child. The term for such an attorney is a guardian ad-litem.

Consider children's wishes and desires, but make the custody decision based upon the needs of the children.

Child rearing is physically and emotionally draining. Therefore, sharing that responsibility takes pressures off the parents. One way to share is to have each parent assume responsibility for raising children.

Joint custody can be successful if the parents have a strong desire to try it. They need to be committed to this form of parenting. They must trust each other and be able to be flexible and cooperative.

Another factor that lends to a successful joint custody arrangement is where the parents' residences are near one another.

Recommendations for the Stepfamily

Go slowly. Recognize that this is a period of adjustment for everyone. Allow some time in between the announcement of the marriage and the actual date. Children need time to prepare for this new change of family status. If the remarriage comes as a surprise, children may feel left out and resent their parents.

Be realistic about the future. One father, filled with joy, anticipating his forthcoming marriage, told his daughter how happy he would be. They would move near the mountains; she'd have her own horse and, best of all, a new mother to care for her. The daughter broke into uncontrollable sobbing and threatened to run away if he remarried.

A better way to pave the way for a successful remarriage is to express both positive and negative aspects about the new stepfamily. One might say, "I know there are some things you don't like about my future wife and your step mom. After all, there are things you don't like about me either. I understand that we're all going to have to show some special effort to work things out for a while."

If possible, start the new family in a new home. Provide children with their own beds, dressers, bedrooms, pajamas, and so forth. Whether children visit every weekend or are living with you, they need to feel they belong.

Establish clear ground rules for the new family. These can be agreed-upon rules that allow everyone to know what is expected of them. Whether it is setting a specific bedtime or completing specific chores, children actually feel better if they understand what their parents want from them. This avoids the trap of "But Mom (or Dad) does it this way." When children express that thought, a good response from the stepparent might be, "I know things are different now. We are all getting used to new rules in a new home and family."

Be cautious of calling the new stepparent Mom or Dad. Children are the best guides in establishing what to call the new parents. Forcing the child can only create resentment. Some children are quite comfortable with the name switches. The best rule is to ask children what feels best, always recognizing that the name is subject to change. What is really most important to a new stepparent is not what children call you, but how comfortable they feel about you.

Recognize that when children express their anger they may be reacting to other feelings about the biological parent. Don't take this anger personally. Understand the source of the hostility, allow the feeling to surface, and remain as supportive as possible. Granted, this is no easy task. In time, children will see that the stepparent is not a threat and, thus, family tension is reduced.

In matters of discipline, to the extent possible, allow problems to be handled by the biological parent. The stepparent needs time to establish an affectionate relationship with children before an atmosphere of trust can be established. Later, discipline can be a responsibility shared by both adults. This may prove to be a difficult matter for males, who are often thought to be the ones who handle discipline. Strive to hold back from any need to assert control right from the beginning.

Include children in as many family activities as possible. While the newly married adults desire time alone together, they need to be sensitive to a child's feelings of being left out.

Some Concluding General Recommendations for Parents

There are some recommendations that all parents need to consider for the children of divorce.

Don't be ashamed to seek professional help for the parents or children trying to cope with divorce. It may be especially important to seek professional help before a marriage. Or, if the children are experiencing difficulties with eating, biological functions such as bowel and bladder control, or in radically altered sleep patterns, these may be taken as signs that children need more help than they are getting at home.

As a general rule, when adults seek to find answers to their problems, they at the same time encourage their children to search for answers too. Parents who try to hide feelings prevent their children from expressing feelings as well.

Try to maintain a daily routine for children. If the routine is stable, that allows children to not have to worry about insecurities caused by never knowing what any given day will bring.

Don't criticize, insult, demean, or denigrate the other parent in front of the child. No matter how much you dislike the other parent, remember that the child is one half of that parent.

Allow the child to grieve for the lost parent. It is natural for a child to miss the parent who left the home. Don't misunderstand and jump to the conclusion that the child loves the parent who left more than the one who stayed. It is just that they miss the one who is not at home.

Encourage the same sex parent to attend functions at school and elsewhere that are appropriate. For example, if it is fathers' night at school, to the extent possible, have Dad go. If it is mother's night at school, encourage Mom to attend with the child.

Don't insist everything is going to be better than it used to be. Allow the child his or her pain and allow them to work through it as best they can with adult support. None of us knows the future; that is why there is always hope. Hope, however, is different than knowing things will be better. Encourage the child to keep talking about fears, doubts, and concerns. In this way, children can tell their parents what they, the children, need help with.

Notes

1. Cantor, D. W. "Divorce: A View From the Children." *Journal of Divorce.* Summer 1979. The Haworth Press. Pp. 357-361. Reprinted by permission.

2. Gardner, R. A. "Children of Divorce—Some Legal and Psychological Considerations." *Journal of Clinical Child Psychology.* Summer 1977, pp. 3-6.

3. Wallerstein, J. S. and Kelly, J. "Effects of Divorce on the Visiting Father-Child Relationship." *American Journal of Psychiatry.* Dec. 1980, pp. 1534-1538.

4. Allers, R. D. "Helping Children Understand Divorce." *Today's Education.* November-December 1980, 24GS-27GS.

4
STRESS
from Peers

Friends, friends, friends
Most friends are good friends
but bad friends are no friends
that is why I like all my good friends. *

David Ryan Welch
(1971-   )

For most children, peers (friends and other kids roughly the same age) can at the same time be a source of pleasure, profound learning, and stress. Children enjoy each other's company; that is apparent from the amount of time they spend together. Children most decidedly learn from their peers, observing different ways of behaving in various social situations such as parties, school, and other public gatherings. They also learn how to be a friend; how to form a close, caring relationship with another person; how to give and take; how to compromise when they can't always get their own way. It is in peer relationships that most children learn the social skills that can lead to success in adult life.

Perhaps most importantly, children learn much about themselves from peers. Whether children feel capable and worthwhile can in part depend on the messages and reactions they get from their peers. Many of the relationships children have with their peers revolve around comparing

*David Ryan Welch. "Friends." Reprinted by permission of Author.

94

themselves with others. The results of these comparisons can have a crucial effect on children's self-concepts, whether they feel positively or negatively about themselves. Peer relationships are the foundry where children's identities are forged outside the home.

As the source of a child's identity outside the home, peer relationships can be a source of stress for many children. Certainly the great majority of us want to be liked, to be accepted, and to feel capable and worthwhile. There is even the possibility that such needs may be biological in origin. Whatever the source of such needs, most children experience them strongly. Wanting to be liked and accepted is natural and necessary. The possibility of not being liked and accepted is a source of fear for a good number of children. Children, especially older ones, worry about having friends and being accepted. They will do what they can (or what they have to) to insure this acceptance.

Peer relationships are extremely important in another, more long term sense. Adults' long-term adjustment to life, how happy and healthy one's adult life is, seems to be directly related to healthy peer relationships in childhood. Children with no peer relationships, or with unhappy, unhealthy ones, are more likely to become involved in juvenile delinquency and more likely to have disabling emotional problems as adults. Children who are more socially isolated are more likely to attempt suicide as adults. One of the best predictors of a healthy, happy adult life is satisfying peer relationships as a child.

Thus, peer relationships are crucial to both the long-term and short-term lives of children. They can make a child's life happy or miserable and can set the tone for the child's entire life. With this in mind, we have set out to provide information and suggestions to increase parents' awareness of peer relationships and give easy-to-follow ideas to improve a child's chances of developing satisfying peer relationships.

Children's Relationships

Before offering suggestions, we want to provide some information about children's relationships. This will enable parents to better understand what is going on in their children's peer relationships and, we hope, better know how to provide what might be missing that their children need.

Much recent research has "discovered" what parents have known for a long time. Friendships and peer relationships have different meanings to children of different ages (Reisman and Shorr 1978; Bigelow 1977). In earlier ages, from about three to seven, relationships with other children seem to be based on geographical closeness and utility. Good friends or playmates are those who happen to be around. Attractive toys also help build friendships at this age. Often relatives such as cousins substitute for peers because they are close by. Later in this period, peers are befriended if they will do what another child wants them to do. If they don't do as another child wishes, they are likely to be described as "not *my* friend." The personality of peers seems less important as a criterion for friendship in this stage. Children's intellectual and emotional development in this period does not lend itself to much more than who is a source of fun. If someone will give a child something, be in the vicinity, and do what the child likes, he or she is likely to be considered a friend.

In later years, from about seven to twelve, things change somewhat. Utility—what someone can do for a child—is still important, but the personal characteristics of peers become more important. Whether one is nice or not becomes more important, as does whether one is accepted and liked by another. A sense of fairness also seems to prevail during this period. If a child does a favor for another, a favor is expected in return. If a child is accepted by another child, there is acceptance expected in return. The principle of utility still operates in this period. Admirable qualities—such as attractiveness, athletic ability, and owning nice things—become more important.

At about twelve years of age, the personality characteristics of people become much more important. Fair exchange of favors is no longer enough. Children seem to value a sharing and support of personal concerns. Qualities such as understanding, the potential for intimacy, and common interests and values help in deciding who will be friends. It is as if children were picking friends who would be acceptable counselors, people in whom they know they could confide. Many of the same qualities that adults look for in friends are apparent here, although admirable qualities such as athletic ability, attractiveness, and wealth are still important.

With the above information and their own knowledge of children, parents can begin to become more aware of their children's peer relationships. They can begin to look more closely at their children's social interactions and decide whether their children's needs are being met. They can look for signs that peer relationships are satisfying or are a source of stress. If they decide that their children are experiencing undue stress over unsatisfying relationships, the following suggestions may prove helpful.

This section will contain suggestions for developing certain social skills which research has shown to be important in developing and maintaining satisfying peer relationships (Gottman et al. 1975). Most children develop these skills in their ordinary day-to-day interactions with others. However, some children don't develop these skills to a sufficient level to succeed in relationships.

Decentration

Perhaps the most important skill in maintaining social relationships is decentration (Gottman et al. 1975). In commonsense, everyday language, this means the ability to know how others feel. It means being able to go outside of oneself and to know or imagine what the experience of another is like. Only if one has an idea that someone else has feelings and some idea of what those feelings are can one take the other's feelings into account. Research clearly shows that children who have decentration skills have more successful peer relationships than children who don't (Rubin 1973).

In order to help children learn to place themselves "in another's shoes," parents can read or tell stories to their children. At various times during the story, stop and ask what a certain character is feeling or what the character is likely to do. Ask the child why the character feels that way or is likely to behave in that way. If the child's response seems inaccurate or inappropriate, offer a more appropriate solution in a non-judgmental manner, such as "Do you think he might also be feeling . . . ?" or "Do you think he might do . . . ?"

Parents can utilize the same approach while a child is watching a movie, a TV show, or even a cartoon. In addition to helping children learn how others might feel, this approach can aid in developing an active, inquisitive mind, as opposed to the passiveness evident in so many children watching TV. Again, ask what certain characters might be feeling or what they might do next.

Another suggestion is to blindfold a member of the family. Build a maze out of chairs, tables, furniture, walls, and doorways. Have children guide the blindfolded person through the maze, using only verbal directions. In order to guide a blindfolded person through, around, over, and under such an obstacle course, it is necessary to put oneself into the blindfolded person's shoes.

Participation

This skill refers to making the effort to be around other children so that other social skills may be employed. Parents can plan an outing to a movie, a park, a ball game, the museum, or anywhere. Have the child invite one or a few other children to go along. Possibly have the child invite a schoolmate or two over a short while after school. The particular activity is less important than the practice the child receives in initiating and participating in activities with peers.

Encourage children to join one or more of the many groups and organizations in existence, such as scouting, athletic teams (see chapter on sports), drama or musical groups, photography clubs, 4-H, FFA, and so forth. There seems to be no limit to the available groups. Again, what matters is that the child develop participation skills. When children express interest in an activity that will require interaction with others, reinforce them for their interest and participation. Show them your interest and pleasure in their participation.

Cooperation

One of the great lessons children learn from interacting with other children is cooperation. This includes offering help to others, sharing, taking turns, and learning to compromise instead of always demanding one's own way. Children who have mastered these skills are certainly more likely to enjoy satisfying peer relationships.

Parents can encourage cooperation by paying attention to and reinforcing children when they practice cooperation skills at home. If a child shares with a brother, or helps a sister with a chore, pay attention to it. Give recognition to the child for it, stating precisely what the child did that was so good. A sentence such as "I really like the way you shared your toys with your brother" can go a long way toward making such sharing happen over and over again.

A fun way to teach cooperation is to create family stories. One person starts the story and after a while stops. At this point another person takes over and continues making up the story. Give every family member several turns and a chance to end a story. Parents can also let children help in the serving of dinner. If the children are old enough, let them take turns asking who would like what to eat and how much. Then let them help serve the food to other family members.

If children are given chores to do, consider some type of special reward if they finish their own chores and then help others to finish theirs. Make sure not to take anything away from the person receiving the help. The above suggestions are all designed for the home. Whenever instances of cooperation, sharing, helping, taking turns, or compromise are seen outside of the home, make sure to mention and praise them.

Communication

Children who have good communication skills are known to make friends more easily and have better peer relationships. Communication involves being able to listen carefully to someone and being able to understand what that person means. Again, these skills can be learned and developed through practice. An excellent exercise is for a family or a group of people to engage in a discussion. Before anyone can speak, they must accurately summarize what the last speaker was saying. If they can't, the last speaker repeats the message and the speaker-to-be again attempts to summarize the meaning of the statement. Another simple technique is to converse with children for a while and then stop and ask them to show that they listened and understood by repeating back, not the exact words that were used, but the meaning of what was said.

Communication also involves speaking clearly and to the point. To increase children's ability to communicate accurately, let them silently read a paragraph or section of a story, or of a newspaper or magazine. After finishing the reading, have the children explain what they read, in as few of their own words as possible. If anything is unclear, ask questions and have the children answer them, again in as few words as possible. The goal of this exercise is to build clarity into children's communication. Choose a wide variety of reading materials, such as news, sports, novels, travel, science magazines, and papers. For an interesting twist, invite children's friends to try this exercise.

Validating

This means letting another person know his or her presence is recognized and appreciated. The skills involved here are simply looking at a person (eye contact), smiling, and making initial conversation such as "Hi, how are you?" The recognition that comes from being looked at, smiled at, and spoken to is the most basic type of social reinforcement a person can receive. It makes most people feel important and good. They are, thus, more likely to want to be around persons who have made them feel good.

A simple way to develop these skills is for parents to model them for their children. This means making a point of looking at children while speaking to them. Maintain eye contact when speaking. When children get up in the morning or come home from school or somewhere else, be sure to smile and say hello. Ask how they are doing. In addition to modeling these skills, parents should reward children when they do make eye contact and offer greetings. Let children know these are important things to do.

Parents can also suggest that their children observe other children who are successfully using these skills. Give children a chance to practice eye contact, smiling, and greeting at home. Parents can play the part of another child and have their children practice these skills. After the practice attempt, let children know how well they did and how they might improve. If they wish, parents can demonstrate first and then switch places, letting the child practice.

Approval

In addition to eye contact, smiling, and greeting, an important social skill is showing approval to another person. It is the icing on the cake, the cake consisting of the more basic skills mentioned above. Approval is simply mentioning to someone something one really likes about him or her. It may be something personal ("I love your hair style"), something the person has done ("Thanks for the card. It was nice of you"), or some personality characteristic ("You're really generous, helping people with their math"). It is easy to understand why a person who has this skill will be liked and thought of as friendly.

The most effective way for parents to help children learn this skill is to model it for them. Take opportunities to mention children's positive characteristics to them. Don't just make them up, because children will see through that. Rather, find truly enjoyable and admirable characteristics and point them out. Children will learn to do the same.

Parents can also use magazines, novels, movies, or TV shows to help children practice this skill. Have children pick one or more characters they like and make up approval sentences for these characters. The children should state what it is they like about the character and then make several different statements for the same desirable characteristics. Thus, if the character is a sheriff on a TV show and he or she has just saved someone from a gang of outlaws, the following statements might be appropriate:

- "You sure are brave, sheriff."
- "I like the way you outsmarted those outlaws."
- "I'd sure feel safe if you were the sheriff of our town."

Pay especially close attention to stories and movies that have characters near the same age as one's children. In this way practice can be directed toward making statements that may actually be used.

Another sample exercise is to have a child name his or her best friends and those they might like to have for friends. Then the child should state what it is he or she likes about these people, finally making up several approval statements for each of the desired qualities.

Self-disclosure

Self-disclosure means sharing information about oneself with another person. This sharing may include factual information such as where one lives or how old one is. It may cover preferences for musical groups, clothes, or food. It may also deal with wishes, hopes, or dreams children have. In its deepest form it may involve sharing the pain surrounding the divorce of one's parents or the breakup of a relationship with a boy or girl friend. Self-disclosure shows a potential for intimacy, a quality in friends that is highly valued by adolescents and adults. If one person discloses information, others are more likely to do so. After people have shared information with one another, they usually report liking each other more. Thus, self-disclosure is very important in building satisfying peer relationships.

The ability to self-disclose is a skill that can easily be learned. Parents can start early in a child's life by supporting the open expression of preferences and choices. Let children choose between foods to eat, clothes to wear, books to read, or activities in which to engage. Even as simple a choice as taking a larger or smaller helping of vegetables or wearing blue or brown pants can help in this area. Parents can also encourage the expression of feelings. If children are obviously happy or sad or afraid, talk to them about it. Let them know it is good and healthy to share such feelings.

A little game may prove very helpful. It is called "Right Here and Now"; any number can participate. Players simply take turns starting a sentence with the words "Right here and now, I feel . . ." and then complete the sentence. It is especially useful in teaching children how to express their feelings in a simple, direct manner. Try to make sure players use words that describe feelings or emotions to complete the sentences. Parents might consider going first to demonstrate how the game is to be played.

Schedule regular periods to be used for the entire family to share feelings and personal information. When children engage in self-disclosure during their ordinary day-to-day routine, pay close attention and show interest. If self-disclosure skills are developed at home, they will flourish in the peer world.

Recognition of Nonverbal Cues of Emotion

Thus far, most of our discussion has revolved around verbal or speaking skills. Another very important social skill is being able to recognize nonverbal signals of how a person feels. The way people sit, stand, or walk, and the look on people's faces can all give clues as to how they are feeling. Not surprisingly, then, children who have such skills are more likely to develop and maintain satisfying peer relationships.

Parents can engage in several activities with their children to help develop skills in this area. First, occasionally turn the sound off while watching a TV show. After a minute or two, ask the children what one or more characters are feeling. When the children have guessed, ask them what they saw that influenced their decision. Turn the sound back on and see how accurate the guess was. The same exercise can be done with pictures from a magazine. Although there may be no way to check for accuracy (unless the story or caption names an emotion), a consensus may be sought from among the participants. The basic goal, to develop an interest in and an awareness of nonverbal cues, is well served either way.

A modification of the game of charades may also be used. Instead of just doing movies, books, or songs, add emotions or feelings to be acted out. One way is to pick a saying that contains a feeling, such as "mad as a junkyard dog," or "happy as a hog in mud." Another way is to match a feeling with an animal word (sad duck), a type of food (happy eggs), or any other type of word. Make them as crazy as possible. The crazier the better. This will stretch everyone's creativity. Develop as many words as possible to describe feelings and emotions. Another game is to get people in a circle and have someone name an emotion or draw one out of a hat. Everyone then takes a turn acting out that emotion with their bodies and their faces. Encourage children to use their whole bodies, not just their faces. If the tendency to use only the face is too strong, put a towel or bag over the person's face and concentrate on using the body.

Another excellent game is to have children convey some message to another person without talking. The messages may be factual as well as emotional. Examples of factual messages are "It's cold outside," "Groceries are really expensive today," and "A football game is on TV tonight." The possibilities are almost limitless. Messages may also be about feelings and emotions, such as "I like you," "I don't like your dress," "This dinner is great," or "I *really* like you." The possibilities are, again, almost limitless. Children often love to play these games on their own once they learn them, so parents need only get them started.

Shyness

Another important factor in peer relationships is shyness. Relatively recent research suggests that nearly 80 percent of adults see themselves as having been shy during their lives (Zimbardo 1975). Further, 40 percent of adults report that they still consider themselves shy. Many persons seek counseling for shyness because it affects so many areas of their lives. Difficulty in expressing opinions and feelings, feeling afraid to talk to friends and strangers, and inability to make and refuse requests are only a few manifestations of shyness which seriously hamper the development of satisfactory peer relationships.

If parents think their children are overly shy, here are several suggestions. First, play a game called Silly Speeches or Crazy Conversations with children. To play, have each player think of as many crazy, far-out topics as possible. Write each topic on a separate slip of paper and place all of them in a paper bag (or hat). Each player, in turn, picks a topic from the bag and then proceeds to talk about the topic for sixty seconds. Since the topics are so silly, no one holds expectations of a polished speech. Rather, the goal is simply to get used to talking (about anything) in front of people. Examples of topics might be radio dials, popsicle sticks, trunks of cars, shoe laces, lint, soapsuds, dirt, or string. Anything is okay; the crazier the better. Extend the game to include children's peers. Kids love to play this game once they get the hang of it.

A second suggestion is for parents to help children explore and think about any irrational beliefs which may be leading to shyness. There is usually some mistaken belief, often exaggerated out of proportion, behind shyness. For example, children often think it would be "horrible" or the "end of the world" if someone rejects them and doesn't like them or want them for a friend. As a result, such children choose not to try to interact socially rather than suffer the "horrible" result, rejection. Parents can help children realize they may not be rejected. That's only one possibility. Even if they are rejected, it's not the end of the world. There are other people who can be friends. All a rejection means is a particular person chooses not to befriend another. It may be cause for some sadness, but it is not the end of the world. The sadness will pass and others may be sought out as friends.

Another suggestion is for parents to find a book on assertiveness. There are many such books available in bookstores and supermarkets. *Your Perfect Right*, by R. Alberti and M. Emmons, and *Asserting Yourself: A Practical Guide for Positive Change*, by S. Bower and G. Bower, are two fine books with practical exercises to help people learn to become more assertive and less shy.

In conjunction with a book on assertiveness, parents can help children with rehearsal or practice of non-shy behaviors. Together with children, parents can identify and describe what behaviors would be more desirable. Then a parent might set up a situation (asking someone for a date, asking a person over for lunch) and the child can practice making appropriate responses. Parents can then observe the child's rehearsal and make helpful comments. Or parents might demonstrate first while children observe, and then switch roles. Finally, Philip Zimbardo's book, *Shyness: What It Is, What To Do About It*, may also provide valuable suggestions.

The following section contains suggestions directed not toward developing social skills in children, but rather designed to increase children's contact with peers, allowing natural developmental processes to guide the acquisition of social skills.

Increasing Peer Contact

Perhaps the simplest yet most powerful suggestion is to allow children the opportunity to interact with peers. For most children, merely spending time with others their own age can lead to the fun and learning mentioned at the beginning of the previous section. Left to their own devices, most children will learn the basic social skills necessary to form satisfying relationships with their peers and give them a good start on a happy, well-adjusted adult life. Keep an eye on children for any signs of trouble in peer relationships, but trust in children's abilities to handle peer relationships. Most can do quite well. Dancing, parties, movies, playing electronic video games, concerts, and sporting events are all popular activities with children which allow the development of social skills and peer relationships.

Walking or riding a bus home from school are natural skill-development activities. So is just "hanging out" together, doing nothing special. Remember that even though nothing earthshaking is happening, kids are always learning from their peers.

Dealing with Peer Influence

An important concern for many parents is the apparently increasing influence of peers and declining influence of parents on children as they grow older. Parents worry that children with different ideas and values will influence their own children's ideas and behavior for the worse. Although this is certainly possible, there is good news for parents. Research suggests that as children approach and reach adolescence, parental influence remains the strongest influence in their lives (Berndt 1979). There definitely is pressure to conform to peer values; this happens to a significant degree. There certainly are arguments resulting from conflicts between parental values and peer values. But through all of this, children report that their parents are the strongest and most important influence in their lives. Furthermore, even when there are conflicts, children report liking their parents much more than they like friends and peers. By the time high school ends, most conflicts between parental and peer influence subside and most children adopt parental values to a significant degree.

It is important for parents to recognize these temporary conflicts and disturbances for what they are—temporary. Most conflicts seem to center around the instrumental role parents play. Parents must make rules and decide what to do when these rules are broken. Parents must make important decisions for their children who are too young to make these decisions for themselves. All parents carry this burden. Conflicts arise in adolescence when parents begin to urge their children toward more independence, while at the same time they continue to make rules and enforce them, keeping children from acting independently. The result is that children often see their parents as critical and strict, often arguing with parents over these conflicting values of independence-dependence. By the end of adolescence, however, parents view children as more capable of directing their own lives, and much of the conflict disappears.

Our suggestions here center around recognition of the temporary nature of these conflicts. They will pass. Parents should realize that children are exploring and learning in their peer relationships. By meeting different people, being exposed to different ideas and values, and possibly even adopting different values for a time, children are exploring and learning. This exploration is a necessary step in the development of effective social skills. Even if children do argue with parents about new ideas and values, it doesn't mean they don't like or love their parents. In fact, when children reach adulthood they report gratitude to parents for the imposition of rules and values, if the rules and values were applied fairly and consistently. So we again urge patience: The conflicts will pass. Children need to explore different ideas, customs, and values in order to develop necessary social skills. We are not suggesting that parents ignore what their children do. Rather, we suggest giving children the chance to explore and grow.

Parents should also keep in mind that once children reach high school age, they probably have already internalized whatever parental values they will. Becoming stricter in the hope of "protecting" children from exposure to different ideas and values won't work. Children can't be isolated from society and the world. They will interact with other children before, during, and after school. Television, radio, magazines, and newspapers will carry information about other ideas and values. We think parents' best bet is to clearly and consistently express their beliefs and values while children are young. Then when adolescence arrives, children can explore what's new and different, feeling secure in their own values. Keeping children away from peers with different ideas may only serve to raise children's curiosity and make off-limits ideas or activities more mysterious and more attractive. Parents should trust the job they have done of raising their children. The lessons learned by children in fourteen or fifteen years of daily living with parents won't be readily or easily discarded for persons known only a short time. Research shows what is most likely is that adolescents will keep most of their parents' values.

Improving Peer Relationships

If children seem to be having problems developing peer relationships, parents can initiate conversation about this topic. It is easy to use TV shows, movies, books, or music as a starting point for the conversation. When a part of a TV show, movie, or song deals with friendships or relationships, ask a child, "What do you think about that?" Notice that the questions do not directly ask "How are your peer relationships?" Rather, they ease into the general area of relationships, making it easier for children to talk about a subject which may be touchy and a private matter.

Once the conversation is going, parents can use the child's answer to get around to what may or may not be going on in the child's relationships. For example, if a TV show depicts a person giving a gift to a friend, a parent could ask, "What do you think of that?" "Have you ever given (or been given) a present like that?" or "Which of your friends makes you the happiest?" The rest of the conversation can flow naturally from such a beginning.

At other times children may initiate conversations, especially if they are having some problem relating to a specific person. Children often wonder what they can do to make someone like them or be their friend. So, we suggest another approach. Spend time guiding children through values-clarification-type exercises. These are designed to help people learn what is important to them, what values and beliefs they hold, and how these values and beliefs influence their behavior. All that is needed is to identify a person's reactions to a situation and then ask a series of "why" questions.

Assume a child says, "Mary doesn't like me. How can I make her like me?" Parents should first attempt to identify what the child is feeling about this situation. The child might answer, "I'm *sad.* I want her to like me and be my friend." Parents can then begin a series of gentle "why" questions.

1. "Why do you feel sad?"
   "She doesn't like me."
2. "Why does that make you sad?"
   "She is so neat and is real popular."

3. "Why would that make you sad?"
   "If she would be my friend, other people would like me."
4. "So you would like others to notice you and pay attention to you?"
   "Yes, sometimes I feel like no one knows I'm around."

At this point a basic value, being recognized or paid attention to, is seen as important and a motivator of behavior. Parents can now help the child explore what other means might be taken to get notices or receive others' attention. Suggestions such as participating in sports, music, or drama may emerge. Discussion of ways to meet people and start friendships may also emerge. All can be worthwhile. The values-clarification approach can be used with any peer relationship problems that arise. Just remember to identify the child's reaction and then ask the gentle "why" questions. The book *Values Clarification* by Simon, Howe, and Kirschenbaum contains an excellent introduction to values clarification and many excellent activities parents can do with their children.

A final suggestion is for parents to ask teachers, coaches, scoutmasters, bandleaders, and others how their child interacts with peers. They will all have a different view of the child. Such conversations may set parents' minds at ease. These people may also have noticed some of the same things parents have and may offer helpful suggestions.

In this chapter we have attempted to increase parents' awareness of the importance of satisfying peer relationships. These relationships can also exert a profound influence on the adjustment adults make to life. We have made concrete suggestions which, if followed, can increase a child's chances of developing and maintaining satisfying peer relationships.

5

STRESS at School

If God had only known
what schools were going to be like,
He would have made children different.

Anonymous

If there is a major myth about schools in our society, it is that all children are eager to go. A childhood friend of one of the authors tells the story of his first day at school. The teacher kept trying to get him to tell her his name. He refused time after time. Finally, exasperated, the teacher demanded why he wouldn't tell her his name. He said, "Because I'm not coming back tomorrow."

Children know better than adults that schools can be places of stress, fear, and even pain for children. They know it and they communicate it to one another. It doesn't take much contact with the preschool class to know what next year's kindergarten teacher is like. Or the first grade teacher. Or which sixth grade teacher is good and which makes the children cringe when they discover they have been assigned to that room.

Aside from the knowledge that a particular teacher may be un-appealing to a child, there is, among certain children, a general overall fear of school itself. Those fears may be real or imagined. Whatever the case, the effect is the same. For too long we have assumed such fear was only a problem of an individual child. Our assumption has prevented us from looking at the school itself as the problem. The point of this chapter is that it might very well be the school itself, the organization and its assumptions, that create needless stress for children. Much of what is contained in this chapter may be viewed as harsh by school personnel. However, it is not the authors' intent to attack teachers or other school staff. It is indeed rare to find a person in school who is intentionally cruel to children or whose primary goal is harming children. Nevertheless, schools, chiefly in their organizational structure and the assumptions under which U.S. schools were founded, are a major source of stress for children.

Consider this as a typical description of a U.S. school. A visit to a school will find children sitting, listening, and isolated in a chair or at a desk. Then consider how closely that describes any normal child. Children do not characteristically sit, listen, and isolate themselves. Children jump, shout, and socialize! It is, then, not unfair to characterize the school as unhuman. Notice we did not say *inhumane*. Teachers are, in the main, good and decent people who genuinely care about the children they are charged to teach. They operate within a system, however, that seemingly has little to do with the characteristics of children.

When the organization of a large institution does not match up at all well with its clients, then the result is stress for everyone involved—in the case of this book, most notably, this means children. Combine this with a general societal assumption that children really want to go to school and what you have is a blaming of those children who do not and who, therefore, suffer at school without any supporting sympathy at home. This is an equation tailor-made for stress. What are the assumptions of the U.S. school system that lead to stress for children?

An Authoritarian Model

The U.S. school system is based on the idea that large numbers of children have a right to education. This grand experiment is still in progress. Whether any nation can educate all of its citizens to a predetermined level of literacy at public expense is still a question that has not come to a final conclusion. The great experiment in the U.S. was founded on an authoritarian model and has, to the greater extent, been supported and sustained by authoritarian models (Cremin 1964).

Any such model must have at its base a system of rewards and punishments to control the people (in this case children) whose own interests, desires, motivations, and concerns are more of a problem to the school than a benefit. In fact, motivation in the schools is often defined as getting children to do things they don't want to do, but that the school authorities have decided are important. It is a system more noted for its criticism of children than for its praise of them. The most dangerous of these controls is corporal punishment.

Whenever the issue of punishment arises, it carries with it a simultaneous concern of abuse. While much has been written about child abuse in the home, concern for abuse in the schools has received scant attention. The courts have been helpful in supporting child-abuse legislation regarding the mistreatment of children in the home, but have not been helpful in preventing mistreatment of children in the school. In a recent decision the Supreme Court of the United States ruled that a beating (a word not unthinkingly chosen) so severe the student involved was hospitalized was justified. The court also ruled that children were not guaranteed the rights of due process before they could be punished.

In the 1960s, a Black activist claimed that "violence is as American as apple pie." It may well be he was right. Corporal punishment is widely praised and widely practiced in the United States. Our schools reflect this cultural assumption. It is widely praised and practiced largely because of two myths. A myth is something people believe but which is untrue. The first myth is that corporal punishment is a tried and true method that produces an obedient child, contributes to sound morality, develops character, and results in self-discipline. The second myth is that in the schools, physical punishment is needed to protect the teachers. Both are essentially false—the first because while physical punishment may be a tried method, it is far from being a true one. Research, in fact, points to just the opposite conclusion (Clarizio 1975). Physical punishment has not demonstrated itself to lead to a reduction or elimination of disruptive behavior. Further, it actually models aggressive and violent behavior for children to imitate. Finally, research has revealed that there is a relationship between physical punishment and deviant behavior (Gilmartin 1979). The second is essentially false because, so far as the U.S. public schools are concerned, far more physical punishment is used in the primary grades (Clarizio 1975). While attacks on teachers have risen dramatically in the last few years, it is difficult to imagine these increases are coming from kindergarten, first and second graders. An unanswered question is whether or not the early physical attacks on children by teachers are repaid in the later years. Have we, in fact, taught our children to be violent by the physical discipline techniques used in our schools? Coupled with the effects of television violence and violence in the home, it may very well be a contributor.

The word *democracy* is often used in U.S. schools. It is, however, seldom practiced. Children—and, for that matter, parents—have little say over the curriculum, books, or methods of the public schools. Outside of fringe groups that are well organized and well financed for political or religious causes, parents are not well organized or well financed, and their concerns as individuals can be ignored. Children have no say in their schooling.

Democracy is a concept which holds that people (children are people too) have a right to have a say in the affairs directly affecting their lives. This concept is given lip service in the schools, but it is denied in practice. Much contact with the schools makes one doubt whether there are many adults there who even understand the concept of democracy. One of the authors is familiar with a public school administrator who told the faculty of a junior high school, "These kids have got to learn to live in a democracy where somebody calls the shots." That is probably a fair indication of how that particular school is run, but it is not an accurate reflection of the concept of democracy.

It may be that the authors of this book have misunderstood the basic tenets of the U.S. democracy. We hope not. Certainly we have grave doubts that the democratic ideal can be taught in an authoritarian institution. Unquestioning obedience to authority is poor preparation for citizenship in a democracy. Students tend to view themselves as they have been viewed by the significant adults in their lives and act accordingly—else, what is the point of school? We need to consider that the next time we allow teachers, principals, or other school personnel to use sarcasm or ridicule, humiliate, or demonstrate a general lack of respect for our children.

A Climate of Fear

Let us remember, first of all, we are discussing children. It is a point that is often lost in the discussion of schools. We live in a society, perhaps more than any other, in which a person's worth is determined, to a large extent, by how he or she does. While this is a difficult enough rule to live by as an adult, it can be disastrous for children. Children are increasingly judged not by their human qualities but by their accomplishments. Years ago, one of the authors saw a cartoon pinned to the door of a college professor's office. It showed a father sitting in an easy chair talking to his small son of about kindergarten age. He said, "You had better enjoy this year, because next year the pressure starts." It is no longer uncommon to see kindergarteners dressed in caps and gowns, graduating into the first grade. Cute, and also symptomatic of the pressures we are placing on children early in their school life. Before too long, grades and competition become the reasons for school itself. A host of other educational values are lost to these two reigning monarchs of educational practice.

We live in a time when the schools are under attack from all quarters. If we have presented a case that the schools are based on an authoritarian model, then there are others in our society who think that our schools are too soft. They are crying out for more discipline, harsher discipline, a return to the "good ol' ways." If there is a charge that sends fear through the educational community, it is that academic standards are low. Heads will roll in any academic setting should anyone raise the fear that children are not made to work hard enough. The outcome of all of these charges and countercharges is children going to school in a climate of anxiety. Principals are afraid; teachers are afraid. Fear is contagious. The children are the end of the line of scapegoating. They are the ones who are the dubious benefactors of the fears of the adults who surround them. The danger is, of course, that schools become more concerned with their own image than they are with children. Teachers become more concerned with the diplomatic handling of parents than they are with any particular learning problem a child has. Recently, one of the authors was talking with a teacher in a large metropolitan area. The teacher was telling about a child who was a discipline problem, who had run out the door and down the hall. The teacher said, "I didn't want to run after him. It would just reinforce his running away. But I had to. The kid might get hurt and I was responsible. I wasn't concerned about him; I was concerned about me. I could be sued if that kid got hurt." All of this in a moment of recognition that the values for which that teacher entered the profession had all somehow, over the years, been distorted. The teacher recognized there was no longer any desire to protect the child, only a desire for self-preservation. Let us be clear about this fear in the school. Fear in the teachers and staff results in fear for children.

We live in a time when there is increasing pressure on children to achieve. The curriculum seems to be steadily creeping downward. Things that were once taught in higher grades are being introduced in the lower grades. There are pressures to learn to read earlier and earlier. Earl Kelley, an author and educator, once said, "I sometimes think the only reason people have children is so that they can have a good reader in the family!" Our system of grading, promotion, and mastery all blame the child for any lack of performance. There is a formula for producing fear in children in schools. It is this: Create a climate in which academic achievement is more valued than individual worth, in which blame is more common than praise, and in which the opinion of others is always more important than one's own. Add to this the following: In the U.S. we have created a school system in which *failure is expected and accepted.* Can it be any wonder that school is not a joyful place to be for many of our children? They must sit quietly, learning what others believe is important, without challenge, sometimes to be physically attacked by adults charged to teach them, and sometimes humiliated, ridiculed, and insulted with no one to protect them in a society that believes if they fail, it is their fault. Yes, it is in a climate of fear that many of our children attend school.

Math Anxiety

Math class! No other class strikes fear in the hearts of children like this one. Adults still shudder in the night with the very memory of those long, boring, fear-producing hours spent in math class. Is this scenario overdrawn? Perhaps.

For many of us, however, it is not, and that is the shame. For many children, especially girls, the description may even be pale. (Tobias 1978; Tobias 1980). When called on to go to the board to do long division (ye gads!) chills run up and down their bodies—everyone in class will know how stupid they are. Everyone.

Why should one subject in school be separated out as the most fear producing? What makes it so frightening? Why are many adults still incompetent at even simple math problems? Why are females seemingly more affected than males?

The answers to these questions lie more in the realm of myth than in the world of fact. What do we believe about math?

Myths about math

If you are good at math it's because you were born with a special gift or talent. Unfortunately, there are even educators who are running around with this antiquated belief. Who knows where it came from? Nevertheless, many believe it. What it takes to set it off is an early failure and then some adult to reinforce it. "Since I don't have the raw material, I'll never be any good at math." Then, there begin the long years of dread and avoidance.

This assumption is false. Math is a skill, especially adding, subtracting, dividing, and multiplying. At the elementary school level, it is no different from any other subject. It is no different from learning the rules of grammar or the rules of jump rope! It is different only in the fear it generates in many of us.

If you are good at math, then you can solve problems fast (Tobias 1980). Many of us believe people who are good at math are good because they can solve problems fast. This is a myth that grows out of evaluation techniques rewarding quickness rather than thoroughness. These tests have little to do with the ability to understand and compute. We have left out the quick ones who fail when we engage in this myth. The authors of this book are personally confused about the source of, or the need for, such timed tests. In spite of the arguments against them, they persist. One result is that a thorough, careful student may come to believe he or she is not good at some subject when, in fact, that student is just the sort of serious scholar we later claim we want to produce.

Boys are better at math than girls. Somehow, genetically, boys are given genes that make them better at math than girls. It is natural for boys to be better at math. It is a subject that really requires thinking, and we all know that girls are not good at logical thinking. Obvious trash, yet many subscribe to this line of reasoning. It is usually followed by some other trash, such as "Girls are verbal. Boys are mathematical."

Again, aside from the sexist implications of such reasoning, the authors do not have the slightest idea where this belief came from. In fact, through the sixth grade, girls actually outperform boys in math (Fiske 1980). Math anxiety exists for all students, but somewhere along the line females begin to take on more fear. There may be many reasons for this. Girls are no more or less susceptible to cultural biases, and so many come to believe the myth about boys being better at math (a self-fulfilling prophecy). Girls may become convinced, for some reason, that intellectual skills are not feminine, a strange, but not uncommon, belief. Whatever the reasons, they need to be encountered in our society and defeated. The loss of individuals and to society as a whole is useless and unnecessary. There is no solid evidence we know of that proves intellectual skills are given more to one gender than to another.

There are indications some environmental influences can be blamed for female attitudes. A recent study of elementary math textbooks revealed those books presented males in positive roles and females in negative roles. In a word, they were sexist. Males were represented two thirds of the time, and they were represented in positive roles in math and science. In contrast, most females were represented as blundering, confused, and stupid (Donady and Tobias 1977).

Elementary teachers provide role models for children. Their attitudes toward math are transmitted to their students daily. When one of the authors was teaching in an elementary school, the following conversation took place between two teachers in the teachers' lounge. One female teacher was overheard to say, "Well, math's not my thing. I try to squeeze it in at the end of the day, but some days we don't do math. I sure love those days!" Since most elementary teachers are female, it is not improbable to believe many suffer from math anxiety in the way the teacher described above did. As a result, those teachers may fail to create a positive, healthy image toward the subject of math.

Parents may also provide a negative image for female children in the ways in which tasks are divided in the home. Mothers tend to help with arithmetic up until about the sixth grade. After that, fathers take over in many households. In many families, fathers assume the financial responsibilities and pay the bills, do the taxes, and so forth. Successful female role models are hard to find. How many female accountants do you know? While flip, that question may remind us of how much the mathematical functions have been given over to males in our society.

The point of all of this is to show that math anxiety comes more from a series of myths, and from the way in which it is taught, rather than from any gender-related or subject-specific problem with math. Since this is the case, it is possible the problem of math anxiety is one that can be alleviated by a thorough examination of our attitudes. That approach holds more promise for us than any direct attack on different teaching methods to help females overcome some real or imagined math incompetencies.

"Jennifer, you're late. The school bus will be here in fifteen minutes and you're not even dressed. Get moving!"

As Jennifer sat on the edge of her bed, her hands trembled. She felt dizzy and sick to her stomach. Just thinking about riding the bus and walking into her classroom filled her with terror. "There's *no way* I'm going to school today."

She crawled under the covers and pulled the sheets tightly around herself. "I don't feel very good. I guess I'll stay home from school today."

At first glance, this scene may not appear to be much of a problem. After all, most children at some time during their twelve years of formal education find staying at home more desirable than going to school. Those familiar "I-don't-want-to-go-to-school" blues, is a fairly common refrain, especially at the end of the never-long-enough summer vacation. In a matter of days, these negative feelings about school are forgotten.

Unfortunately for hundreds of children like Jennifer, those feelings don't go away. They intensify. The fear of attending school becomes so great these children create physical symptoms, like migraine headaches and abdominal pains, when there is no organic cause for these symptoms. They will tolerate the most severe forms of punishment rather than experience the emotional terror evoked by going to school. The agony of a young boy is keenly felt as he told his father, "I don't care what you do to me. You can take away all my games and money, but if you make me go back to school I'll kill myself."

The child was suffering from a condition known as school phobia or fear of school. This is a misleading term. While some psychologists suggest this condition is a result of some specific school-related situation, most of the research indicates school-phobic children are not frightened by teachers, blackboards, or the school building itself. Rather, their fears are caused by separation anxiety. They are terribly afraid to leave home or to leave their parent(s) (Whiteside 1974).

Who are these frightened young people? Usually these children are the youngest or eldest in the family. The average age of school-phobic children in the U.S. is eleven. Prior to the onset of this condition, most of them have had positive school experiences.

While these children are anxious when away, at home they may be controlling and manipulative. Parents who are anxious themselves may contribute to the child's separation anxiety. Still, this is a difficult connection to make, since a child's fear of school may appear after many years of successful school experience. Many parents are shocked to learn of their child's fear; in this instance, teachers are unable to provide any insight, since the child's anxiety is probably not tied to any real event, situation, or person that could lead to a concrete solution. In fact, these are often children who are having no academic problems in the school and could, in many cases, even be considered successful at school.

School phobia can result from many situations in the child's life. Its appearance may be triggered by moving to a new town, changing schools, a death in the family, or divorce. All of these, of course, directly attack a child's sense of security and safety in the world. All of these present some form of loss, and the child may be clinging to home as a stable place in the midst of rapid changes over which he or she has no control. Whatever the initial cause, these children cling to a mistaken belief that their parent(s) either emotionally or physically need them at home. They feel they have to protect Mom or Dad from some perceived threat, danger, or worry. If the child stays home, then things will be fine. In one extreme case, a daughter thought her mother would starve to death if the daughter didn't stay home and prepare lunch. It is in the face of such irrational responses that many parents find school phobia so difficult to deal with.

What may be frustrating for a parent, as well, is that the condition may continue undiscovered until the fear has become so severe the child is unable to go to school at all. It is not a problem of reluctance, of being tardy, or of missing from time to time; it is a problem of a compelling fear which will not allow the child to go to school. While school phobia begins gradually, with subtle warnings, it is often not until a final dramatic fear and refusal that many parents recognize the severity of the problem for their child. These subtle signs may include a general irritability, crying for no apparent reason, fitful sleeping patterns, and a refusal to visit a friend next door or down the block.

Although there are many causes of school phobia, what these children share is an all-encompassing, overpowering fear. This is not pretend fear. It is real. It is only the source of the fear that is ill-defined. These children aren't trying to trick their parents; they are genuinely afraid. So far as children are concerned, the longer it takes for a parent to recognize the problem, the more difficult it is to treat. It is a problem that can persist over months and, unfortunately for some families, over years.

School phobia is a serious problem for families. Therefore, it is not one parents can deal with themselves or one the child will grow out of.

The problem will not go away by itself. It is one of those problems that demands professional help.

Suggestions for Overcoming the Fears of Children About School

Despite the nature of our schools, there is nothing that prevents us from changing them. There is nothing that prevents parents from insisting that schools be places where their children feel safe and protected. If there is a formula for creating fear, then there is a formula for creating well-being. Let us begin to replace the formula for fear with a formula for success.

A beginning for our entire society is to stop using adult concerns, fears, and standards as a basis for evaluating children. While it is entirely correct to have academic standards for engineers, physicians, attorneys, accountants, or other professionals, these concerns have little to do with the elementary education of children. The notion that the academic achievement of children is crucial, life-directing, or ultimate is, of course, nonsense, and has much more to do with adult fears than it has to do with the lives of children. One need not be a psychologist, an educator, or a curriculum specialist to know children are eager learners. One doesn't have to search outside one's own experience to know tasks of one's own choosing hold more interest and are mastered more readily than those forced upon us. Children are no different. It is only the child haters among us who would have us believe that children need to be forced to learn. They, of course, need fear as a weapon. Most of us do not.

We have three sets of recommendations for helping children deal with the fears they have about school. There are recommendations for parents. There are recommendations for teachers. There is *a* recommendation for the school system.

Parents

Take the pressure off the child. Do this by valuing the child rather than the child's achievement. Easy to say; hard to do. One way of doing it is to change the way most of us give praise. Most of us have learned to praise products. We might say, for example, "Oh, Daniel! What a good story you have written." Now, by and large, there is nothing wrong with such statements. Notice, however, the praise is actually for the story rather than for Daniel. Over the years, a lesson is learned. It is the products that count, rather than the producer. Another way to praise could be to say, "Daniel, I can see how pleased you are with this story" or "Daniel, you had the biggest grin on your face when you brought me this story. I'll bet *you are* pleased with it." The overall effect of this slight change is to create an atmosphere of warmth rather than one of evaluation.

Conspicuous availability. Create a home in which the children know there is always time to talk. Parents might even begin to initiate conversations about school. One of the authors learned the hard way that children do not respond to direct questions about school. Parent says, "Tell me what you did in school today." Child says, "Nothing." Dead end! Parent tries again: "Listen, Pardner, I'm the sheriff around this ole corral and I need some information on what the hired hands are a'larning down at the new school." Result (especially for little children)—child blabs all over the place! Using cues and patience, parents can teach their children to talk about school and any fears they may be encountering. If parents are there, then the child can learn that his or her opinion really counts in the family.

Be a teacher. Don't be afraid to teach children skills, knowledge, or competencies. The teachers and the schools are not the only sources in society where children can learn. Help children learn to read, write, or do math. Teach them about the parents' jobs. Teach them to build, ride, jump, climb, draw, dig, or create operas! Teach them what you know. Learning counts. Help children with homework. Don't do it for them, but always let them know you are ready, willing, and reasonably able to help. If you don't know what the child is doing, then learn along with him or her.

Be an advocate. In disputes with the school, don't be too ready to take the school's side. The school has plenty of support; the child only has you. It doesn't matter if the child is "guilty" of the "crime"; she or he still needs a good "lawyer" (Mom or Dad) to argue for due process, fairness, and justice—even mercy.

Be a protector. Despite a general denial on the part of schools and a general lack of belief on the part of the public, teachers are still hitting children in the schools. As a parent, you can help reduce the fear children face at school if you are vocal, and firm, about not allowing school personnel to physically punish your children. Make it clear you do not approve of teachers or principals hitting children, and should any one of them hit your child you will first insist upon a full investigation by the school board and, if necessary, go to court to protect your children from such behavior.

If you are of a political mind, you might begin a campaign to have corporal punishment banned as a method of discipline in your school district. There are many organizations willing to help in various states. In fact, many local teachers' organizations have themselves tried to have corporal punishment banned in schools and can be a source of help. One national organization that can be of help is End Violence Against the Next Generation (EVAN-G). Its address is:

EVAN-G
977 Keeler Avenue
Berkeley, California 94708

Teachers

The teacher in the classroom is the person at school who can do the most to reduce fear in children. He or she is in total charge behind the classroom door.

Reduce the climate of fear. If any person can reduce the climate of fear based on judgment by achievement, it is the teacher. It is possible for teachers to have at least one unacceptable behavior in any class—failure. If failure is unacceptable, then the teacher can move forward creating success. Insist upon it and create it.

Teach. Remember, the job is to teach. It is not to sort, classify, or grade children. Resist the impulse to label children and thus create self-fulfilling prophecies of failure for children.

Confront one's own fears. Teachers are faced with an incredible number of jobs they have to do and for which they are held accountable. This is both frustrating and anxiety producing because often they interfere with the job and might even determine whether the teacher is rehired. Those fears are real. And the children had nothing to do with their formulation or implementation. Don't take your fears out on the children.

A rule. As a general rule, remember: A child is always more important than reading, writing, and arithmetic.

Schools

There is one recommendation for schools. Change the system. Nothing less will do.

Stop the fear-creating, learning-hindering system of comparative evaluations which characterize our schools. We have created a system in which we insist at least some of our children fail all of the time. We have a national system of evaluation in which the scoring creates 50 percent failure all the time! That is an absurdity. Voltaire once wrote, "People who believe in absurdities commit atrocities." He must have had the American system of standardized testing in mind. A former government official in the field of education is quoted as saying, "Our goal is to have every child in America above grade level in reading." What a worthy goal— the problem is that it is impossible. Grade level is defined as the point at which 50 percent of the children can read and comprehend and the other 50 percent cannot! Yes, you are right, that's a dumb way to measure things, but that is the way we do it. Failure is not only expected and accepted, it is created.

There are other ways to measure achievement which are not competitive or comparative. There is the concept of competence. There is the concept of mastery. Both of these systems are simply measures of whether or not someone knows how to do something. It doesn't matter if someone else already knows how. The only time speed counts is when speed is the skill to be mastered.

Another way is to use the child himself or herself as the basis from which change is measured. For example, if today Julie knows one letter and tomorrow she knows two, then there is absolute proof that she has grown/learned. Consider this formula if one were to make a judgment of a child in the sixth grade that many might call slow in a comparative system. What would the child's achievement look like if it were measured in terms of absolute growth from grade one to grade six? Different, no doubt. What would be the fear in school if children were continually presented with evidence of their own absolute growth/learning? It is a question that needs to be asked more frequently and with more force of our nation's educators.

Suggestions to Help Children
Overcome Math Anxiety

The following suggestions are divided into two parts. First, there is a section for parents. Second, there is a section for teachers. While these concrete suggestions can be helpful, it will be even more helpful to begin an examination of attitudes, at home or in the school, that are contributing to anxiety on the part of children.

Parents

The suggestions that follow are meant to help parents confront both the attitudes and behaviors of children. It is entirely possible, as one gains skills in an area, that one's attitudes toward that area will change as well.

Play number games with children. For example, when traveling with children, play a number of games with license plates of cars. Have the children take turns adding up the numbers on the plates. Or, point out any unusual plates. (For example, 3 6 9 12 or 81 9 3—the first is a series; in the other, 9 is the square root of 81 and 3 is the square root of 9. What about ABC 123?). Allow children to compute mileage from one city to another if a trip is planned and then figure out the actual mileage upon arrival. While these may seem too easy, they do have the advantage of unconsciously teaching that numbers can be fun and can be mastered. Further, they teach that parents care about numbers and their children's learning.

Provide opportunities for girls as well as boys to tinker with old clocks, radios, and other mechanical objects. Encourage them to take them apart and put them together again.

Play games with children which develop visual and spatial relations. For example, games such as three-dimensional tic-tac-toe and tangrams (a game of different-shaped pieces which can be assembled into many different geometric forms) can be played with children. Further, such outdoor games as volleyball, baseball, basketball, tennis, and so forth also help develop perception and coordination. The importance of this recommendation and the previous one lies in the fact that research has revealed a relationship between such visual and spatial skills and math.

Be sensitive to your own attitudes and behaviors as a role model. For example, insure that children see both parents doing bills. Make sure children observe both mother and father balancing the checkbook. Whenever one parent finds himself or herself saying something that demeans the ability of one gender or the other to perform some skill, it is not too late to say, "Did you hear what I said? Isn't that silly? We know that boys and girls can both do that."

Read newspapers together, pointing out graphs, ratios, percentages, and so forth. We might even learn something ourselves! Show how math is used in everyday life and common experiences such as baking, building, measuring, and deciding where to hang a picture.

Finally, encourage one's daughters, as well as sons, to continue in their math education in spite of the anxieties they feel. Encourage them to do it for the experience rather than for the grades. Encourage them because it appears our future is leading us toward a world in which working with calculators, computers, and other math-related hardware will open up new areas of work and play in which anyone with a limited mathematics background will be seriously hampered.

Teachers

Here are some suggestions that can be used by teachers to not only reduce math anxiety, but to teach the subject better overall. Try some of these in the classroom to see how children respond. Also, there is nothing to prevent parents from using these suggestions as well.

Confront your own fears in math and work to reduce them. One way of doing this is to talk about them in class with students. Tell them you can understand how some students in class feel about math because you are anxious about it too. Search out any number of books with math games. Do not allow it to become a subject that is put off until the end of the day. Use math as a basis for the construction of games and activities in the classroom.

Be sensitive to the fears of children. Support the idea that math is difficult and what it takes to master it is practice and effort. (Don't tell children something is easy. It ruins the experience for everyone. Consider this:

If it is easy and you get it, what have you done? If it is easy and you don't get it, then that really means you are dumb.) Point out those times when children say things that put themselves down. Take those opportunities to tell them all they are struggling with is a skill, and that is no reason to think less of themselves as persons. People are more important than math.

Reconsider giving speed tests. Think over what point is proven if one child is relatively more rapid than another. Try to move toward a concept of testing to find out if children have a skill. Test in the same way you teach. If you use a hands-on approach to teaching, then don't test using paper and pencil. Those are two different skills.

Foster a classroom climate where the emphasis is on success. Encourage peer cooperation. Have groups of children work together to solve particular sorts of problems. Allow the children to teach each other. Create some kinds of problems that are easy and others that are more difficult. Teach children to search as well as to answer. If you have a particularly good rapport with a class, give them some problems that are impossible. If they say they are impossible, ask them to explain why.

This is an excellent place to introduce the concept of calculators. Children are fast becoming more comfortable with calculators than many adults, teachers included. There are many calculator books on the market that are both fun and educational. This can become an excellent way to have individuals work alone while the teacher works with others in the class.

Take the focus off "right answers." Begin to concentrate on the procedures children use. Increasingly, ask students how they did what they did. Begin to ask, "Are there other ways to work this problem?" The fact of the matter is, math is not as concrete, black and white, as many of us learned.

Further, it is entirely possible for children to arrive at "wrong" answers using the proper procedures. A simple indication of right and wrong answers may simultaneously teach a child that a procedure which is workable is wrong. Teachers can avoid this kind of teaching mistake by integrating in the classroom a desire to build creative thinking as well as analytical thinking. Take the time to give credit for creative and imaginative solutions to problems as well as for right answers. There is an old story of a creative student who, when asked to use a barometer to figure out how tall a building was, said she would find the owner of the building and say, "I'll give you a good barometer if you will tell me how tall your building is." Mathematically it isn't too sound, but it is a heck of a solution to the problem!

Suggestions for Helping the School-Phobic Child

The suggestions that follow are divided into sections for parents, teachers, and school. While the most important recommendation for the school-phobic child is to seek professional help, there are things parents, teachers, and the school can do.

Parents

Listen to behavior. Children often talk in circles. They are not always able to explain how they feel in concrete ways understandable to parents. Therefore, watch their behavior closely. If they begin to show signs of fearfulness, complain of physical symptoms, and avoid leaving the house for school, these can be an early signal the parents can evaluate to determine if a more serious problem exists (Whiteside 1974).

Examine parental behavior. Make certain there are not subtle messages in the family that communicate to the child one or both of parents is somehow dependent upon the child. The pressure for this sort of dependence is greater in divorced and single-parent families. As adults, our own emotional pain and confusion often prevent us from providing a strong support system for our children. As silly as it may seem, reassure children that parents are able to take care of themselves. A parent might say, "Thank you for being concerned about me. I want you to know that I don't think anything bad is going to happen to me while you are away at school." It is also helpful to share specific activities parents will be doing in a day to reassure the child.

Allow the child to call home. This may involve many phone calls in the beginning. The calls will decrease over time as the child grows more confident and secure that things at home are safe.

At the first sign of separation anxiety, be firm and insist the child return to school. Most school-phobic children remain at home with their parents' knowledge and approval.

However, in severe cases, this force should not be used. This is a case where professional help is most needed. In such cases, making the child go to school will probably result in a runaway child. Consult a professional; then become involved in treatment. Remember, this is not a problem a child has alone—it is a family problem.

Teachers

Self-concept. Many school-phobic children suffer from a problem of poor self-image. Just as it is important for all children to see themselves in positive, self-enhancing ways, it is important for the school-phobic child to learn he or she is a worthwhile child. The classroom can be a place where this sort of image is built and reinforced.

Contract for attendance. It is possible a school-phobic child can learn to come to school again a bit at a time. For example, a teacher might contract with a child about what part of the day will be spent in school. It is possible the child could have a tutor for other school subjects missed while out of school. Finally, such a contract can have the effect of fostering independence and responsibility as the child learns he or she is gaining control over his or her life.

Home visits. The teacher may shift the classroom to the child. It is possible that the teacher and members of the class might visit the child at home. They could encourage the child to come back to school the next day. If one visit doesn't work, visit again.

Recognize that the purpose of the visit is not to create more pressure for the child. If the child doesn't respond and appears to become more anxious, then do not continue the visits. This home-visit program is most effective early, perhaps when a child has missed a week but not more than a month.

School

School climate. School personnel can work to create a supportive and encouraging climate at school. It is especially important for the school-phobic child's return to school to be welcomed and wanted. This child in particular needs to know that he or she won't be ridiculed for the avoidance behavior.

Flexibility. In order to facilitate the return of a school-phobic child back into school, the rules might have to be bent. Allow the child to make calls home as many times as necessary for reassurance. Allow the child to arrive at school at different times, if necessary, to encourage coming when the child believes he or she can manage.

Inform school personnel concerning school phobia. Provide all school personnel with information regarding school phobia; especially inform them of any particular child so there is no accidental ridicule or inappropriate discipline. In this way, a climate can be created that actively works to encourage the child back into school.

6

STRESS
in Sports

The battle of Waterloo
was won on the playing fields of Eton.

Probably never said by the
Duke of Wellington

For many children, playing sports is a relaxing, enjoyable activity. It is a healthy, worthwhile way to spend time. However, this isn't always so. Consider an instance related to the authors. A young boy was participating in a Little League baseball game and made an error, allowing a ball to roll through his legs. His father was so enraged at him he locked his son out of the house after the game. Sports were less a source of relaxation and enjoyment for this youngster. While admittedly an extreme example, this instance does raise the possibility that organized athletics may be a source of stress for some youngsters. We have found stress to be produced by five different causes: (1) parental attitudes, (2) coaches' attitudes, (3) psychological factors, (4) physical injuries, and (5) sociological factors. After examining how the five causes produce stress, we offer concrete suggestions to prevent or reverse the stress associated with the causes. It is not our intention to criticize sports. Rather, we want to inform parents about possible sources of stress which may be connected with participation in organized athletics. The suggestions, if followed, will enable children to enjoy athletics and experience the many benefits athletics can offer.

Perhaps the single most powerful factor that leads to stress for children involved in organized athletics is parental attitudes about sports. The most harmful idea parents can convey is that winning is the same as success and losing is the same as failure. We will often talk about self-concept in this chapter. Basically, self-concept refers to what persons believe about themselves. Do they believe they are competent, lovable, and worthwhile, or do they believe they are not very skilled, not lovable, and not worthwhile? The first set of beliefs may be called a positive self-concept and the latter set of beliefs termed a negative self-concept.

Parents who overemphasize the importance of athletic competition run the risk of distorting their children's self-concepts (Gerson 1977). The idea "Winning isn't everything; it's the only thing" can have serious effects on young, developing children. Seeing the importance some parents place on winning—the disappointment, disgust, and even anger parents experience when children play poorly or lose—you can be almost certain children will make these ideas part of their self-concept. If they play well, or win, they can come to believe they are competent, lovable, and worthwhile. If they lose or play poorly, they can easily come to believe they are incompetent, unlovable, and not worthwhile. Winning comes to mean success as a person. Losing comes to mean failure as a person. Since everyone wants to feel loved and worthwhile, the pressures to win and perform well in sports can become overwhelming. Making an error or dropping a pass can become signs that a child is a failure as a person. The overemphasis on winning and performance will often have negative effects. Even when a child almost always wins, the pressure is there the next time. People expect him or her to win, and losing becomes even more dangerous.

Another parental attitude that leads to pressure for children is the meaning parents place on sports and athletics. For children, games are primarily a source of fun, something to enjoy. Games also are a way for kids to release energy, both physical and creative. Finally, games give children a chance to test their developing abilities, to compare themselves to other kids and form an impression of how skilled they are. The main source of enjoyment in spontaneous playing comes from the playing itself. Winning or losing seems less important to children. However, for a variety of reasons, adults who organize athletics for children have imposed their own values on kids' games. They see children's games through adult eyes. The businesslike ideas of adults—that there should always be a reason for things, that there should be goals which are worked toward, that success is important—replace the reasons for which children naturally play games. Parents may adopt a *product* approach. Winning and achievement are important. Children, if allowed to play naturally, adopt a *process* approach (Dubois 1980). Playing is fun. Winning and achievement are secondary. By changing the way play and games naturally occur, by organizing sports and insisting on winning, children are deprived of an important part of growing up. This adds to the pressures involved in organized athletics. Kids do compete when they play in a natural, spontaneous manner. Even simple games such as tag or kick the can have "winners" and "losers." However, there is little stigma in being tagged and becoming "it." Being "it" also changes from moment to moment. Youngsters are less likely to think of themselves as failures after a game of tag than after losing a ball game. A spontaneous game of tag offers competition and fun without the stigma of failure or success.

There may also be relationships between the decline in spontaneous play in American children and increased participation in organized sports. In addition to having less time for spontaneous play, organized sports may bias children toward competition and winning and losing. Kids may come to think that all play is supposed to have a goal—winning. They may become predisposed to seeing play through the adult or product view, that there must be a reason or goal (winning) for playing games. If this is so, children may not be as able to create their own games. They could be getting trained out of the natural tendency to create their own games and to play them for fun (Smoll et al. 1979).

Another parental attitude that can lead to pressures on children is the idea participating in organized athletics is always good. Most often this is an idea that is never questioned. Parents simply assume organized sports are good for children and then ship their children to the ball park. Little, if any, thought is given to the many ways in which organized sports may be harmful. Because the parents assume athletics are good for children, they may push their kids into sports when, in fact, the children would rather be involved in music, camping, or Christopher Robin's favorite thing to do— nothing, as in when Mother asked, "What have you been doing all day?" and you answered "Nothing." It is this blindness to the possible negative aspects of organized sports that allows other pressures to build up. Related to the idea that organized sports are good is the idea that once children start playing on a team, they should never quit. Since competing is thought of as automatically good, quitting is thought of as automatically bad. Many times it was the parent who wanted the child to play in the first place. The parents buy equipment, provide transportation, and attend games. All of this investment of time and energy makes it difficult for children to say they aren't interested in continuing. In other instances, children decide they would like to try a sport. After a while they discover the practices, games, and the pressures are not enjoyable and decide they no longer want to continue. Again, realizing how much their playing means to their parents, they find it difficult to quit. Parents may even quote such sayings as, "Nobody likes a quitter." The message is clear. The wishes and feelings of the child don't matter. It is what Mom and Dad want that matters most. The pressure of having to do what someone else wants, to keep others happy, can begin to mount and take its toll (Bruns and Tutko 1978).

Finally, participation in organized athletics has been found to be a source of competition between children in the same family. Often, family organization is disrupted by the logistics needed to keep a child on a team. Traveling to and from practices and games requires time, time away from other family members. Other children may have to accompany parents while a brother or sister is transported to and from games and practices. If several children are playing on different teams, the question arises as to who will watch what game—a computer may be needed to help organize the whole affair. Equipment bought for a child participating in sports or dinner table discussion of a game may both be sources of jealousy on the part of nonplaying brothers and sisters. If one child is more successful at sports than another, the attention given to the more successful child may come to be resented by the less successful one. The transportation and monetary aspects of keeping children may come to be resented by parents, especially in times of economic hardship and uncertainty. All in all, such situations are filled with the possibility of developing high levels of stress.

How parents deal with children's fears, disappointments, and complaints is another factor that can lead to stress. The risk of injury is real in organized youth sports (Burke and Kleiber 1976). There is sufficient evidence that injuries suffered as a child may affect a person throughout adult life, yet parents so often deny the seemingly minor injuries children report. The idea that it is "manly" or "tough" to keep playing, even when injured, is widespread. How often does the TV resound with the phrase "he can play with pain"? The TV, of course, fails to mention the athlete is being paid enormous sums of money for competing. The TV also fails to mention how many retired athletes there are who have "played with pain" and are permanently disabled. Still, parents will minimize the child's hurt, saying, "Oh, that's not so bad. You'll get over it. Just tough it out." Children have fears about playing sports. These are real. Parents, forgetting they are dealing with children, minimize the fear and impose adult standards.

Children also experience sorrow and disappointment over losing. Often they feel like crying. Just as often parents will not recognize these feelings. Rather, they will tell children to stop crying and then begin talking about the next game or what can be done to correct any mistakes that might have been made.

All the situations mentioned above have in common the denial or lack of recognition given to children's feelings by parents. The message that comes across to children is that their feelings aren't important. They shouldn't have such feelings as fear, hurt, or pain. If children believe that their feelings are unimportant, it follows that they may think they themselves are unimportant. The seeds are planted that lead to the belief that their ideas and feelings don't count. Only by pleasing others can they find acceptance. Only by being a person who is unafraid and doesn't cry can they be lovable in the eyes of their parents. They have to become someone they are not. The pressure of such a double life is damaging.

Coaches' Attitudes

Child athletes spend a good deal of time with adults other than their parents, most often with coaches and managers. Just as parental attitudes can have a profound effect on children's development, so can the attitudes of coaches (Parkhouse 1979).

Many coaches' beliefs are similar to and reinforce those presented by parents. The Lombardian philosophy, "Winning isn't everything, it's the only thing," is far too common among coaches of youth athletic teams. Coaches who see winning as the ultimate objective of youth sports only add to the pressures already mentioned. Coaches can be seen to rant, rave, and scream at their players in an attempt to "motivate" them to perform better. They convey the familiar message that winning means success and superiority, and losing means failure and inferiority. Performance on the athletic field is again translated into a message of personal worth. In order to prove to themselves and others they are, indeed, worthwhile and okay, children may try extremely hard. The pressure of having to prove that every time they are on the field can become unbearable and can be very damaging.

Coaches love to win. In order to win they often have to make coaching decisions that can have emotional effects on children. Coaches who are overheard to say, "I'll put Johnny in right field, not many will be hit out there" or "Billy and Tommy, you two take everything you can reach and help Bobby out" may be making game-winning decisions. They are also sending messages to children that they can't be depended upon and are not skilled and competent. Coaches also promise children that they can play "later" in the game. When the game is a close one, "later" never comes, and the bench warmer continues to sit on the bench. The game may be won, but the child loses much more in terms of self-confidence and self-respect. The message is clear; the pressure of not being "good" or dependable continues. The problem is, coaches treat children as objects or pawns in their own game of winning. Coaches can be either unaware or careless about the effects their moves have upon thinking children. All that matters is winning. Coaches may also believe winning or losing is a reflection on their own competence and ability. Their motivation is to prove themselves. The instruments of that proof may be children who are suffering emotional and physical damage.

Many coaches also believe participation in sports is always beneficial. Just by appearing at practice and playing in games, good things are thought to happen automatically. This belief makes it easier to scream at children, sit some children on the bench, direct physically exhausting practices, and ignore or look down upon complaints of injuries, fatigue, or hurt feelings. Children are dressed in uniforms like adults and are then thought to possess adultlike physical and emotional qualities. Children are not miniature adults. They don't have the physical and emotional skills of adults. To expect them to behave as adults is to place too much pressure upon them.

Psychological Pressures

Self-concept

One of the most obvious stress factors on children participating in organized athletic competition is the attitude they have learned about winning and losing. Parental pressure, a win-at-all-costs attitude of a coach, and having to perform in front of large, emotional crowds can all combine to create a dangerous situation for children. They can come to believe winning means they are okay and worthwhile and, worse, losing means they aren't okay, that they are inferior and worthless. Since no one, including children, wants to feel inferior and worthless, striving to win becomes a striving for self-respect. The stakes change and the purpose of participating in athletics is no longer to have fun or even to win; it has become a matter of preserving self-respect.

Psychologists have discovered that self-concept, how persons feel about themselves, has a powerful effect on how successful they are. Persons who believe they are unimportant and incapable can have great difficulty in even attempting, let alone accomplishing, relatively difficult challenges. They fear failure because that will be further proof they aren't capable or worthwhile. In order to avoid failure, and the bad feelings that accompany it, they avoid new, challenging situations that could result in failure. They stop growing psychologically and become much less than they have the potential to become.

Thus, the message that winning means one is okay and losing means one isn't okay can place incredible pressures on children. The need to please one's parents, to please other adults, and to be accepted by one's peers all combine to add importance to the winning of a game. Some children may be able to handle such pressure, but most can't; the damaging effects of such pressure may last a lifetime.

Another source of stress for children is more subtle than the meaning of winning and losing. Participating in organized sports can restrict the opportunities to develop creativity, initiative, and self-direction over one's life. Children who participate in organized sports most often have to do what they are told, do it when they are told, and do it in the way they are told. Little is left for them to decide. Research has shown that one of the purposes of play is to allow children to use their creative abilities, and that the exercise of creativity is important in the healthy emotional development of children. With the rise of organized athletics there has been a decline in the amount of *spontaneous* play in American children. Children are spending less time making up their own games with their own rules. The opportunities for learning to make a game work and for learning to get along with others are thus lessened. Children no longer have to (or *get* to) think for themselves. Rather they follow a schedule designed by someone else. Nothing seems left to the child's imagination.

The results of this decline in creative play may include, then, a reduced ability to think for oneself and to make one's own decisions.

The authors have observed numerous college athletes who, in effect, have their coaches register for them. They are told what courses to take, when to take them, and what teachers to get. In some cases coaches or other students actually walk through the registration for the athlete. In some cases the courses are easy, introductory ones which are chosen because they are easy. They are chosen to keep the athlete eligible for participation in sports. The fact that such courses may not lead to graduation or prepare a student for a career is lost to the athlete. He or she is so used to doing what coaches and officials say it becomes automatic. Initiative and directing one's own life take a backseat to following the directions of coaches, managers, and other officials.

Closely related to the lack of initiative and self-direction that may develop from organized athletics is the inability of children to be the source of their own satisfaction. Children can come to depend on others, usually on adults, to make many of the decisions they could and should be making for themselves. This dependence may even extend to the evaluation of their own performance. It is a common occurrence to see children looking to a coach or a parent for some sort of praise or signal their performance was satisfactory. Instead of deciding if their own performance was satisfactory and feeling happy about it, children often learn to wait for some praise or credit from others. Making a successful play or trying hard for an entire game are events that should be sources of pride and satisfaction without having to wait for words or rewards from others. One of the authors clearly recalls coming home after a Little League game in which he went three for four and his team had won. When he shared this with his father, his dad's response was, "You could have gone four for four." A three-for-four game, surely worth feeling good about, was suddenly not worth feeling so good about because an *adult* had decided it was not so good. Always looking to others for approval can be a continued source of stress.

Perhaps nothing contributes to this problem as much as the use of rewards for winning or playing well. Although rewards such as trophies, money, or other prizes may help motivate children in the short run, such rewards can have negative long-term effects (Meehl 1978). Playing and trying hard come to depend on the presence of a reward. No longer do children play because they want to or because it is fun for them. They begin to play to win the trophy or the money or whatever the reward is. Intrinsic motivation—doing something because persons want to, because it's fun and makes them feel good—begins to disappear. The sport itself becomes less important; what can be gained becomes important. Thus, an important source of pleasure and satisfaction is again removed from the child and placed in the hands of coaches, parents, and league officials. The long-term effects can be when the rewards are no longer present, interest in the activity disappears. Thus, the likelihood of staying active in a sport or in athletics in general may be lessened. The importance of physical fitness in leading a healthy, productive life is obvious. If children lose interest in sports it may be more difficult for them to stay involved in physical activity as adults, when the rewards aren't money or trophies. The rewards of fun and good health may not be enough to hold their interest.

Fear

There are a number of common fears which, while they may not prevent children from competing in organized sports, can certainly increase the stress associated with competing (Lipsyte 1980). The first of these fears is the fear of being ridiculed. Ridicule may follow a poor performance; the fear that others will laugh at or make fun of one's errors, mistakes, or poor play may lead to increased pressure on children. They can begin to worry more and more about making mistakes. Even if their own parents don't ridicule them, they may see a teammate or an opposing player being publicly ridiculed by a parent, friend, or coach. This alone can instill the fear in a child. Research suggests that worrying about mistakes instead of concentrating on the correct things to do will increase the chance of making mistakes. A circle of worrying leading to mistakes leading to more worry leading to more mistakes can be formed. That is a short-term effect. A long-term effect can be a child who is afraid to try because failure may lead to ridicule.

Another fear is that of disappointing one's parents. Parents, often unwittingly, by their intense interest in their children's sports, their emphasis on participating and winning, their constant support in terms of transportation, equipment, lessons, and so on, can set up a situation in which the child is afraid to lose because it will disappoint his parents, who are so involved. *They* will be disappointed, and that means the child must try even harder to avoid letting them down. After all, they have put so much into helping him become a better player. The fun of playing disappears and is replaced by the fear of disappointing loved ones. Someone once said, "When parents are concerned with winning, children lose." This quote suggests that trying to please parents and not disappoint them can take the fun out of playing for kids. It is hard enough for children to handle their own disappointment after losing without also being responsible for their parents' disappointment.

Another very common fear is that of getting hurt (Bruns and Tutko 1978). The high rate of injuries sustained in youth sports does not go unnoticed by youthful competitors. In Little League baseball one can be hit with a pitched or batted ball. In youth league football one can be tackled or hurt while tackling. In youth soccer one can be kicked or hit with the ball. Having these fears causes pressure on kids. Often, these pressures are combined with parental and coaches' attitudes that only "sissies" are afraid. Being afraid may be seen as letting Mom and Pop down. The pressure may build to intense levels.

All of these fears can add to the stress experienced by children in organized athletics. This stress can be compounded by adult attitudes, which make it difficult for children to admit and discuss these fears. Kids have trouble dealing with these types of stress and need all the help they can get.

Finally, there is a pressure, which, while not affecting most children who participate in organized athletics, is nevertheless real. Children who are exceptionally talented and those who have the promise of developing into good athletes face this unique situation. They are often protected, excused, and admired because of their special talent or promise. They may be asked to only do well enough academically in order to be promoted. They may be given grades unfairly. They may not be expected to do chores around the house so that they can practice or rest for a contest. Because of their talents and accomplishments they come to be admired by parents, coaches, peers, neighbors, and so on. These and other examples can lead to a distorted sense of importance. Too much of the child's sense of self-respect revolves around athletics. In a sense, such children may be prevented from normal development because of the special attention and rules that govern their lives. They don't have to deal with many of the same problems which the majority of less talented children must learn to solve. As a result, they may end up feeling helpless and lost except when involved in matters related to their sport.

Another related pressure is that resulting from these protected, excused, and admired children simultaneously experiencing negative feelings from others. While treated like kings and queens by some people, they may be despised and envied by many others. The special treatment they receive, the easy road they seem to be able to travel can be a source of many negative feelings from those who don't receive such special treatment. The result is a feeling of being pulled in two ways. The attention and admiration are wonderful, but the price can be steep in terms of the envy and rejection that can go along with them. Also, spending so much time in sporting activities can make it difficult for children to spend time with the kids they would like to socialize with. They may be forced to associate with other athletes who happen to be around most of the time.

Physical Injuries

Not all the stresses related to organized youth athletics have psychological causes. Recent research suggests that physical injuries are more common than previously believed and seem to be on the increase. Little League elbow was the first sport injury to receive much attention. One study found elbow and bone abnormalities in each of eighty players aged eight to fourteen who were pitchers in youth league baseball (Bruns and Tutko 1978). Only a small percentage of nonpitchers had this problem. Other studies have isolated a common epiphyseal injury which occurs in children aged nine to fourteen in the knee area as a result of landing from a jump such as in basketball (Burke and Kleiber 1976). Yet another study found significant cardiac contusions resulting from spearing in youth league football (Silverstein 1979). Spearing, although illegal, continues to occur; it has been cited as responsible for 30 percent of youth league football injuries. Recent evidence also has discovered a condition known as Little League shoulder. The evidence seems clear that serious and chronic injuries may result from organized youth sports.

The fears children have about being hurt while playing have a basis in reality. Pressure can thus be created. If a child is injured, it can be the source of additional stress. If parents and coaches have stressed the importance of playing with pain and ignoring minor injuries, children can feel they aren't tough enough and don't measure up. Children who suffer serious sports injuries can also experience a fear of not being able to compete effectively again. If much of their praise and worth centers around playing sports, they can fear not being accepted by their parents in the future. Not knowing what else is as important to their parents as sports, they may feel lost as to how to please their folks. Children with injuries may also feel pressured to return to play earlier than is medically sound, thus risking even more serious injury. In short, athletic injuries may set up a wide variety of pressures that can prove stressful.

Sociological Pressures

The prevalent attitude in American sports is to win at all costs. This attitude may be found from the professional level down to the youth leagues. One of the byproducts of this attitude is that coaches search for talented youngsters and, thus, concentrate on fewer and fewer kids at earlier and earlier ages. The increasing number of children not selected face the danger of turning away from sports, then from exercise, and finally from physical health (Bosco 1977). Further, the tremendous public exposure given to youth sports has set up a situation where it is very easy for children excluded from these sports to feel left out and unimportant.

Critics of organized youth sports have pointed out that sports have been taken away from the participants and used to teach certain values. The main value which is taught, critics say, is to subordinate one's own wishes and desires to those of the sports organization (Sage 1978). The league organization, the team, and their representative, the coach, all become more important than the individual. Where and when children will play, what children will play with which other children, how they play, what rewards they can receive, how they will dress, and other decisions are all made by the organization. Any ideas that individual players may have are subordinated to those of the organization. Youth sports organizations may reach down to five- and six-year-olds and reach up until graduation from college. During all of this time, an active sport, which is allegedly engaged in for fun and for the development of the participants, is kept out of the hands of the participants and in the hands of a few powerful organization personnel. Parents should consider the possibility that many youth leagues, originally organized for the good of children, may have changed and may no longer be operating for the same reasons. It is quite possible that the few relatively powerful persons who control various youth leagues may be more concerned with promoting their own personal values rather than those values parents would like to see. As one example, some children have even had to go to court to achieve the "right" to play sports in some youth leagues. The authors firmly believe that all children have a right to participate in athletics. Any organization that attempts to prevent children from participating should be closely scrutinized. The values such organizations promote and teach might not be what parents are hoping for.

The organization of children's play begins to resemble the adult world of work. There are bosses who tell people what to do and people who must do what they are told. Why shouldn't youth sports resemble the adults' world? Youth sports are run by adults, with adult values and adult goals. The problem with this arrangement is that children are deprived of the carefreeness, creativity, spontaneity, and fun of their play. The most important benefits of play, the growth experiences it can provide, are subordinated to the values of obedience to an organization and subordination of the individual's will to the group will. The child's own expression of creativity and choice is stunted, and a valuable opportunity for growth is lost. As mentioned before, when persons are not exercising their potential and abilities, a stressful situation is created. The stress may be more subtle than most mentioned in this chapter, but it is stressful nevertheless.

Suggestions for Reducing Stress in Sports

Parental Pressures

Our most important suggestion to parents is simple. Remember that children are not adults. They are different from adults physically, intellectually, and emotionally. They aren't as strong, as fast, or as coordinated as adults. They don't think in the same ways and their feelings don't always work in the same ways. Keeping this in mind, we offer the following two guidelines: 1) Let children be what they are; 2) Let them be the athletes they can be, not the athletes we, as parents, would like them to be. The simplest way to follow this first guideline is to make sure that children want to participate in organized sports. Sometimes we try to influence our children to play sports without really knowing why. We believe we are doing it because we think it is good for them. However, we might have some other motivation. One of the authors has a son who was ten years old. Summer was approaching and Dad wanted to know what baseball team the son wanted to play on that summer. The son said he didn't want to play baseball that year. For several days Dad kept asking what team the son wanted to play for. For several days the son kept saying he didn't want to play baseball that summer. His dad finally figured out that all his questions about baseball had to do with his own appreciation and love for the sport. Dad hoped that his son would also love baseball and get as much pleasure from it as he had. Dad's motivations had little to do with building character, health, self-concept, or what-have-you. Dad wanted the son to play baseball because Dad liked it! The son took up swimming.

Ask children if they really want to play. If children are already playing, ask them if they are having fun and want to continue. Ask them simply and in a straightforward manner. If they answer yes, then they probably do want to play. At this point parents should follow the second guideline and ask themselves some very important questions. "Am I trying to make my children into the athletes I want, winners and champions? Am I more concerned about whether my children win and play well or are my first thoughts about whether they had a good time?" Parents can ask children whether anything they do makes the children feel uncomfortable or embarrassed. These types of questions can give parents clues about their motivations in having their children play sports. Every parent would likely want their children to do well and win. But to insist on winning, to place athletic performance above the child's life, can lead to high levels of stress.

A second important suggestion is one on which physical educators, sports psychologists, and just about everyone else involved with children seem to agree. Parents should recognize and praise effort, not winning and losing. What should matter and what children should learn is that it is important to do one's best. That is all anyone can do. When a game or match is over, make some comment about the fact that the child participated and tried hard. Tell children that trying hard makes their parents happy. A smile and a hug after a game, especially after a loss, will help ease the pain of losing and let the child know that trying is what is expected and that they are loved both when he or she wins and when he or she loses. If a child has just won, it is always important to mention and praise the child's effort. Discuss and share the child's happy feelings over winning, but make sure they know they are cared for regardless of the score.

Another suggestion for parents is to treat their child athletes as people, not as X's and O's. Realize that children are more than pitchers, quarterbacks, or backstrokers. They are persons with feelings, sometimes intense ones. Treating a child as a person means to recognize that: 1) children have their own feelings, and 2) they have a right to feel that way. Children's feelings can often be observed by watching them. If a parent isn't sure how a child feels, then talk to the child and ask. Once the parent knows how the child feels, it is important to accept the feelings. The child has a right to those feelings. Acceptance of these feelings can be conveyed by discussing the child's feelings with the child. Avoid statements that deny or dismiss the child's feelings. "Don't feel so bad. You almost won." "You have no reason to be embarrassed. It wasn't your fault." "It's only a game. Forget about it." "It's only a bruise. It will heal quickly." All of these statements tend to deny or dismiss the feelings a child may have. It would be much more helpful to make statements that recognize and accept the feelings. "You're pretty sad, huh? You almost won and then they beat you. I know that's really disappointing." "I know you feel bad. You don't like to lose and you really wanted to win this game." "I'll bet that bruise is pretty sore. I know it sure hurt when I used to get skinned up." The second set of sentences recognizes the child's feelings and conveys the message that it is acceptable to have the feelings. This is a good first step toward treating young athletes as persons.

Another suggestion for parents is related to their motivation for having their children participate in sports. Parents should take great care to make sure kids are playing sports for their own pleasure, not their parents'. This is one way to avoid producing unnecessary stress for children. At the same time, a healthy goal for parents would be to stimulate and maintain an interest in lifetime sports for their children. Medical, physiological, and psychological evidence all seem to point to the fact that by remaining active and staying fit, one's health may be kept at higher levels. Exercise has been shown to make persons more resistant to stress.

Therefore, it makes sense for parents to stimulate an interest in sports so that children will want to continue participating throughout their adult lives. Lifetime participation in sports is a desirable and beneficial goal. To help achieve this goal, parents could do at least two things. One, avoid giving rewards such as money, trophies, prizes, and so forth for athletic performances. Research suggests that even if children enjoy doing something just for fun, presenting rewards will change their motivation. They soon may want to perform only when there is some reward to be gained (Meehl 1978; Gerson 1977), Then, in the absence of a reward. little, if any, effort is made. A child who loves to play a sport may soon lose interest if there is no financial or material reward to be won. Lifetime sports have to be intrinsically motivated. This means the person does them because they are fun or because they lead to health or something else important to the person. At present there are very few rewards or prizes provided by other people for staying fit and competing in lifetime sports.

By giving rewards to children for playing sports we may be making it more difficult for them to continue playing these sports as adults.

Second, in addition to organized sports, try to stimulate an interest in sports that can be played for a lifetime and have a definite health value. The traditional team sports offer some of this, but football and baseball are not great conditioners. Consider jogging, swimming, and bicycling as sports in which to involve children. These are all excellent sports for maintaining health and can all offer competition for adults. If persons don't want to compete against others, they can always compete against themselves or the clock in these sports. The more of these activities children become involved in, the more likely it is they will be able to stay fit as adults.

City recreation programs often offer the opportunity to participate in athletics at a less competitive and potentially damaging level. Without the elaborate uniforms and organization of many youth leagues, recreation programs begin to look more and more like the games children used to organize themselves. A T-shirt, a cap, and a glove instead of a flannel uniform with spiked shoes and large vocal crowds may make it easier for kids to relax and enjoy themselves.

The easiest way for parents to stimulate interest in lifetime sports is to set an example for their children. Do these sports together as a family. Being with their parents and having fun is rewarding enough for most kids to keep participating in these "nonglamour" sports. In addition to motivating children toward fitness, such activities can build closeness and communication in families.

There are several other suggestions that may prove very helpful to parents. One is to help children learn to evaluate their abilities clearly. Children do this naturally when they play in a spontaneous, relatively unorganized manner. Children know who is talented in what areas and they seem to accept this quite well. But when adult values about being a winner and being number one become internalized, it is not so easy to admit that others are more talented. Psychologists point out one of the signs of a healthy personality is the ability to accept negative information about oneself. It takes a strong, healthy self-concept to admit "I'm not very good at tennis. But that's okay. I can do other things and I'm a pretty good person."

Parents can help children reach this high level of adjustment. Helping children admit they did the best they could and the opponent was probably better, at least on this day, is a step in the right direction. There is nothing wrong with not being the best. There is something seriously wrong with not being able to accept it, with always having to make excuses for not winning, with feeling bad about oneself after a loss.

Parents can also help their children to reach this high level of adjustment by encouraging them to engage in as many different sports and nonsporting events as possible. If parents decide their children will be a major league shortstop and concentrate the child's efforts and training in this direction, they are putting all their eggs in one basket. The child may not have the skills and temperament to reach this goal. However, the child may have abilities in swimming or track or some other sport. The child may be very nonathletic and have talent in music, drama, or woodworking. The point is, by concentrating on only one or a few activities, the child may never discover skills, talents, and enjoyment in other activities. There is little chance that such a child will be able to say, "It doesn't matter that I'm not a great shortstop. I can still play piano well and I'm a pretty fair swimmer." So our suggestion is to encourage participation in as many sporting and nonsporting activities as is reasonable.

Some children are not talented athletes and won't get to play often. They are the substitutes or bench warmers. Special care should be taken with such children, as they may be especially vulnerable to stress (Bruns and Tutko 1978). Sitting on the bench may come to mean that the child lacks talent and is "inferior." The child must play this role in front of parents and friends. Because substitutes don't play much, they don't get much of a chance to improve; this can lead to feelings of disappointment. Seeing one's friends becoming more skilled and oneself standing still can lead to children feeling isolated from their teammates and friends. In some cases, unskilled coaches will often pick on the substitute when things aren't going well on the field. Research has found this to be a much-too-common occurrence. All of these factors can lead to mounting stress for a child who is a substitute. Parents should be especially sensitive to such a child's plight. Many of the suggestions made earlier apply doubly in this situation. Let children know you understand how they feel. Accept those feelings. Make sure children know their worth has nothing to do with how much or how well they play. Emphasize this with statements such as, "Gee, I'll bet it's hard to just sit on the bench and not play much. I know how much you'd like to get into the game" or "It's hard to see your friends playing and not get to play yourself, isn't it? I'm sure proud of the way you go to practice all the time and still keep trying hard." We think it will be helpful for parents to know research shows children would much rather play a lot for a losing team than sit on the bench for a winning team. Most parents also would rather see their child play for a losing team than to be a substitute for a winner (Bruns and Tutko 1978). Winning is less important than playing. So, try to find a situation where children will be able to play, even if it's for a less talented team. Children will appreciate it, and since pressures will be reduced, parents can also enjoy games much more. If at all possible, try to set up some time when such children can play. An informal game with friends or family on a nonpractice day might be helpful. Above all else, make sure the children know they are accepted and loved independently of what happens or doesn't happen on the field.

Coaches

Parents can take action to be more certain their children will have a coach who does not place unnecessary pressure on their children. First of all, no parent has to let their child play for a coach they think may be harmful. There are always alternative activities in which children can practice. If the child wants to participate in a youth sport and there seem to be problems with a particular coach, go to league officials and insist the child be allowed to play under another coach. If nothing can be worked out, remember: An alternative activity may be far less stressful and harmful, although initially disappointing.

Before allowing a child to play on an organized youth sports team, go meet the coach. Meet him or her firsthand, in person. What does he or she seem like? Is he or she comfortable to be around? Does he or she answer questions to the point? While meeting the coach, ask at least the following questions:

1. What is his or her attitude about winning? How important is it? If winning is too important to the coach, look elsewhere.

2. If the coach says winning isn't the main goal, ask what is?

3. If he/she says building cooperation or teamwork or developing character is the main goal, ask how he/she goes about doing that. What does he/she actually do to try to teach teamwork and sportsmanship?

4. Ask about his or her policy of playing time. Does he/she let everyone play in every game and about equally? If not, why not? Be alert to subtle hints that winning may be overly important.

5. Ask the coach what he or she does to make practices and games fun for the children.

6. Ask the coach how he or she stresses effort and trying and how the importance of winning and losing is minimized. What are some of the specific ways the coach recognizes and rewards effort and trying hard? How is teamwork rewarded? Ask for specific examples. How does the coach feel about using extrinsic rewards such as money, prizes, and treats to motivate athletes?

7. How important is individual improvement to the coach? How does the coach show the players that their individual improvement is important and not winning or losing?

8. Explain to the coach you would like your child to be the athlete he/she can be and not what the coach wants. Ask the coach what that means to him/her. What can she or he do to attain that goal? Ask the coach to be specific.

If the coach's answers seem satisfactory and in line with your own wishes, feel more comfortable with the coach. But go to at least one or more practices and games to see if the coach's actions match the answers that were given. If there is some discrepancy, be cautious. A coach's behavior should be believed above any vague philosophy or promises. Remember that a coach can have a powerful effect on children, and this effect may be positive or it may be negative. Choose carefully.

Early in the season, ask how a child likes the coach. Are practices fun? Are games fun? Talk to the child and find out if the coach's philosophy seems to be working well for the child.

Psychological Factors

The most important suggestion we have for parents is to make special efforts to help their children learn to handle winning and losing. Take time to learn what winning and losing mean to a child. Sit down and talk with children about what they feel like after a game. Are there feelings of extreme sadness, disappointment, indifference, happiness? Whatever the feelings that are expressed, investigate the reasons behind them. Emotions reflect the meanings we place on events and situations. By discovering why a child feels a certain way, it is possible to discover what winning and losing mean to that child. There are several guidelines to help explore feelings. People who study this process have found certain types of statements can help people explore feelings, while other types of statements don't help. Here is a short lesson in how to help someone explore their feelings.

Acceptance Rules

There is no such thing as a bad feeling. Don't criticize children for their feelings or tell them not to have such feelings or thoughts. Avoid saying things such as, "Don't be sad and pout around this house" or "I told you not to get so mad."

Feelings belong to the person who feels them. Don't deny the feelings of a child. Don't tell them they don't feel the way they feel. If a child says "I hate my coach" (or the umpire or a teammate), don't say "Now, Bobby, you don't really hate the coach. You mean you dislike him very much, don't you?" Don't deny feelings; accept them.

How to Explore Feelings

Listen. Don't plan what you are going to say while the child is talking. Try to hear exactly what the child is saying.

Empathize. Ask yourself this: "How would I have to feel to say what the child is saying?" Don't just keep this sentence in mind. Actually ask yourself. This will help put yourself in the child's shoes. Empathy means understanding how another feels. So, if after losing, a child says, "I don't want to play any more," ask "How would I have to feel to say that?"

Respond with the feeling(s) you have identified above in 2. Respond by saying something like, "You feel really sad because you lost the game" or "You're mad because your team lost." Identify the feeling and state the reason you think the child feels a certain way. This should help the child know someone understands; it will make it easier for the child to continue discussing feelings. If these guidelines are followed, then the chances are children will better be able to talk and cope with their stress.

If it appears the child is equating winning or losing with personal success or failure or with personal worth, take the time to make it clear that you, the parent, don't feel that way (Bruns and Tutko 1978). Say it clearly. Tell children they are loved and important regardless of the score of the game. A simple statement about their worth to you and a hug can go a long way toward relieving the pressure to perform and win. Let children know having fun is what you hope they get out of sports. If they have dreams of further high-level competition, that is fine. But make sure they know that their success or failure in reaching these higher levels has nothing to do with how much they are loved or how much they are worth as persons. Some additional suggestions which may help in this process involve providing children with alternative meanings for winning and losing. Winning is good, but losing is not a disgrace. What is important is for the child to participate and have fun. If a child knows just playing is pleasing to parents, regardless of winning or losing, much of the pressure can disappear. Another idea is to stress the importance of trying one's best. Ask the child what might have been done differently or better. Suggest working on that particular aspect before the next contest. Above all, make it clear trying—trying hard—is what really matters. This is a value that is important and doesn't lead to unnecessary pressure.

The play of children doesn't mean the same thing as adult play simply because children and adults are different. Children are not miniature adults. They differ in physical, emotional, and intellectual ways. Therefore, some ideas should be kept in mind about children's play. The first is that children's play is not an accident. Play is meant to serve several important functions in the lives of children. First, and perhaps most important, play is important in helping children learn to think creatively. Translating ideas into physical action helps children learn to play ahead and carry out their ideas. Organized sports limit the ability of children to think and act creatively. The when, where, and how are all decided by adults. Once the child chooses to play, many decisions are already made. Before the rise of organized youth sports, children decided when and where they would play, and they made up their own rules. They were also responsible for enforcing their own rules. In order to do all these things children had to learn to cooperate, to give and take, to get along with one another. These opportunities are lessened by organizations which make most decisions for children.

In order to give children an opportunity to exercise choices and creativity, insure that organized sports don't make up a majority of a child's play. See that they make or have time to play with other children in spontaneous, relatively unsupervised situations. Let children make up their own games and just play.

Therefore, it is important not to model children's play after adults' play. Giving kids adult uniforms with adult rules and adult expectations for play and conduct may prevent them from obtaining the benefits play can provide. Modeling children's play after adult play may lead to stress instead of reducing it.

A second idea to remember is that one of the reasons children play is to have fun. Play, although it may be vigorous, is fun and, ultimately, relaxing. So it is most important to make sure that children are enjoying playing in organized sports. Are they having fun? The easiest way to find this out is to watch a child. Does the child appear to be having fun? Do you see a smile and a carefree, loose appearance? Or does the child appear tight, tense, with a serious look? Parents know their children well enough to know if they are enjoying themselves. If a child doesn't appear to be enjoying a sport, it is time for a talk. Sit down and talk and find out why the fun and zest seem to be missing. Ask the child what activities are fun. What about these activities is different from the sport that isn't fun? If there is something that can be done to make the sport more fun, consider doing it. If there doesn't seem to be anything that will make the sport fun, consider having the child find something else to do.

The National Association for Sport and Physical Education developed a Bill of Rights for Young Athletes. Here is a summary of the rights to which children are entitled. These rights are based on the most up-to-date knowledge available from physical educators and child workers. The ten rights all children should have are:

1. The right to participate in sports.
2. The right to participate at a level that matches the child's maturity and ability.
3. The right to have qualified adult leadership.
4. The right to play as a child and not as an adult.
5. The right to share in the leadership and decision making of their sport participation.
6. The right to participate in safe and healthy environments.
7. The right to proper preparation for participating in sports.
8. The right to an equal opportunity to strive for success.

9. The right to be treated with dignity.

10. The right to have fun in sports.

If these ten rights are observed, parents need not worry about excessive stress on their children while playing sports. Instead, children will be able to get most of the positive benefits available from organized sports and avoid most of the negative effects.

The problem of depending on the judgment of others for satisfaction can be overcome in at least two ways. The first suggestion is to avoid giving external rewards such as money, prizes, and so forth for positive performances or for winning. It has already been mentioned that this can lead to the loss of intrinsic motivation, doing something for the fun of it. Secondly, instead of giving something to a child, let the child decide if the performance was a good one. Ask the child what he or she liked about the game and his/her performance. Ask what he or she didn't like about the game and his/her performance. At this point, let the child decide whether he or she believes the performance deserves a treat or some reward. No one knows better than the child how hard he or she tried. If you are willing to provide a reward, allow the child to evaluate the performance and decide what, if any, reward is appropriate. The difference between giving a reward and letting someone reward himself or herself is a subtle but very important one. Giving a reward places the reward and sources of satisfaction outside the child. Allowing a child to reward himself or herself places the source of satisfaction where it belongs, inside the child. Another idea is to provide a treat after every game, regardless of winning or losing.

Sports should provide a release from, not a source of, tension and frustration. If it appears that tension and frustration surrounding sporting events are becoming excessive, it is time to do something. Take the child aside and have a talk. Try to learn what about the sport is causing the frustration or tension. What is the source? Once that is established, try to work together with the child to develop a plan for reducing the tension and frustration. Sit down and try to figure it out together. The tension and frustration are unpleasant for the child, and he/she will be motivated to eliminate them.

Fears

We have several simple, straightforward suggestions for parents to use in dealing with the fears children may have. The first is to recognize and accept that the fear exists. Remember that viewed from an adult point of view, a situation may not be very frightening. But through a child's eyes, things may be very scary. So, sit down and allow the child to admit the fear. Listen carefully to what the child says. Recall how you felt when you were scared. It is likely the child feels in a similar way.

The second suggestion is to encourage (not force) the child to talk about the fear. Once the fear is admitted, it should be easier to discuss. Talking about the fear can help to lessen its severity. By relating times when they were afraid, parents can help the child not feel alone and isolated. A child will not have to feel he or she is the only one with a fear. To know that someone they love and respect was afraid as a child and at times still is, even as an adult, can be comforting. Children can learn that it is normal and acceptable to be afraid.

Another suggestion is to use certain communication techniques that have been popularized recently. *Between Parent and Child* by Haim Ginott and *Parent Effectiveness Training* by Thomas Gordon both show in detail how to use these techniques. Basically, the method involves listening to what the child says and reflecting back to the child the meaning of his or her sentences. The main value of these techniques is in letting the child know the listener understands what the child has said. They also seem to help get conversations going and can lead to deeper, more helpful discussions.

In summary, the goals in dealing with children's fears should be to: 1) allow the child to admit the fear; 2) encourage the child to openly discuss the fear; 3) help the child understand that everyone has fears and that he or she isn't alone.

Sociological

See to it that children read books that accurately reflect what is going on in sports. Too many books are written that idealize sports and athletes, painting a rosy world in which everyone gets along well and there are few major problems (Lipsyte 1980). One need only read books like Jim Bouton's *Ball Four*, David Meggessy's book on pro football, *Out of Their League*, James Michener's *Sports in America*. All of these books give an insight into the more negative side of professional sports. If a child is going to devote a major part of his or her life to a sport in hopes of making the pros, parents have a duty to let children know what they are heading for. Give them a realistic picture of what professional sports are like.

Parents may also schedule professional athletes to come and speak to the youth teams in their area. Firsthand reports of the pressures of constant traveling, loneliness, drug and alcohol abuse, boredom, fear of failure and getting old, the constant pressure to reach and stay on top, the nagging injuries which will probably become chronic are all facts with which children should become acquainted.

It has already been mentioned that the overorganization of children's sports by adults is helping to mold children who look to others for satisfaction and who are being socialized to do what organizations tell them to do. Their own individual choice is being blunted. In order to counteract this, children should be encouraged to create their own play. Whatever sport they want to play, let them plan the games. Let them decide on their own rules, let them select their own teams and choose when and where they will play. Drop all the red tape. It only ties kids up and prevents them from developing fully. Allow children to begin to develop a sense of control over their own lives. When the time comes for them to make their own decisions, the more practice they have had, the better decisions they will make. Let children play sports as they play any game. They will enjoy the games more and will experience far less stress.

Injuries

The clear-cut evidence of frequent and, often, serious injuries incurred during youth sports activities should be the concern of every parent. What is important to know is that by following some simple guidelines the chances of being injured can be dramatically reduced. Fully 66 percent of youth injuries could likely have been prevented (Goldberg 1979). Some suggestions are:

Encourage children to report any injury, no matter how slight or minor it might appear at first. Don't let the fear of being branded a sissy prevent a child from reporting an injury. At first the injury may not be serious, but with repeated playing it can get worse and may become a major, chronic (long-lasting) problem.

If there is any question about the seriousness of an injury, seek qualified medical or professional help. Remember that most coaches are not qualified to determine the seriousness and nature of a sports injury. Don't wait to see if the injury will get better. Be especially mindful of head and joint injuries, including neck, shoulders, knees, elbows, and ankles.

Make sure the physical and emotional requirements imposed upon children are matched with their developmental level (Burke and Kleiber 1976). In other words, don't let children be pushed into doing more than they are physically capable of doing. Again, be careful of coaches who say that extremely strenuous workouts are "good" for the kids and will make "men" of them. They are children, not adults. They will be adults soon enough. Also, make sure excessive emotional requirements are not placed upon children. A game should be a game, whether it's for first or last place. Don't let children assume responsibility for a game that is obviously out of their control. Besides getting hurt feelings, children, due to stress, may try to do things they aren't capable of, thus risking an injury.

Equipment should be modified to match a child's developmental level. Equipment designed for older children or adults should be avoided. Make sure equipment fits as it was designed to, because 18 percent of reported injuries are equipment related (Silverstein 1979). This includes ill-fitting equipment and failure to use equipment. Make sure the child wears the equipment.

Encourage your child to participate in sports with fewer chances of injury. Football and skateboarding appear to lead to the greatest percentage of injuries (Chambers 1979). They are also among the most popular sports. On the other hand, while less popular, tennis, swimming, cross country running, field hockey, and soccer seem to lead to far fewer injuries. In terms of cardiovascular health they are also far superior (Martin 1979; Burke and Kleiber 1976). Consider having children participate in more of the latter group of sports. They are safer and can lead to greater health. Their relative lack of popularity can be overcome by encouraging participation and setting an example by participating in them with the children, if possible. All of the second group of sports offer a chance for competition if that is desired. And most of them offer the chance to measure a child's progress against himself or herself rather than against another child.

If there has been an injury, don't let the child return to competition too soon. Almost 25 percent of injuries are due to inadequate rehabilitation (Goldberg 1979). The affected area was not allowed to heal, or it was too weak to support the activity required. No game should be important enough to risk a permanent, disabling injury.

Insist on having a qualified medical person or trainer available at games. Immediate diagnosis and treatment can prevent the worsening of injuries and reduce much of the associated pain. Insist that the league have coaches receive training in basic sports injuries and some sort of emergency treatment training. Immediate attention to an injury can make a difference.

7
STRESS
of Hospitalization

*To be a child in America is to be powerless,
controlled and devalued as an individual.
Hospitalization magnifies this experience.
It is a training ground in learning helplessness.*

Anonymous

Bobby lies in a bed in a strange room surrounded by adults who are wearing masks and strange clothes. They are speaking words he does not understand. He knows they are going to take out his tonsils, which are in his throat. How can they get to his tonsils without slitting his throat? He knows that they will soon cut him open and thinks he may die. Oh, if his mom and dad would only come and take him home! But they left him here. Maybe he was bad and they are punishing him. Maybe they just don't love him anymore. Whatever the reason, he is alone now and they are sticking a large needle into his arm. They say it won't hurt, but it hurts a lot. They are lying to him. Maybe they are lying about his feeling better in a little while. Maybe they are lying about his parents coming to see him soon. Maybe he is going to die.

The above scenario, while it may seem incredible, accurately reflects the type of thinking and feeling that occurs in many children who are hospitalized for surgery or serious illness. Research suggests that such

156

hospitalization is almost always a source of stress for children, especially younger ones (Peterson and Johnson 1978; Goslin 1978). Because of their limited intellectual development, they are not able to understand what is happening to them. They often develop misconceptions about why they must go to the hospital and what will happen when they get there. Stress, which can reach damaging levels, may be experienced as a result.

Mary Robinson is child life director at Children's Hospital National Medical Center in Washington, D.C. She says:

> While it is true that many children will "get over it" in the sense that they will not commit suicide, go to jail, or be committed to a mental hospital, a large percentage of children, particularly young children, will have endured a period of significant suffering.[1]

Judith Viorst writes:

> This suffering may be revealed in eating and sleeping problems; in nightmares or temper tantrums or wetting the bed, in withdrawal or depression or dependency on phobias or fears. This suffering, if it lasts too long ... may mark his character permanently and *cripple the ways in which he is able to live and the ways he is able to love for the rest of his days.*[2]

In this chapter we will discuss the major sources of stress for children who face hospitalization for serious illness or surgery. We hope this will help parents to become more aware of stresses due to hospitalization in their children's lives. In the second half of the chapter we offer suggestions to help parents reduce their children's stress associated with hospitalization.

The most common fear among children, especially those below four years of age, is the fear of being abandoned, of losing their parents (Zager 1980). Separation from parents can be an extremely stressful situation; the mere thought of it can upset children. The incomplete knowledge that strangers may be sticking them with needles, taking out their blood, or cutting them with sharp knives can be terrifying. Being separated from Mom and Dad, their main source of protection, can lead to panic. The fear of separation from parents can magnify and intensify whatever other fears might be present. Closely linked to the fear of separation is the fear that the separation may be forever, that the child may be abandoned. For a relatively helpless child whose main source of strength and protection is parents, such an idea must be truly terrifying.

The second most common fear among hospitalized children is fear of the unknown (Masthoff 1979). They will be going to a place where they probably don't know more than one or two persons, if any. They will be subjected to procedures of which they know very little, if anything. Questions such as "What will happen to me?" "Will it hurt?" "How long will I be there?" "Will the doctors and nurses be nice to me?" "What will the hospital smell like?" "Where will I sleep when the hospital closes at night?" "What will I get to eat in the hospital?" all reflect a desire to know more about an unknown and, therefore, frightening situation.

Further adding to the stress surrounding hospitalization for children is their limited ability to understand the language used to describe medical procedures. For example, the simple phrase ". . . take your blood pressure" meant to one child that the staff was going to take his blood, all of it. Children seem to have a built-in idea of the importance of blood, and anything that suggests they will lose this blood can be frightening (Lewis 1978). Children often take words at their literal meaning. Thus, a child who hears, "She doesn't look too good . . . she's not getting much better" can interpret this to mean that she isn't being good. Children want to please, and such a misinterpretation could lead them to believe they aren't pleasing their parents or other adults. This can be a source of stress.

The fear of being mutilated, of losing some part of the body, is very common in children facing surgery (Viorst 1977). Explanations of surgery to children often describe a small "hole" being cut into them. The concrete thinking of many children can lead them to visualize a "window" remaining after the operation. Children's primitive knowledge of body parts and their location can also lead to misconceptions about what might happen. Removal of any body part, even hidden ones, can be the cause of much anxiety for children.

There seems to be an almost universal fear of needles among children (Lewis 1978; Zager 1980). Thus, the taking of blood samples and the use of IV procedures to administer medications and fluids can be especially threatening to children. Children are usually fully awake, not anesthetized, when needles are used. Most often several strangers are around, as are parents and other patients (children). Thus, there can be the pressure of having one's behavior scrutinized by others. Children can translate needles into images of darts, vicious animals, arrows, and knives or other malevolent objects. Poetry by children written about their injections with needles clearly shows the anxiety they experience in such situations[3]:

The needle is so long that it looks like a skinny man that's so
    mad it could go through my body.
Inside me it fights the bones like a snake throwing his poison.
The needle is like an animal, fighting another animal.
It scratches my bones and it's not nice to me.
It's too mean to me.

Another child wrote:

  ... It feels like she gonna push it all the way in and leave
    it in.
And leave all my brains out broken and terrible.

Yet another wrote:

  ... When the doctors give the shots they don't know how it feels.
They say it's not gonna hurt only because it doesn't hurt them.

Again, the fear of losing too much blood also accompanies the use of needles and can add to the existing stress (Lewis 1978).

Many children, especially those of school age, also experience fear of losing control (Viorst 1977). In their everyday lives their activities are proof of their increasing ability to do things on their own. They have begun to make decisions and to dress themselves. Attempts to do things for them are often met with resistance or anger. They no longer think of themselves as children, but see themselves as little adults, competent to do their own thing. Being ill or needing surgery is something they suddenly can't control. Nothing they say or do can change the fact they must be hospitalized. Once hospitalized, medical staff members will decide what they can and can't do. Doctors may probe them with sticks and needles, may cut them with knives and decide when they can finally go home. The pouting or tantrum behavior of many hospitalized children may be seen as an attempt to regain a lost sense of control. Such outbursts are directed toward getting adults to give in and do something for the child, toward controlling their behavior. Negativism toward suggestions from hospital staff may also be attempts to regain control. Children's emerging sense of control over their lives is threatened by hospitalization; stress can be the result.

Children also fear the pain they know will be associated with a stay in the hospital. Attempts at reassurance, such as "It won't hurt too much" do little to remove the fear. They may, in fact, reinforce the idea that there will be pain. Widespread watching of TV has implanted the notion of pain and suffering occurring in hospitals. People don't go to hospitals unless they are sick. While in the hospital they are poked, jabbed, and cut. Children know there will be pain and they fear it.

Children also commonly have a fear of death upon entering hospitals. Death means different things to children of different ages, but most children fear it. Children have expressed this fear in various ways. One child was crying because he was going to be "put to sleep" for an operation. The child's pet had been "put to sleep" recently and the child feared he too would soon be dead. Another child expressed that the only way to avoid the pain of surgery was to sleep so hard that he would be dead. Another child, overhearing she would be injected with dye, believed she was going to be injected with "die" and thought she would soon be dead. Familiarity with deaths in hospitals as seen on TV shows also raises this fear for many children. The fear of death can be extremely stressful.

Another source of stress for children is the idea that they are ill or are being hospitalized as a punishment for being bad (Viorst 1977). Statements such as "God makes children sick because they misbehave" or "I caught this sickness from another bad boy because I'm a bad boy" suggest that children's explanations of their illness and/or hospitalization revolve around the ideas that they have been bad and are being punished. Unable to medically understand what is happening to them, they construct an explanation that fits with their experience. Punishment is unpleasant and follows misbehavior. Illness and hospitalization are unpleasant and are punishment. Being sent to one's room following misbehavior is common. Being sent to a hospital comes to mean the child was especially bad to merit such treatment. As illogical as it seems, children can believe such ideas. The result can be extreme stress at disappointing Mom and Dad and being separated from them.

Another cause of stress for children who are seriously ill or who need surgery is the anxiety experienced by their parents (Goslin 1978). Most often this anxiety is due to the parents' own fear of the unknown and their fear of death. Being relatively ignorant of the medical profession and its procedures, they—just like their children—begin to imagine what might happen to the child. The pain and suffering their child may experience is magnified, and this frightens parents. The possibility their child might not survive frightens parents. The cost of medical care worries many parents. All of this worry is sensed by and transmitted to the child. It is added to whatever other stress the child may be experiencing.

Another source of stress for many parents is the belief they are somehow responsible for their child's illness (Rothstein 1980). They may believe that something they have done or something they haven't done is causing the illness or injury. The result is that they feel guilty and anxious. They feel guilty over being the "cause" of the illness and anxious over what might happen due to their inadequate parenting. Some parents are so anxious that they don't eat enough to maintain their strength. Others feel nauseated, find it difficult to move their arms or legs efficiently, or suffer from insomnia or dizziness. Others, more seriously affected, feel isolated from their spouses and children, preferring to remain by themselves. While some of the above symptoms are extreme, they are symptomatic of feelings that most parents who love and care for their children have. The feelings are the normal result of caring for, protecting, and loving children. The problem arises when the symptoms become so severe they increase the child's own anxiety and stress.

In many cases, the parents feel so guilty they begin to relate differently toward their child. As if to atone for their "mistake," which "caused" the illness, they become overprotective. To insure they never again do too little for the child, they do too much. The child is forced to become more dependent on the parents, thus stunting psychological growth and leading to more stress. In other cases, the parents' behavior becomes so markedly altered, so different from what the child is used to, that the child becomes uncertain and confused. The child is experiencing unfamiliar and possibly frightening situations due to illness. The child depends upon the stable, well-known relationship with the parents for comfort and security during the time of illness. If this relationship suddenly is changed and markedly different, the child experiences further uncertainty and confusion. The net result is increased stress.

Suggestions to Help Children Cope with Hospitalization

While estimates (Peterson and Johnson 1980) have been made that up to 90 percent of children who are hospitalized without proper preparation can suffer extreme stress, evidence also exists that being hospitalized does not have to be a negative, harmful experience. In fact, there is growing evidence hospitalization can be a positive, growth experience for children (Zager 1980). By facing a stressful situation and devising their own strategies for coping with the stress, children can come to be more confident, feel they have more control over their own lives, and be a source of pride and satisfaction for their parents.

In this section we will make suggestions which, if followed, will lessen the stress surrounding hospitalization for both children and parents. The suggestions are in three major sections: What can be done before hospitalization, what can be done during hospitalization, and what can be done after hospitalization.

Before Hospitalization

One of the best approaches to reducing stress during hospitalization is the preventive one. Do whatever can be done before the child is sick or injured. Take the time to call a local hospital(s) and set up an orientation tour for your child or a small group of children (Pomarico et al. 1979). This may also be done through groups such as the Girl Scouts, Brownies, Cub Scouts, and nursery school and early elementary school classes. Many hospitals, especially pediatric hospitals, now offer such services. By taking such a tour before a child is ill and anxious about being hospitalized, the child can learn about the hospital and its staff in a relaxed, enjoyable manner. In this way much of the fear of the unknown can be removed prior to hospitalization. The effectiveness of this preventive approach cannot be underestimated.

If a preventive tour isn't practical or if a child has to be hospitalized before a tour can be set up, there is still much that can be done. About 75 percent of pediatric hospitals offer some type of prehospitalization orientation tour as a regular part of their procedure. If your hospital doesn't offer such a tour, talk to your family physician and request that one be set up. Research conclusively points to the effectiveness of such tours (Wessell 1979). A well-organized tour would include trained personnel who conduct the tour as well as a slide show presenting the major people, equipment, and procedures children are likely to experience. A walking tour of the hospital is often conducted. During this time children meet doctors, nurses, and technicians. This is especially helpful in reducing children's fears of strangers who will be poking, probing, cutting, and taking care of them. During the walking tour children may be encouraged to look at and touch some equipment. They may even be allowed to pretend they are using the equipment and having it used on them. They may try on masks, lie on tables, try on gowns, and do anything else that might reduce the unfamiliarity with the hospital and its staff, procedures, and equipment. Many orientations will have a break for refreshments and then allow children to explore more equipment. Children can handle thermometers, take their own temperatures, use stethoscopes to listen to heartbeats or use tongue depressors to see the tonsils of a friend. Finally, a question-and-answer period can end the orientation. The reduction in stress that is gained by familiarizing children with a hospital and its unknown procedures, machines, and people is significant.

There are additional ways to provide information for children and reduce fear of the unknown. In place of or in addition to an orientation trip to the hospital, parents can give a narrative explanation to their children. This means telling children exactly why they must go to a hospital, what will happen there, how long they will likely have to stay there, how much pain there is likely to be, how long it will last, what type of food will be available, whether or not they will be able to play at the hospital. In order to do this, parents will probably have to consult a physician—the surgeon, if there will be one—or nurses who will be working with the child (Salk 1978). Find out in as much detail as possible about the procedures and equipment to be used. Even mentioning the color of the rooms can help prepare a child for a stay in the hospital.

The cardinal rule to remember when giving narrative explanations is to *always be honest* (Costello 1980; Salk 1978; Viorst 1977; Brazelton 1976). One nine-year-old wrote it this way: "The baddest thing, is to lie to a kid. It's much badder to lie to me than to scare me by telling me the truth. To lie to a kid is the baddest thing of all."[4] At no time should parents lie about what is going to happen. Trying to keep children relaxed and unafraid is a loving gesture, but trying to do it by keeping information from the child is the worst way to do it. First of all, the child will soon enough experience pain, separation, and other things that the parents lied about. The inevitable result is the child will then begin to worry about what else might happen that Mom and Dad lied about. "Maybe I won't get to go home after all and maybe Mom and Dad won't come to see me" are common worries which may arise because of lying. This additional worry will slow down recovery. Worse, the bond of trust between parent and child will be weakened. Often it is this very bond, the belief that Mom and Dad will be protective and can be trusted, that provides the confidence and strength that aids a child's recovery. The bond between parent and child should be a source of strength and confidence, not a source of worry and stress. So tell children the truth, the whole truth, and nothing but the truth. And when events come to pass as Mom and Dad said, remind the child you said things would be like this. So, if you have told your child her throat would hurt after a tonsillectomy, remind her you had said it would be so and, just as you said, it will soon feel better, too. Trust will be strengthened by such a reminder.

There are also movies that have been specifically produced to inform children about what will happen in the hospital. Research has shown that observing movies of other children reacting calmly to various hospital procedures can significantly reduce children's stress in a hospital (Goslin 1978). Ask your family doctor or hospital personnel about such movies. Check with your local library or contact the Association for Care of Children's Health (ACCH) for information on how to obtain films. *We Won't Leave You* is one film that has been developed to prepare children for hospitalization. Many books have been written that deal with hospitalization of children. They provide information about what will happen, often in story form. They explain in easy-to-understand language what medical terms mean. Often they have some pictures of hospital situations for children to color. Check with your doctor, hospital personnel, a local library, or the ACCH.

An especially effective technique for presenting information to children is playing with puppets (Goslin 1978; Viorst 1977; Peterson and Johnson 1980). Parents can work one puppet, who will explain to the other puppet (worked by the child) what will happen. The child's puppet can then ask the adult puppet any questions that might be troubling it. Later, parents and children can reverse their roles, with the child working the "adult" puppet, giving the explanations and answering questions. The first phase is helpful in discovering what questions the child has and what fears may exist, as well as for passing on information. The second phase, where roles are reversed, is especially helpful in discovering how much the child has understood and what misconceptions or fantasies might exist. Simply playing and having fun while discussing hospital matters can do much to relieve anxiety.

During Hospitalization

The chief fear experienced by children during hospitalization is of being separated from their parents and abandoned. Fortunately, much can be done to counteract this fear. First, a parent can stay overnight at the hospital with the child. Hospitals are beginning to encourage parents to stay overnight for several reasons. Part of this is undoubtedly, first, for the support children receive during this time of stress. Having a familiar person present can help reduce the fright, confusion, and boredom children often experience in hospitals. The result is that recovery seems to be quicker and more complete. Secondly, participation such as overnight stays can do much to strengthen the bond between parents and children. The sense of trust a child feels toward parents can be further solidified. Third, research suggests children will receive more thorough care if parents are present (Mason 1978). Nursing personnel, overburdened with duties, may forget to bring a food tray or remove it when the child hasn't eaten. Parents can help prevent such oversights. They can also do much to encourage the child to cooperate with hospital procedures which might be unpleasant.

So, a most important suggestion is to consider staying overnight at the hospital. Parents do have a right to do so. If the hospital doesn't have accommodations, arrange for a cot to be moved into the room. If a hospital refuses, shop around and find a hospital that will allow overnight stays. Prior to hospitalization, discuss staying overnight with your child. Give your child a choice of whether you will stay or not. Some children will prefer not to have Mom and Dad stay overnight. That should be their right. If your child does want you to stay overnight, plan to do so.

During overnight stays, it is often possible to prepare meals for the child. As long as home-cooked food meets any dietary restrictions, there should be no problem in serving it to a hospitalized child. Some hospitals make facilities available for cooking meals. If not available, meals may be cooked at home and brought to the hospital. If this is impractical, most hospitals will allow a parent to eat hospital food with the child. The advantage of home-cooked food is its familiarity to the child and its ability to bring back good feelings from home. This can do much to reduce stress and anxiety for children.

Another suggestion is to allow your child to bring clothes and pajamas from home. Again, familiarity will help to reduce the stress associated with being in a strange place. Pajamas may especially help at night, a time when fears and loneliness may be intensified. Toys brought from home may also prove helpful.

A relatively recent trend in hospitalization for children is the scheduling of one-day surgery. Basically, this means that the child will go home shortly after an operation. Other names for this approach are outpatient surgery and ambulatory surgery. Not all surgery is amenable to this approach, but estimates are that as many as 80 percent of surgical procedures may be performed on an outpatient basis (Mason 1978). One-day surgery has several major advantages. First, because the period of parent-child separation is so short, stress is reduced and emotional disturbances are reduced. Second, research suggests there is a significant decrease in the chance of developing postoperative infections if a child returns home soon after an operation. Contact with numerous hospital employees and other ill patients is reduced, which reduces opportunities to develop infections and other postoperative complications. Third, there can be a substantial saving of money with such procedures. Some surgical procedures can be done at half the normal cost. With the continued rise of hospital costs, savings will likely increase. If at all possible, arrange for ambulatory, one-day, outpatient surgery. It can do much to alleviate the stresses normally associated with childhood surgery.

Another suggestion is to arrange to be with your child at crucial stress points in the surgical procedure. Some of these are during the moving of the child to the pre-op room, during the administration of anesthesia, and when the child awakens in the recovery room. This can usually be arranged with most hospitals. Just tell the doctor you want to be with your child during the anesthesia process. Arrange this ahead of time. If there is any difficulty, consider finding a doctor who is comfortable with your being present during anesthesia. Many physicians recognize the benefits of parental presence and welcome it. Find such a doctor. The separation of the child and parent, often stressful during the best of times, can be intensified at this point. The operation is now a present reality and the child will be put to sleep—in his or her mind, maybe never to see the parent again. The presence of one or both parents sharing the child's anxiety reduces the fear and makes the anesthesia process run more smoothly. Research has shown that surgery is less stressful when mothers were present at anesthesia induction (Mason 1978). Even if they were nervous themselves, the mothers' cooperation resulted in children who were much more composed. While in the pre-op room, tell your child when you will see him/her again. If it will be in the recovery room or in the regular hospital room, make that known. Just say "I'll see you in an hour (or two) when you wake up (or when you come back to your room)." We have already mentioned how reduced stress can aid in the healing process. So, accompany your child to anesthesia induction.

Other stress points are when the child is taken to the anesthesia room and when the child awakens in the recovery room. Arrange to be present in these situations also. Every chance to reduce stress should be taken. If it is absolutely impossible to be physically present during these crucial times, make sure you and the child receive stress-point counseling. This means a doctor, nurse, or other staff member will come and explain what is about to happen and answer any questions. Many hospitals now make stress-point care a standard part of their surgical procedure. If your hospital doesn't offer this service, request it. It can be very effective in reducing stress.

If overnight stays or one-day surgery are simply not possible, arrange for extended visiting privileges. Many hospitals, realizing the benefits of parental visiting, have cooperated by allowing parents to stay until the child falls asleep and to be present early in the morning when the child is awakening. Again, if your hospital doesn't routinely allow extended visiting privileges, arrange for them. If they can't be arranged, look for a hospital that will allow you to stay as long as you wish. Nursing staff are often grateful for the help parents can give and the cooperation they can induce in children.

Once the operation is completed and the recovery process has begun, much can be done to reduce stresses that might slow down healing. First, the opportunity to play, especially with a child's own toys, has been shown to be helpful in stress reduction. Many hospitals have playrooms designed specifically for recovering children. If such a room isn't available, a lounge room or the child's hospital room will serve quite well. If the child must remain in bed, games and toys that don't require lots of movement can be used. Allow your child to choose what games or toys will be used. The use of drawings, poetry, and puppet games can be both fun and beneficial to a recovering child. They all are excellent ways to allow a child to express worries, fears, wishes, and hopes. Parents should pay close attention to the feelings expressed in these activities. In addition to the fun the child is having, there may be valuable clues that will suggest things to talk about. For example, if a child's poem seems sad and talks about home and friends, parents can acknowledge that the child misses friends and would like to go home. Discussions of these feelings may follow and can result in lowered stress and a speedier, more complete recovery.

In the section on causes of stress for hospitalized children, we mentioned the anxiety and fear parents experience. If parents are nervous and fearful, this will be passed on to the child and add to whatever stress is already present. Thus, it is very important that parents do what they can to reduce their own anxiety and fear. It probably is impossible to get rid of all the anxiety surrounding a child's impending surgery, but it is possible to minimize it so that it doesn't add to the child's stress. First of all, parents should learn everything they can about the surgery. They, too, will probably have a fear of the unknown and what might happen to their child. Spend as much time as possible learning why your child needs surgery, what will be done, what the results might be, and what the experience will be like for your child. Go to the hospital and take a tour. Ask questions of the staff members. Meet those who will be caring for your child. Read what you can about the procedures and the equipment to be used. One of the most anxiety-provoking scenes for parents is that of their child hooked up to an IV apparatus, especially if it's attached to the scalp (Poichuk and Fraser 1980). Make sure you find out why an IV is being used and what it's like for your child. Be able to describe the colors and sounds and smells of the hospital to your child. What color gowns do the doctors and nurses wear? What color will your child's room be? The more you know, the less anxious you will be and the less of your anxiety will be passed on to your child. Children seem to have a sixth sense about such matters, and it is most difficult to pretend to be calm when, in fact, you are anxious. Rather than try to fool a child, it is better to try to minimize your own anxiety and be honest. So learn as much about your child's illness and the hospitalization process and surgery as possible.

A second cause of parental stress is the mistaken belief held by many parents that they are the cause of their child's illness. Somehow, they believe it is their fault. If it weren't for something they did or something they didn't do, they believe their child would be healthy. Such beliefs are common to all parents, although appearing to different degrees. It is important to know that almost all parents experience guilt and anxiety when a child is seriously ill or in need of surgery. It is normal; it shows care and loving. However, it is important not to let the guilt and anxiety disrupt the parent-child relationship and add to the child's stress. So, our suggestions are: 1) Become aware of any thoughts or feelings about being the cause of your child's illness. 2) Become aware of any marked changes in your eating and sleeping habits or ways of relating to children and spouse. The easiest way to gain such an awareness is to ask those directly involved, your children and spouse. Ask them if you're behaving differently in any ways. 3) Talk to your family doctor about the beliefs you hold. Often, medical information will help to alleviate feelings of responsibility. If they persist, talk to a counselor or pastor or a close friend about the situation. Just expressing the feelings of guilt and anxiety and sharing them with others can help to reduce their intensity. The result will be the ill child will experience less anxiety because parental behavior patterns will be similar to those to which the child is accustomed. Uncertainty and confusion will be lessened, as will the child's stress.

Another important suggestion for parents is to make sure your child does not believe that hospitalization or surgery is a form of punishment for misbehavior or being bad. This is an all-too-common belief among children. When it happens, children feel guilty about letting their parents down. The guilt can lead to fear of abandonment and further punishment. To avoid developing such fears, first attempt to determine whether your child has such beliefs. The use of puppets is an excellent way to do this. As suggested earlier, the child's puppet can be the sick person and the parent's puppet can be Daddy or Mommy. Have the adult puppet ask the child's puppet about the illness, how long the illness has been present, what it feels like, and why the child thinks she has the illness or has to go to the hospital. Pay close attention to the last answer for any hints that the illness is punishment. If such an idea seems to exist, quickly have the adult puppet correct the idea. Sentences such as "No, you aren't sick because you've been bad. Even boys who behave well, like you, get sick occasionally. A germ of some sort is making you feel ill, but it's not because you've been bad. No, you're a good boy and I love you" will help dispel any misconceptions. Puppets are a great idea, but if they aren't available, a more direct question-and-answer session can be helpful. Ask your child how the need for hospitalization or surgery came about. Again, if there is evidence of thoughts of punishment, give as clear a message as possible that this is not the case.

Another suggestion is to encourage visits by brothers and sisters to a hospitalized child. If at all possible, have some hospital worker brief the visitors on what has happened so far and what the hospitalized child is currently experiencing. Encourage brothers and sisters to ask questions so they more fully understand the situation. After the visit, arrange for a nurse or ward personnel to spend a few minutes with the brothers and sisters discussing what they have seen and what their impressions were. A well-prepared visit can go a long way in reducing feelings of isolation and separation.

After Hospitalization

Once a child returns home from the hospital, most of the difficult times are over. However, parents should be alert to watch for signs that might suggest stress may still exist. Any exaggerated change in behavior on the part of the child, excessive crying, excessive clinging to a parent, loss of appetite, continued problems with sleeping, and withdrawal from usual family activities may all be signs of continuing stress. To discover sources of stress, consider the use of puppets again. Have the child's puppet play a person who has come home from the hospital. Have the child's puppet tell the adult's puppet what it feels like to be home, whether it's fun or not, what the child's puppet thinks about during the day and at night. In this way clues may be found leading to the sources of stress for the child.

Another suggestion when a child comes home is to encourage discussion of the hospital experience. Let the child call grandparents, aunts, uncles, and friends to share what the hospital was like. Let the child explain in his own words. Also, encourage children to draw pictures about their hospitalization and to write poetry or songs about it. What was important during the hospitalization will most likely come up; this will help relieve any residual stress.

As soon as it is physically possible, let the child return to everyday routine. Return to a familiar, well-known way of life will aid greatly in eliminating stress. Chores, playing with friends, schoolwork, movies, sports, and TV should be resumed as before. Avoid limiting any of these activities and avoid smothering the child with too many of them. Try to return to normal as soon as possible. Check and make sure this suggestion is consistent with whatever medical advice has been given by hospital personnel and physicians.

Other Suggestions

Throughout this book we have mentioned the importance a sense of control plays in reducing the effects of stress. In this chapter we mentioned the fear of loss of control, especially in school-aged children. Therefore, we suggest that parents do whatever they can to help children develop a sense of control over their own lives. The easiest way to do this is to allow children to make decisions whenever possible. The decisions don't have to be earthshaking. Even relatively simple decisions will aid in developing a sense of control. With regard to hospitalization, there are many decisions that can be left to children. Whether a child wants a parent to stay overnight at the hospital; what clothes, books, and toys to bring to the hospital; whether to cry or not when receiving shots; whether to observe other children receiving IVs or shots; what to watch on TV and what to play at the hospital are all examples of decisions children can easily make. If allowed to do so, children can develop a sense of control over their own lives and become more immune to the effects of stress.

Oftentimes parents may not realize the extent of control they have over what procedures are used on their children. Parents can select the doctor they want. They can also choose the hospital they want. So take your time, if possible, and shop around. Meet hospital personnel and choose the hospital whose policies most closely match your needs and desires. By the same token, choose a doctor whose philosophy or treatment most matches your own. Don't be shy. Ask for what you want. It could mean the difference between a stressful hospitalization and a growth experience for your child.

When checking for a suitable hospital, ask if a hospital has a child-life worker on its staff. These are persons who have been trained specially to deal with emotional issues of hospitalized children such as the major fears we have discussed in the first part of this chapter. If no child-life workers are available, see if nurses or social workers have any special training in dealing with the hospitalization of children. Most hospital personnel don't have this special training, so ask to make sure. Ask whether any nurses and recreation workers are affiliated with the ACCH. Membership in this organization suggests that the particular worker is aware of and interested in the special problems of hospitalized children. Write to the ACCH for information and suggestions on how to reduce the stress of hospitalization. Be prepared—write before your child needs a hospital. The address is:

ACCH
3615 Wisconsin Avenue, N.W.
Washington, D.C. 20016

Hospitalization can be an experience from which children need not suffer unnecessarily, but rather one from which they can grow and develop self-confidence and a deeper trust in and love of their parents.

In this chapter we have discussed some of the major sources of stress for children who face hospitalization for illness or surgery. Our hope is that parents will have an increased awareness of how stressful hospitalization can be.

Notes

1. Viorst, J. "The Hospital That Has Patience With Its Patients." *Redbook*. February 1977, pp. 48-54. © by Judith Viorst. Reprinted by permission.

2. Ibid.

3. Lewis, Nancy. "The Needle Is Like an Animal—How Children View Injections." *Child Today*. January 1978, pp. 18-24.

4. Viorst, op. cit., pp. 48-54.

8

STRESS
of Death
and Dying

Oh, call back my brother to me!
I cannot play alone;
The summer comes with flower and bee—
Where is my brother gone?

Felicia Dorothea Hemns
(1795-1835)

Death is an ever-present reality. Our lives and our families are not protected from the ravages death can deal to the hopes and dreams we hold for the future. Children are the most affected by the untimely arrival of death. They are the least prepared of all humans to be able to deal with death. The death of a parent leaves them without a source of love and protection which is so necessary for them to grow and mature into adults who can cope effectively with the tragedies of life. The death of a friend or sibling leaves them without an understanding of what has happened to their companion. The death of a pet may deprive a child of the only source of unconditional affection in his or her life.

It is said a king once demanded of a visiting sage a gift of supreme importance. The sage is reported to have said, "I could give you no greater gift than that your father die before you and that you die before your children." Most parents would understand. There is no greater pain than the death of a child. We seem to be able to come to grips with the death of the old. Their lives have been lived; their deaths can be understood as the natural progression of things. But a child has barely started life. There is no justice in that, and there is no peace. Add to this another saying—"May you dance at your children's weddings"—and we have a blessing unequaled in the gifts of life. We do not suffer the death of children and they do not lose a parent until adulthood.

It is often this lack of peace and the pain that prevents parents from being able to cope effectively with the surviving children and to deal with the children's lack of understanding and fear. This is why it is important children begin to be involved in discussions of death and dying before such an event occurs in a family.

There are some who would advocate waiting until some natural event occurs that can serve to open up discussion of such a frightening subject as death and dying. Certainly, that is one opportunity, but it may be based on the false assumption that knowledge of and the experience of death is rare in the lives of children. In fact, children find out about death in any number of ways from which parents can in no way protect them. Their questions come earlier than many of us are prepared for and, taken off guard, we answer those questions in ways that can create and reinforce fears about death, ways in which we might not answer if we were given some time to think and to prepare better responses. One of the authors' children once started the following conversation while his parent was driving down an interstate highway. The child asked, "Are you going to die before me?"

"I hope so," the parent answered.

"If you do I want to be buried right on top of you."

The child was four years old.

How Do Children Find Out About Death?

Children find out about death not only from events that occur in their families, but from the larger world too. A child's first experience with death may come from the death of a pet or from a squirrel falling from a telephone line. It could be an accident between the family pet and a automobile. Certainly, these are times to talk about death with children. But we no longer live in a leisurely world where parents have time to wait until some natural events occur that can serve to introduce the subject of death. Television may have destroyed forever the protected naiveté of the recent past. Children now spend more hours in front of television sets than they do in school. It is no stretch of the imagination to realize that before a child even starts the first grade he or she has watched 10,000 hours of television! Obviously, there is danger in this, especially if television continues the trivialization of death in shows that emphasize violence and distort the real effects of violence and death. Those distortions, in evening prime-time shows meant for adults and watched by children, pale before the Saturday animated nonsense in which violence plays so important a part of nearly every cartoon. Violence and death are so fictionalized in these Saturday morning shows that, other concerns aside, it would be virtually impossible for a child with 10,000 hours of exposure to them to have anything at all resembling a realistic conception of death and dying. They may not even know that a hit over the head with a chair hurts or that being run over by a steamroller doesn't flatten people out—it kills them.

Certainly, this distortion has dangers, but it is not the major impact of television. The major impact of television is not in its presentation of fantasy, but in its presentation of the news. Children who are tuning into fantasy on any given Saturday morning are going to receive news of Anwar Sadat, the assassination attempt on President Ronald Reagan, the bombing of Iranian government officials, the MX missile system, the B-1 bomber, the war in Afghanistan, starvation in the Third World, the death of teen idols through drugs or murder, and the use of the death penalty in America. These are some of the realities of modern American life. Parents can no longer wait to discuss death when an event in the life of a family makes it necessary. The world has invaded our homes through the television screen.

Children's Books

One might think kids could go to children's literature to learn about death even if their parents don't want to talk. There are, in fact, many books for children that deal with death and dying. Here it is necessary to point out many of the books dealing with death and written especially for children do not provide accurate or age-specific information that could be helpful to children. There seem to be three major themes in children's literature regarding death (Bailis 1977). First, death is often described as temporary in children's literature. By this it is meant the dead person returns to life or is presented as immortal or living in some afterlife. Second, death is presented as inevitable. That is, in most children's literature it is made clear death cannot be escaped, even though this view is tempered by the view above concerning the lack of the permanency of death. Third, death is not presented as the end of all existence. Children's literature deals mostly with the death of the physical body only and, as discussed above, does not discuss at all the idea that death is permanent and the end of existence itself. Such reservations on the part of children's authors to deal directly and factually with death and dying also contribute to the stress of death and dying for children, since they distort and deny death. (It is true, of course, that some authors do deal directly and factually with death. These will be discussed later in this chapter. However, the general trend in children's literature seems to follow the themes discussed above.)

We Can't Protect Children from Death

Even if television did not exist, statistically, one out of every twenty children will lose one of their parents before they turn eighteen years of age. In a school of 600 children, one child will die every two or three years (Atkinson 1980). The fact of the matter is, as children grow older, the likelihood of their direct knowledge and experience of death increases. Even though this is true, parents continue to avoid the topic of death and dying with their children.

This desire of adults not to involve their children in discussions of death creates other problems. One recent study reported that fully 44 percent of children were not even told of the death of a significant person in their lives (Grollman 1977). Such a death-denying attitude on the part of adults ends up not protecting the child, even if that was the intention in the first place. It has also been reported 34 percent of children between the ages of fourteen and eighteen lived in families in which death and dying were not openly discussed. Another 26 percent reported that even when death was discussed, it was only when necessary, and then with a great deal of discomfort (Wass and Shaak 1976). It seems clear from research many parents are not comfortable discussing death with their children; even when an event occurs in a family that could lead to such a discussion, many adults cannot bring themselves to talk to children about death. Many children are left with their own inadequate resources to reach an understanding of death and dying, having been denied the experience and comfort of the adults in their lives.

It should come as no surprise to anyone that the people who are willing to discuss death and dying most openly are the ones who have the least fearful attitudes toward death (Foster 1981). Those who have somehow come to grips with their own death and, for whatever reason, have no fear of death are the ones who are the most comfortable talking about death with children. Even those parents who do not see themselves as being afraid to talk to their children make the assumption that children know more than children do and, therefore, assume it is not necessary to discuss death and dying with them. Or, in just the reverse circumstances, some parents fear that the mere discussion of death and dying will create problems in their children they would not have had if the discussion had not taken place. They fear the discussion will create fears. We have seen, however, there is no protection in our society from the realities of death. The information, knowledge, and fear many parents hope to protect their children from invades our homes regardless of how silent immediate family members may be on the subject of death and dying. The lack of discussion about knowledge of and fears associated with death and dying do not have visible outcomes such as those shown by the lack of information about sex, which might result in venereal disease or unwanted pregnancy. It can affect adults' later ability to face a concrete reality of life. What are some of the assumptions adults in our society might make that make it difficult to discuss death and dying with children?

Adult Attitudes

Children in our society receive little preparation for death. It is reasonable to ask why, when, as we have seen, death is an inevitable, ever-present reality of our lives. Why, when confronted with a child's questions, do adults avoid discussing death? Why do we even appear reluctant to use the words *die, death,* and *dying* with our children? The answer is at once simple and complex. The simple answer is we adopt the mythical behavior of the ostrich, stick our heads in the sand, and hope that their questions will go away. We hope when they get older they will somehow find out for themselves and we won't have to face the issue.

The complex answer has to do with the fear of death. Many psychologists believe the failure to come to grips with one's own death is a primary source of mental disorganization plaguing modern technological humanity. Whether all of those psychological implications are real or fanciful speculation remains to be demonstrated elsewhere. It is clear, however, that many adult members of our society have great difficulty coping with death. Certainly the death of loved ones causes us great pain. That is natural. What causes problems is not the natural process of grief, which is good, healthy, and necessary, but the inability of some members of our society to enter into the grief process, and, therefore, to never resolve it. Their inability to enter and conclude the grief process creates new unresolved problems. Further, should this person be a parent, it hampers their children from gaining a clear understanding of death, since their parents are unwilling to talk about it. Such individuals are handicapped from entering into honest relationships with others; they resist any discussion of death as morbid (!), unnecessary, and even sick. Their own fears prevent others, especially children, from gaining knowledge and understanding that prepares them for what is an undeniable fact of life. Death is not a pleasant topic. It raises fears for ourselves and for those we love. It is because of that love, both for ourselves and for others, that this difficult topic must be discussed before death takes a member of a family.

One reason for this is that when death occurs in a family, the children are the forgotten ones. Because the adults in the family are now trying to deal with their own feelings, they have little time or patience with a child's natural, but often painful, questions. We may react angrily and sharply, causing the child to feel guilt over the death. Children may even believe they have somehow caused the death and that is why their parent is reacting angrily. Certainly it is difficult to sit down and try to explain the meaning of death when someone close to us has died.

If it is true many adults in our society fear death, it is also true many feel helpless to cope with the grief and loss children feel. While adults are trying to cope with their own grief and loss, it is easy to forget the feelings of children. It is easy to overlook death-related issues and behaviors when adults are caught up in their own feelings. The simple fact of the matter is we can't help our children if we can't recognize they need help. Recognition is made more difficult if some time has not been spent with children discussing the feelings and fears we all have regarding death and dying.

When a death occurs in a family, relatives come to offer comfort and care. While it is a good and positive response, it is also possible relatives can actually hinder children's ability to cope with the death. In their concern to protect the child, they may interfere by preventing children from confronting the death directly. They may tell them not to think about the death, not to worry, not to grieve. They may try to comfort them by telling them myths or even lies ("Daddy's gone to a better place" or "Mommy can be happy now. She is at peace," or, worst of all, "Mommy's gone on a long trip" or "Death is like sleep") to help ease the pain. As we have seen above, this behavior may have as much to do with their own fear as it does with an honest desire to comfort the child. Their attempt to "make it better" may interfere. Another reason preparation is necessary, then, is so children will be better prepared to cope with well-meaning but ill-informed relatives.

Finally, without preparation, adults may fall into ways of treating children that can have long-range damaging effects after a death in a family. There seem to be three primary damaging ways of treating children. First, it is possible the child could be used in ways designed to counteract one's own grief. For example, we might take out our anger at losing a loved one on the children. We might unwittingly blame them. We might transfer more family responsibility to children than they can handle. Second, it is possible children could be used to substitute for the dead person. It is possible, for example, for a parent to tell a child they are going to have to be the mommy or daddy in the family now that Mommy or Daddy is gone. Third, it is possible the child could be given qualities of the dead person. A parent might begin to see more and more of the dead person in the child. ("You look more and more like your brother every day" or "That is just what Jennifer would have said if she was still with us.") The danger is that as this is done, the child has less and less opportunity to develop a distinct and separate personality of his or her own.

All of these attitudes do not help children cope with death and dying. All prevent the child from entering adulthood with the knowledge and understanding that will allow them to continue to grow and develop without crippling fears about the end of life for either themselves or their loved ones.

Nature of Society

If adults have attitudes that prevent them from openly discussing death and dying with their children, where do the adults get their attitudes? Whatever other sources might be mentioned, the one that cannot be ignored is the society in which we live. It is the great teacher of us all. What sort of culture/society do we live in?

We are a death-denying, death-defying culture. As we have seen above, on children's TV the bad guys who were killed on last week's TV program reappear, only to be killed again this week.

One of the ways in which some people try to deny their fear of death is by defying death. There was once a television program entitled *The Thrill Seekers*. These death-defying addicts placed themselves in situations of danger for thrills. Admittedly, they probably did it for other reasons, too—like money. The point of the show, however, appeared to be to emphasize the danger involved.

The predominant religious point of view in America, the Judeo-Christian, emphasizes that death is not permanent. This widely accepted religious point of view teaches children death is physical only and that the most important part of ourselves goes on living forever. There is no death.

Other cultures on the planet teach that life should be lived in the constant knowledge of death and when death comes, people should have it come consciously and with full awareness (Foster 1981). Our Western culture seems to have prevented such an understanding of this relationship between life and death.

It is not only the religious establishment that teaches us not to be concerned with the permanence of death, but the medical establishment as well. In the medical model it is widely held death is unacceptable. It could even be said physicians don't talk about death. All of their training is aimed at the preservation of life. Death is to be avoided, denied. This desire to prevent death is so strongly held, the most "heroic" measures are applied and continued even after it has been demonstrated life is no longer possible and our bodies have been kept functioning long after any hope of recovery is realistic. The physician's entire training is challenged when he or she is forced to "let go."

It has even been suggested that when death education is taught, it has been taught in factual and clinical ways which end up denying the emotional aspects of death and dying. In our emotional efforts we have tried so hard to be objective we may have missed teaching the real needs for which persons enrolled in the class in the first place. Any death education program that is worthwhile will not approach death in so cold and calculating a fashion as to miss the human concerns of the class members.

Finally, it may very well be that the real losers in all of our cultural teaching are the males. While our death-denying culture affects all of its members, another aspect of our culture multiplies the effects on males. In this death-denying culture we also teach that males are not allowed to express the emotions they have about the events in their lives as readily as females. Our boys, then, are caught in a culture in which the pain of death and dying must be met with a stoicism beyond their years. They hurt, and they are not allowed to express that hurt without being criticized.

Euphemisms

People don't die, they pass away, depart, pass on, go to their final reward, meet their maker, go over to the other side, go to heaven, or are simply no longer with us. Some expire. Some are delivered. People aren't buried, they go to their final rest, not in a graveyard, but in a memorial park. They did not have a funeral, but a ceremony, and this was held in a home by a grief counselor in a slumber room. We don't know about you, but we can't wait. It sounds like an experience we don't want to miss!

Arnold Toynbee once remarked that Americans consider death to be un-American! Euphemisms protect us from facing realities by using words that deny the true meaning of an experience. They protect us at our own expense because the fears about death do not go away. We have to invent greater and greater schemes of denial to prevent our fears from entering consciousness.

Not only do these fictions and half-truths prevent us from confronting our own fears, they allow us to appear to be knowledgeable and forth-right to our questioning children. The evasions are discovered only later, after the child has matured and has accepted the denial as right and proper.

In one area this is an especially sensitive and delicate subject. This is the matter of religious belief. While it is absolutely proper for parents to provide religious instruction for their children, it may not be an effective way to talk about death to children, especially young children. When children are told that Mommy has gone to heaven, they are led into a long series of questions that have no concrete answers. The abstractions of religious view are lost on children. If Dad is in heaven, children will want to know where it is and why they can't go visit. If they are told it is God's will, they will want to know why the good God does such cruel things. If they are told God took someone because they were good and God wanted them to be with Him, they might ask if God couldn't have gotten along

with someone else, because they needed Mommy too. Or they may be confronted with an unsolvable dilemma. If the good go to be with God and
they (the children) are alive, it means they are bad; if they are good, it
means they are going to die. While theologians may be able to resolve such
dilemmas, it is beyond the reasoning capacity of children.

Consider the following play, based on an actual event. It represents
the problems adults have when they try to use clichés, evasions, and
abstractions to deal with the subject of death. The cast is Susan, who is
five years old, and her mother.

The Serious Talk[1]

(Susan is bouncing a ball.)

Mother: Susan, we need to have a talk. Sit down. (Susan continues to play.)

Susan: Okay.

Mother: (Shakes Susan) I said, sit down. We need to have a talk. (Susan reluctantly sits down.) Now, that's better. (Mother becomes very serious.) Susan, Grandma died today.

Susan: (With no interest in the conversation.) Oh?

Mother: Do you know what that means?

Susan: (Nodding her head) Uh-huh. Who killed her?

Mother: Susan!!! Nobody killed her! She just . . . died.

Susan: Well, if she died, somebody must have killed her. That's what they do on TV.

Mother: Susan, I don't know what's wrong with you! She just died. She's dead.

Susan: Mommy, what's *dead*?

Mother: Well, dead is like, well, like being asleep.

Susan: (Happily) Can 1 go wake her up?

Mother: Susan!!! You can't wake her up. She's dead!!!

Susan: Well, when Billy plays dead, he wakes up and then he's it, and we all have to run so he won't catch us.

Mother: Susan, Grandma is not *playing* dead. She *is* dead!

Susan: Okay (a long silence) Mommy, if Grandma is dead, where is she? Where is dead?

Mother: Dead isn't a place, Susan. Grandma is in heaven. She is an angel now.

Susan: (Another long silence) Where is heaven, Mommy?

Mother:	Heaven is up in the sky . . . with God.
Susan:	(Claps her hands) Oh, good! We can go visit her! When we go on the airplane for vacation we can go to heaven to see Grandma, can't we, Mommy?
Mother:	We can't go to heaven until we die! Don't be silly!
Susan:	(Thoughtfully) Well, airplanes go up in the sky. If heaven is up in the sky, why can't we go on an airplane to heaven!
Mother:	(Growing more disturbed by the moment) Because we can't, that's why! Stop being so silly! It's time to go to the funeral home to see Grandma. Come on, let's get dressed. (Susan sits and pouts.)
Susan:	(Sits still) Mommy, you said Grandma was in heaven . . . up in the sky?
Mother:	Yes.
Susan:	How can we go to the fun'r'l home to see her if she is in heaven? Why can't I go to heaven to see her?
Mother:	Susan, honestly! Grandma's soul is in heaven. Her body is at the funeral home.
Susan:	(Looks puzzled) Why is Grandma's sole in heaven? How can a shoe be an angel?
Mother:	Susan, shut up! If you don't, I'll put you to bed and you can just go to sleep right now. (Susan begins to cry. Mother attempts to pull her from the chair. Susan cries more loudly.)
Susan:	I don't want to go to bed! Please don't make me go to bed! (Mother drags Susan screaming from the room.)

There is a lesson here for all of us. What serves us best in our efforts to help children deal with death and dying is the truth. What confuses children the most are evasions, myths, half-truths, fables, and lies which are meant to comfort but ultimately create more fear.

Assumptions About Children

We have discussed the problem of talking to children about death as coming from adults' own fears regarding death. There is, however, another cause for this reluctance. It stems from the assumption we make about what children are like. It may be, for example, that some adults feel comfortable with talking about death with other adults, but not with children. They may believe children lack the emotional and intellectual maturity to understand the actual meaning of death. In this belief they are partially right, but largely wrong. Children can understand death even though they understand it differently at different stages of life. Emotionally, they feel with the same intensity as adults. When adults make the assumption children cannot profit from talking about death, they deny them the opportunity to become prepared for one of life's realities. The adult's good intentions condemn the child to a lack of knowledge and understanding.

Other adults make the assumption that talking to children about death will only create fears which would not be there if they hadn't talked about it. This attitude characterizes many of our interpersonal relationships, leading to a host of communication problems, not only with children but in our entire society. A better attitude is to believe that not talking about death creates problems in the same way not talking about any real human concern creates problems.

It may be some adults assume children aren't concerned about death. This fiction is exposed when one spends time with small children. They are interested in death, and this interest comes early in their lives (O'Brien et al. 1978). We have already related the experience of one of the authors with a four-year-old child. It is only a slight exaggeration to say children begin to ask questions about death when they can begin to ask questions. The assumption that children aren't concerned about death probably fits more in the death-denying category than in any real statement about the nature of children.

For some reason, there are adults who believe children aren't affected by death. They believe children are somehow so elastic in their lives they will be unaffected by sorrow and grief. Actually, sometimes it is frightening to view children who have experienced a loss and appear not to be affected. Usually this signals problems for later on, just as it does for an adult who refuses to grieve at a loss. It may be this view comes from those who believe they know what the proper way is to grieve, and if children do not fit that pattern, then it must be the children aren't grieving. Children are as individual in their ways of grieving as adults, and that can be misleading. To assume children are unaffected by death, or that their fears, anger, and pain need not be discussed is to do serious damage to children.

It is entirely possible there are adults, willing and able to talk to children about death and dying, who are simply waiting until a child asks them a question about it. They might believe, for example, the proper time to discuss issues with children is when they ask questions. There is hardly anything wrong with this view—that is a good time to talk with children. The problem with this point of view is that children don't always ask questions about the things that are troubling them or even about the things they want or need to know about life. The belief that the time to provide information is when children ask questions can have the dangerous effect of leaving children unprepared to face a death when it occurs. Often we do not have time to deal with questions when someone has died. A safer route is to provide the opportunity to ask questions and even to set up situations where children can be asked their opinions and concerns regarding death.

Finally, perhaps the worst assumption some adults make about children and death is if a child does ask questions about death, there must be some psychological problem with the child. Some adults have a romantic notion of childhood that holds that children are happy, carefree, and joyous all the time. Any child who raises serious or morbid questions must somehow be morbid, sick, or disturbed. This attitude would not only deny death, but actively punish any child who raises questions about it. It is the most dangerous assumption of all. It is an assumption that creates guilt, shame, fear, and denial in children. If the assumptions above are incorrect, what are children like and what can they understand of the meaning of death?

What Are Children Like?

First of all, it is important to know children are as individual as adults. They feel the effects of death as intensely as adults. They feel the loss of pets or persons close to them in different ways and act differently as a result of those feelings. The grieving process will vary among children for four reasons. First, the age of children will affect how they view death. Second, the relationship children had with the dead person will affect how deeply they feel the loss. Third, children's emotional needs will affect how they are able to cope with the loss. Fourth, children's individual personalities will determine how they respond to the loss. With the exception of age, these same factors apply for adults. These factors should be considered when adults are considering discussing a death with children. They are also important simply because they allow the adult to view each child as a unique individual for whom techniques and plans of action cannot be applied without knowing the individual.

In trying to understand children and their understanding of death and dying, there are three factors that differentiate children from adults.

First, they have a limited knowledge of the world because they have been here a limited amount of time. Second, they have a limited knowledge of the world because they have limited experience with the world. Third, they have a limited knowledge of the world because of their developmental stage. The third factor is the most difficult to understand and the most important. Children do not view the world the way adults do. Their knowledge and understanding of the world is based to a large extent on the development of intelligence, which seems to grow and develop in predictable and natural ways. The identifiable stages of development are roughly age related and carry with them commonly held understandings of life processes such as death. This growing understanding of the causes of events in the world allows the child to come to better and better understand the world, provided something doesn't prevent the natural development of the child. Two things that can certainly prevent the natural development of intelligence are fear and false information. There seems to be general agreement that children progress through a developmental understanding of death that proceeds from an early, immature stage to a later, more mature conception of death. A clear explanation of how children at various ages view death was published by Delphie J. Fredlund and we are indebted to her for permission to use her words at some length.[2]

The Development of a Concept of Death

In the early part of this century most of the deaths occurred in the home, just as most of the funerals did, and also almost all of the births. Children were around—they heard the conversations, they saw the dying person as his disease progressed, they helped in the care, they knew that death was part of life in a very different way than our contemporary children do. At this time the education system also contributed a great deal to children's knowledge about death because many of the school books contained stories and poems about death and burial, often the death and burial of children. For example, one of the books commonly used in educating children 100 years ago, *McGuffey's Fifth Eclectic Reader*, included 57 poems, 27 of which referred to death and dying.[1] Infant mortality was high, many children died from communicable and other diseases, medical technology was not nearly as far advanced as it now is, many mothers died in childbirth, men were involved in hazardous occupations and there were no safety codes. Many children actually were orphaned at an early age, and they regularly experienced the death of other children. There has always been a tendency for writing of any period to reflect the personal and social conditions of the environment.

Many writers have contributed to the literature on how children develop an understanding about death, and there is general agreement that this understanding develops in an orderly sequence from a state of total unawareness in very early childhood through stages to the point where death can be considered logically in terms of cause and outcome.

Under Three

Most children younger than three do not comprehend anything at all regarding death. They can and sometimes do experience grief in response to the loss of an essential person (i.e., the mother) but they are reacting to the separation aspect, and death as an understandable concept does not enter into their thinking.

From Three to Five

In the early part of this stage most children begin to accept that there is an all-powerful force in the universe that controls the workings of the world, and to which they must adjust.[2] If a child experiences a family death as early as three or four, the separation is still the most significant aspect, and his questions reflect this. "Where did he go?" "When will he come back?" "What is he doing?" These questions are very difficult to answer to the satisfaction of a very young child because of this limited frame of reference, and because he does not understand he may react with intense anger and experience severe rejection.

As children grow toward five they regard death as a departure, but they feel that it is reversible and that the dead person or animal will somehow return and go on just as usual, or that he is doing all the usual things when no one is looking, for example at night, or in the attic, or even in the grave they think that life continues. They also have considerable faith in their own omnipotence and their ability to make things happen, simply by wishing. Small children find it easy to wish death of people who interfere with their freedom but their threats of violence are meant to get the interferer out of their way, for the immediate present, so they can do as they please. The reversibility of death serves as a comforting protection to them.[3]

For four- or five-year-olds, immobility is the crucial factor about death, but of course it is reversible. They begin to accept that death happens to people but only when they are old. Most of them do not believe that they themselves will ever die or that children can die.

Neither do most of them believe that they will ever get old; they can stretch their imaginations at age five to personal parenthood, but to grandparents? That is much more difficult.

From Six to Nine

Children begin to believe that death is permanent as they grow toward six. This is associated with the development of the time sense; yesterday, next week, last month begin to have meaning. Many children become exceedingly anxious about death during this stage.[4] Perhaps this is the reason that Ilg and Ames said that children have their worst troubles about death when they are six years old.[5] Children are naturally boisterous and wild during this period and almost always consider death to be associated with violence. Most of them still think of themselves as invincible during the early part of this stage, but as they approach eight they are beginning to accept that death is for everyone. They tend to regard death as a person and use many descriptive names. They associate death with darkness and feel that at night you have to step lively to keep out of his clutches.

By age nine many children have an almost obsessive interest in death and they may sound morbid at times. It is a very scary time for them because they are trying to develop a perspective on what death is all about. They talk to each other if adults won't listen and it really is important that they have their questions answered, even if the answer is, "I don't know." If the questions are ignored, they soon learn to quit asking.

From Ten to Twelve

Children in this age group are ready to deal with the reality of death but they have learned something new which is very difficult for most of them to fully accept. *Death can happen to anybody at any age.* No one is immune for any period of time at all. There was comfort earlier in accepting human death as a phenomenon of aging and therefore there was no need to worry about it or even think about it happening *to them* for a long time. By the time children are ten they know that is not true, and they struggle with developing a philosophy which accepts but still defends them against daily vulnerability. Most children in this age group have outgrown their belief in their magical powers to bring death to a person by wishing it or saying it, but they need to be reassured that they have not caused deaths to happen in their families or to their friends by things they actually did or did not do. Many children feel responsible for such deaths, but too often they can't talk about it, they can't share their fears in order to gain absolution. I think teachers should be very alert to this possibility.

Age ten to twelve is a very anxious period for facing the reality of death, but many children deal with their anxiety by developing an elaborate facade. They joke about and make fun of death, and create fantastic stories about skeletons and ghosts which they swear are true. It is a period of great one-upmanship, and they may laugh uproariously as though the whole subject is very funny. Most of them really don't think it is so funny, they are just trying to protect themselves from a very fearful and very dangerous unknown.

Adolescence

The practice of making fun and joking about death continues into adolescence, but something new has been added and that is a defiance, a kind of "I dare it to happen to me" stance. Many of them have a tremendous need to prove over and over again that they are immune. For example in *Morante's Autobiography of an Italian Boy*, Arturo says:

> The thing I most hated was death. In my own natural happiness I chased all my thoughts away from death.
>
> But at the same time the more I hated death, the more I exaltedly enjoyed giving proof of my own temerity. No game was enough fun if it lacked the element of risk.[6]

The risk-taking behavior of many adolescents, their games of Chicken and Russian Roulette, their driving, drug use, hitchhiking may very well be related to their natural developmental stage of defiance about danger and death.

What this description allows adults to do is to give children an understanding of death from a point of view that is understandable and from which their misconceptions can be confronted directly. They are growing and children. It allows us to see that clear, unembellished truth is the best tool we have in talking to children about death. They have enough fantasies of their own without adults, on whom they depend in great measure for help in understanding the world, adding to their misconceptions by reinforcing fables and myths.

Suggestions for Helping Children Understand Death and Dying

This section is devoted to providing concrete suggestions and information for helping adults help children gain knowledge and understanding of death and dying. There are suggestions regarding the attitudes we take toward death as well as suggestions for specific issues and questions about death and dying.

Helping Attitudes

If there are assumptions that are harmful, then there are others that can be considered helpful.

1. First, and perhaps most important, is to ask, "What can I do to help children cope with death and dying?" Asking this question allows adults to investigate the material available so the information and skills necessary to help children can be developed.

2. Recognize that children are as individual as adults and that they react differently to death. Further, they grieve just as individually as adults. Therefore, do not be too quick to tell a child how to grieve (Kohn 1978).

3. Don't offer children final answers about death, since there are none. It is perfectly all right to answer, "I don't know" (Grollman 1977). It is also all right to say to a child that it is good to remember, to care for, and to love the one who has died.

4. There are no more powerful forces than trust and truth. There are two goals for adults dealing with children trying to cope with an inadequate understanding of death and dying. These are honesty and continuing love and care.

5. If you need guidelines in talking about death and dying, remember— the same commonsense practices you would use in talking about sex apply when talking about death and dying.

6. Use gentle firmness in dealing with irrationality. Doris Herold Lund provides us with this example.[3]

> I remember the day my father died. It was entirely unexpected. Although 77, my father had been active—working, playing golf— so his instant death from a coronary shocked us all.
>
> He was a dashing grandfather to the children, with gentle affection for them and a charming wit. Lisa had loved him very much. Now through flowing tears, Lisa said to me fiercely "I won't believe it. He can't be dead. I'm going to go right on writing letters to him. I'm going to put his name along with Gramma's on every envelope."

"No, you're not, Lisa," I said firmly. "That wouldn't help Gramma and it wouldn't help you. She's going to miss him and we will too. But we have to begin getting used to the idea that he is gone. We have to accept it somehow."

7. Children are tough and resistant as long as they receive care and attention. Grief leaves scars, but it also provides the opportunity for coming to understand a reality of life, the fact we all must die.

8. Don't forget, children should share in the joys *and* sorrows of family life. Children should be treated as respected members. Don't exclude them from family grieving or protect them from grief.

9. Don't be surprised if children do not appear to be grieving. Sometimes they are trying to control their feelings. Encourage them to talk and to share.

Talk to Children

The secret of talking to children about any sensitive subject is to use any excuse to talk to them. Use television programs as an introduction to feelings of any number of subjects; use the death of a pet or a national figure to talk about death.

In talking to children, use the descriptive truth in talking about death. Children actually do respect those adults in their lives who do not act out the charade of denial. What we must understand is that silence deprives children of opportunities to share their feelings, fears, and sadness. Adults can learn to talk about death as permanent without using euphemisms, myths, half-truths, or fables; they can begin to talk openly, naturally, honestly, sincerely, and plainly in simple, clear, concrete, and direct language. An example might be as follows

Child: What is it like to be dead?
Adult: I don't know. But I do know that dead people don't breathe, eat, or drink. It's not like sleeping or going on a trip. It isn't like any of those things.

If we are going to talk to children about death, it is best to try to be truthful, understanding, and useful in what we tell them.

If you select materials to help you explain death and dying to children, pay some attention to age and intellectual development in selecting the material.

Encourage children to talk about death and dying. The real question is not whether we should talk to children about death and dying but when and how.

When you talk to children about death and dying, remember any talk should also include feelings. Do not be afraid to cause tears in talking about the death of someone or something the child loved.

Remember to talk about the future and emphasize the continuing care of those who are still living and the hopes we all have for the future.

Listening to Children

There seem to be four goals for listening to children.

Why

1. If we listen to children, we can gain some personal insight into their perception and understanding of death and dying.
2. We can help clarify their feelings.
3. We can help clear up any misconceptions they may have.
4. We can help them through their grief.

How

1. The basic skills of listening involve trying to really understand what the other person is meaning, and sharing our own real feelings.
2. Listen carefully for feelings and accept the feelings, whatever they are.

What

1. Get children to talk about past memories and experiences.
2. Allow children to ask their puzzling questions in an atmosphere of acceptance.

Sharing

1. Listen for the chance to share your own fears, feelings, and fantasies.
2. Listen for the chance to share your own sorrow.

Preparing for Death

There are at least three reasons for trying to prepare children for death and dying. First, since it is impossible to protect children from experiences with death, it makes sense for adults to try to help children in understanding the meaning of death. Second, since there are many needs that are created in dealing with death, there can be many ways to meet those needs if children are prepared. Third, it is unwise to try to help children cope with death only after a death has occurred. If we are to help children cope with death, we as adults will have to confront and cope with our own feelings of death first.[4]

It is better to risk explaining too much than to omit explaining death and dying entirely.

Make a special effort to explain that death and sleeping are not the same. Make a special effort to explain that death is not a place. Make a special effort to explain that death and going on a trip are not the same.

Reassure the Child

Children depend on adults. If we desert them, they have no one to turn to for help with their confusions, doubts, and fears. They count on us for support.

Therefore, do not ignore death. Especially, do not ignore children when a death occurs. Adults should be available to comfort a child even if it appears the child is unaffected by death.

Remember, it is more frightening for a child to be sent away than to stay and see a parent or other adult cry because of some anguish. If you believe you are unable to comfort a child because of your own grief, get someone who can comfort the child. Don't try to deal with the grief of a child if you can't deal with your own.

Reassurance is both physical and verbal. Do not be afraid to hold children in order to comfort them. Verbalize your caring. Tell your children of your affection for them. Reassure them it is all right to cry and to feel sorry for themselves. It is okay to talk about the fears they have about death. It is all right not to hide the way they feel.

Check up periodically on how children are coping with their loss. Ask them directly if there is any help you can give. Finally, if you offer help, follow up on what you say you will do.

Strive to recognize when children are in pain. Death hurts, and children need to be comforted and reassured. There is a beautiful example of how one person did this. Bridget Moore writes of when her father died.[5]

> I suddenly missed my father. Suppose he came back? He wouldn't know where we were. I knew he was dead, but still he might come back. . . . I walked round and round the church, touching familiar bushes and flowers. I went to a corner of the building and leaned against it. I cried as hard as I could. I hadn't cried before and the strength of the sobs hurt, but I couldn't stop.
>
> I felt a hand on my shoulder and Jim, the old sexton who let me ring the bells on Sunday, drew me into his arms. He had tears in his eyes. I knew he had loved my father as much as any of us had. He rocked me and held me close. I told him I couldn't leave because Daddy might come back. "Don't worry, my house is on the other side of the church," Jim said, "I will know if your father comes back. I'll tell him where you are. But, he said, "you know he won't come back."
>
> "I know," I said, "but just in case."

From the quiet reassurance of a living friend, Bridget Moore made peace with the death of her father. This is a gift we can give to all of our children.

Helping the Child to Cope After the Death of a Loved One

1. The most important thing to do is to talk about death over and over. One serious talk is not enough. Mourning takes a long time.

2. It is equally important to realize it is unkind to children to allow them to continue to believe falsehoods. They must be encouraged to

talk about fears, feelings, and beliefs so that any irrationalities can be confronted.

3. After a time, turn the talks to the constructive future. Begin to discuss the positive changes that are taking place and the hopes you have for the future, too.

Pets

There are two recommendations regarding the death of a pet. First, don't deprive the child of the grieving process simply because it is an animal that has died and not a person. Second, do not replace the pet immediately, because if you do you deprive the child of the period of mourning that can teach him or her something important about a significant experience of living. It is possible that replacing the pet immediately trivializes death and teaches grief can be overcome by simply seeking out a new puppy. The problem comes when we try to replace a dad, mom, or grandparent.

Funerals

While a funeral may be a way for persons to enter and effectively deal with their grief, it is a misconception to believe funerals are automatically good for children. Children need a relaxed, loving, and evocative discussion regarding funerals so they can either decide for themselves whether they want to go or so that parents can decide whether the child should go.

Roughly, if children are under four years of age the parents should decide; if children are over four, they can decide for themselves (Wessell 1981). For children under four, the parents need to answer this question: Will this be helpful for the children? For children over four, the parents need to provide a clear, straightforward description of what goes on at funerals and insure that the child is accompanied by a non-grief-stricken adult.

If these guidelines are followed, a reasonable decision can be reached for each child regarding attending funerals.

Children's Books

Selecting materials for children is more difficult than it would at first seem. This is so because the books designed for children often don't meet the criteria of age or intellectual development they are designated for. This makes it difficult to simply pick a book off a bookstore shelf and be assured that it is a good book for your child. The articles below are recommended for two specific reasons. First, they are good for looking at the cultural or societal assumptions that are common in children's literature. Second, they examine specific books and make recommendations for books and authors considered appropriate for particular ages.

Lawrence A. Bailis. "Death in Children's Literature: A Conceptual Analysis." *Omega*. 1977-78, pp. 295-303.
Discusses the themes that are common in children's literature after examining forty children's books.

Joanne E. Bernstein. "Literature for Young People: Nonfiction Books About Death." *Death Education*. 1979, pp. 111-119.
Reviews a number of nonfiction books on death.

Robert G. Delisle and Abigail S. Woods McNamee. "Children's Perceptions of Death: A Look at the Appropriateness of Selected Picture Books." *Death Education*. 1981, pp. 1-13.
Six picture books are evaluated in terms of their appropriateness for dealing with the concept of death.

Carol C. Ordal. "Death as Seen in Books for Young Children." *Death Education*. 1980, pp. 223-236.
This article evaluates twenty-two children's books for their usefulness in helping three- to nine-year-olds understand and cope with death.

Carol C. Ordal. "Treatment of Death in Selected Child Care Books. *Death Education*. 1979, pp. 121-130.
Twenty child-care books are examined to see if they contain any useful information to help children cope with death. Recommendations are made.

Hannelore Wass and Judith Shaak. "Helping Children Understand Death Through Literature." *Childhood Education*. November/December 1976, pp. 80-85.
Presents an overview of the concept of death and dying and reviews several books that are considered appropriate for different-aged children.

Death Education

The importance of death education has been stressed throughout this chapter. We conclude this chapter with specific recommendations concerning death education.

1. Any school program of death education should include three areas. First, it should include discussions of children's feelings. Second, it should include therapeutic treatment, if necessary. Third, it should provide information. The best programs will involve open communication in groups involving feelings and will use honest terminology. Any good program of death education cannot simply be factual about death.

2. It is important death education not be confined to schools. A program, in order to be effective, must involve parents as well as teachers and counselors. This might involve a class in death and dying for the parents.

3. An effective death education program needs to teach there is strength in the expression of honest feelings. It should be emphasized that grief is an honest feeling.

4. An effective death education program cannot be devoted to any one theory in explaining children's behavior. It cannot be effective if professionals try to impose their religious beliefs on children, teachers, and counselors, especially in public schools. Such a program needs to realize and respect the rights of individual children to their own beliefs. Certainly, in any public school program, the religious beliefs of teachers and counselors cannot be imposed on children.

5. Two prerequisites to an effective death education program for children should be knowledge of children and the teachers' self-awareness. Teachers in children's death education programs should provide themselves with four necessary information bases (Atkinson 1980). First, they should understand the developmental needs of children. Second, they should understand the developmental levels of thought about death and dying. Third, they should be informed concerning children's possible grief reactions. Fourth, they should be aware of signs of interest or distress.

It is also crucial that teachers in death education programs also clarify their own feelings, fears, fantasies, values, and doubts regarding death (Atkinson 1980). This examination should be done before the class is taught, but it is entirely possible in teaching the class a teacher could discover previously unknown attitudes or values. It is then that a strong, mature, and sensitive adult is most needed. Death education is a necessary part of life. In an effective program, children can grow in awareness, knowledge, understanding, and strength to move into adulthood well prepared to face what for many is the most frightening aspect of human consciousness—the fact that we all die.

Notes

1. McLendon, G. H. "One Teacher's Experience With Death: Education for Adolescents." *Death Education.* 1979. 3:56-65. Reprinted by permission.

2. Fredlund, D. J. "Children and Death From the School Setting Viewpoint." *The Journal of School Health.* November 1977, pp. 533-535. Reprinted by permission.

Notes from Fredlund Articles

1. *Symp II, Group for the Advancement of Psychiatry, Death and Dying.* New York. Mental Health Materials Center, Inc. 1965, p. 661.

2. Plant, J. S. *The Envelope.* New York, The Commonwealth Fund. 1950, p. 41.

3. Page, H. *Playtime in the First Five Years.* New York. J. B. Lippincott, 1954, p. 125.

4. Feifel, H., ed. *The Meaning of Death.* McGraw-Hill Book Co. 1959, pp. 22-23.

5. Ilg, F. D. and Ames, L. *Child Behavior.* New York. Harper and Bros. 1955, pp. 311-313.

6. Talbot, T. ed. *The World of the Child.* Garden City, N.Y. Doubleday and Co., Inc. 1967, p. 336.

3. Lund, D. H. *Parents.* February 1975, pp. 42, 66-67, 72. Reprinted by permission.

4. Nelson, R. C. and Peterson, W. D. "Challenging the Last Great Taboo: Death." *The School Counselor.* May 1975, pp. 353-358.

5. Moore, B. "When I Was Nine . . ." *Reader's Digest.* January 1981, pp. 143-144, 146. Reprinted by permission.

Appendix:
Calming Techniques
for Children

*A child's life is like a piece of paper
on which every passerby leaves a mark.*

Ancient Chinese Proverb

Since each parent-child interaction is a unique combination of the individual personalities and circumstances, parents need to select antistress activities that best suit their situation. If your children are especially active all the time, you may wish to begin by introducing them to a more active relaxation activity to get them used to the idea of listening to their bodies and calming themselves.

This section includes examples of a variety of antistress activities possible for parents and their children. Additional references are listed for your benefit.

Quieting Reflex—A Choice for Children

We often ask children to listen, be quiet, or pay attention without acknowledging that they may not know how to produce the results we demand.

This Appendix was written by Clydette Stulp, Mark Disorbio and Debra Carver.

Teaching children to relax with the *quieting reflex* (Kiddie QR) is giving them a tool to facilitate any activity or task they are asked to perform. The pride in being able to calm oneself is a significant step in building self-esteem. A secure self-image not only facilitates learning, it is vital to aliveness and well-being!

The Kiddie QR is the children's version of a technique devised by Dr. Charles Stroebel, head of research for the Institute of Living in Hartford, Connecticut, and further developed by Elizabeth Stroebel. The Kiddie QR is a step-by-step six-second process of relaxing and calming the body, undoing inappropriate stress responses before they become a way of life.

Each time a child has a stress response to such things as fear, worry, anger, pressure, and so forth, the QR becomes a reflex to replace this response. The steps to the six-second quieting reflex are as follows:

Quieting Reflex

Step 1: *Awareness*—Become aware of worry, fear, or anxiety that creates a stressful feeling.

Step 2: *Smile*—Make a smile (allow eyes to sparkle).

Step 3: *Inhale*—Inhale an easy, natural breath. (We recommend that people inhale imagining that the breath comes in through the hands and arms to the chest.)

Step 4: *Exhale*—While exhaling the breath, let the jaw, tongue, and shoulders go loose, feeling a wave of limpness, heaviness, and warmth flowing to the toes as the breath is exhaled down through the body and out the feet.

Step 5: *Calm*—Say to yourself inside, "My body is calm."

Step 6: *Resume normal activity.*

A QR breath can be taken any time, any place throughout the day. The more frequent the QR, the greater the calmness and the more dramatic the ability to focus attention and be creative.

Here are a number of good times for children and parents to use the QR (six-second calming breath):

BEFORE . . .
> meals . . .
>> going to school . . .
>>> tests . . .
>>>> starting a new activity . . .
>>>>> checking out books in the library . . .
>>>>>> doing homework . . .
>>>>>>> going home . . .
>>>>>>>> a family discussion . . .
>>>>>>>>> going to sleep at night . . .
>>>>>>>>> etc., etc.

> DURING . . .
>> meals . . .
>>> confrontations . . .
>>>> class . . .
>>>>> tests . . .
>>>>>> moments of high tension . . .
>>>>>>> homework . . .
>>>>>>>> a family discussion . . .
>>>>>>>>> any other time it fits . . .
>>>>>>>>> etc., etc.

> AFTER . . .
>> meals . . .
>>> tests . . .
>>>> doing homework . . .
>>>>> playing outside . . .
>>>>>> a fight . . .
>>>>>>> recess . . .
>>>>>>>> going to a new activity . . .
>>>>>>>> etc., etc.

Rag Doll

Autogenic training was developed over seventy years ago in Germany. This relaxation method has been extensively researched and is gaining wide applications throughout the world for many stress-related afflictions. The following exercise, the *rag doll*, developed by Beata Jencks, is an adaptation of the adult version of autogenic training designed for children.

Parents are encouraged to do this with their children, following the directions closely.

The following should be read aloud or, after you are familiar with the procedure, it can be acted out in thought, silently.

For the first few days, heaviness of the limbs alone should be practiced. Then, one by one, always after a few days of practice, the other exercises should be added. If the total series becomes too long, heaviness of the limbs and warmth of the limbs can be abbreviated.

Since the subject closes the eyes for the rag doll and may relax fairly deeply, a good "waking up" procedure is needed to end the relaxation, unless it is used before falling asleep. The simplest method for waking up is to act like a healthy person after a good night's sleep: to stretch the arms and maybe also the legs, to yawn and inhale deeply and refreshingly, and to open the eyes and feel refreshed and full of vigor. This waking-up procedure should be followed after every practice session.

Repetition in the exercise instructions are indicated by dots. Different choices of imagery are offered to increase the possibility of suggesting the one that works best. Those that are unpleasant or do not evoke the adequate psychological and physiological reactions should be disregarded.

The exercises should be done in a quiet place, at a comfortable temperature. The child should be comfortable and well supported in a symmetrical lying or sitting position. Tight clothing should be loosened.

Approximate wording (speak slowly and calmly):

Heaviness of the Limbs

Lie down and make yourself comfortable. Allow your eyes to close. Then follow my instructions: Lift up one arm a little, and then just let it drop. Let it drop heavily, as if you were dropping one of those Raggedy Ann dolls: Flop! You know, like one of those floppy dolls or animals. Choose one that you like in your imagination. It might be a doll; or an old, beloved, soft, terry cloth teddy bear; or a soft, velveteen rabbit; or anything you fancy; and lift the same arm again, and drop it! Let it rest there a moment. Think again of dropping a limb of one of those floppy toys, and lift the arm, and flop! . . .

Now think of your arm again, but don't lift it in reality, just in the imagination. Lift it in the imagination, and think that you are dropping it again, and do this while you breathe out. Your one arm just goes limp like a rag, flop! while you breathe out.

And now work with the other arm. Use either your imagination or really lift it at first. It does not matter. But do not lift it too high, just enough to feel its heaviness, and let it again go flop!, but gently and relaxedly. Learn to do it more and more in the imagination only. And when you breathe out again, let it go flop! again, just gently and relaxedly, flop! . . .

Next lift both arms together, and let both arms together go flop!, simply relaxed like an old rag doll, one of those old ones that has been used for a long time and is very soft . . .

Lift one leg. Lift it only a little, and let it just go flop!, just flop! . . . Do this always when you breathe out. Don't lift the leg too high, so that it does not hit too hard; or better yet, lift it only in the imagination. Do this a few times in your imagination only: Just let it become heavy and relaxed . . . .

Now do the same with the other leg. First lift it a little—lift the leg of the imagined rag doll a little—and while you breathe out, let it go flop! Let it relax. Let it go soft like a rag. Feel free to move your legs or any part of your body to a more comfortable position any time you want to do so. Just flop! Relaxed and limp . . .

Now both legs together, flop! Relaxed and limp, relaxed and heavy . . .

Now all together, both arms and both legs, all together, limp and relaxed, like a rag doll you put down in a sofa corner or on the floor: flop!, just in the imagination: flop!, heavy and comfortable, well supported by the chair, the sofa, or the floor.

Warmth of the Limbs

Next imagine that you put your rag doll in the sun. Let the doll be warmed by it. The rag doll is lying very relaxed. Feel how the sun is shining on it. Feel it on one arm first, and then on the other. Put the rag doll so that its head is in the shade, but all the limbs are sprawled out in the sun. Imagine the rag doll, and in your imagination touch one of its limbs and feel the warmth, and then let your arm become as warm as that of the rag doll's—warm and soft and relaxed. Be that rag doll and feel that arm. And then do the same with the other arm. . . . And then let one leg be nicely warmed by the sun. . . . And then the other leg, nicely warmed by the sun. . . . And then remember again, you are the rag doll, and you are lying in the sun. All your limbs are nice and warm, but your head is lying in the shade and is comfortably cool.

Warmth of Breath

Now put one hand to your mouth and breathe into its inside. . . . Feel the warmth of your own breath. Such warmth is within you all the time. Then put the hand down again, and imagine that you breathe this same kind of warmth into your own inside. . . . While you breathe out, imagine that you breathe that warmth down into your throat, down into your chest, down into your tummy. . . . Just become nicely warm inside. . . . Or you can imagine that you are drinking something that really warms you nicely inside, or even that something like a warming, glowing ball is rolling around within you. Allow it to warm your inside, so that it becomes all soft and relaxed.

And now just lie there and relax completely for a while and think of the rag doll with its body warmed comfortably, relaxed in the sun.

(*Note:* Omit the following if child is supposed to go to sleep.) And now it is time to end this playing with the rag doll and get up! Stretch the arms and maybe also the legs. Yawn and breathe in deeply and refreshingly, and open your eyes! Look around and breathe in once more, and then sit up and go back to play!

Jumpy Ball

Jumpy ball is a child's exercise game designed to simulate strenuous physical effort and deep breathing. The length of the exercise is determined by the reaction of the child. Do not push or force the exercise to a point where it becomes unpleasant. The duration of the exercise can be extended a little bit each day to increase the physical conditioning and to retrain the child's breathing to a more relaxed rhythm.

Parents should carefully monitor the child during the exercise for signs of breathing distress, such as labored breathing, coughing, or noisy breathing. When such signs occur, the exercise should be ended and the child led into a passive relaxation method.

A small rubber ball, approximately one and a half inches in diameter, is preferred for jumpy ball. It is small for the preschooler's hand, and it is light so that when thrown, it will not hurt others or damage property. It should have lively bouncing action. Jumpy ball can be played alone or in groups.

To play the game:

Show the ball to the children and tell them it is a special ball. It is jumpy ball. When you drop it or toss it in front of you it will "Jump, jump, jump." (Demonstrate by saying "Jump" each time the ball bounces.) Caution them that it is not a thrown ball, to discourage them from throwing the ball vigorously. Some children would sometimes rather do throwing than jumping.

Tell the children that they are going to play like they are jumpy balls.

Demonstrate tossing the ball in front of you, and then jump in the direction of the ball each time it bounces on the floor. Jump so that you land on both feet at once.

Next, distribute balls to each of the children and instruct them to begin. Make it fun. Encourage effort. Praise them for good performance. The enjoyment of the game is enhanced when a small group of children is playing jumpy ball. The balls fly in all directions and children are jumping and running to recover their balls. Repeat the performance.

By letting each child play the game to the level of his or her physical capacity, it teaches the child to monitor his or her physical effort and to stop when necessary, even though others may continue to play. Following jumpy ball, sit calmly with your child or children and do some deep breathing with eyes closed.

Massage

Massage is a natural, soothing way to calm oneself. You can massage your children or teach them to do self-massage. Following is an example of a head-self massage to teach your child. You can both do the activity at the same time.

SELF-MASSAGE—THE HEAD You can use these suggestions to design your own method of self-massage and to teach self-massage to your children. Remove glasses or contact lenses. Let your body tell you what needs attention and what feels good.

Sample directions for demonstrating a self-massage process to your children:

1. Begin by rubbing your hands together. This helps your hands create energy and become warm. Play with the hands a little, shake them out, and allow yourself to really feel them.

2. Now place the palms of your hands on your face. Hold them there for a few seconds. When they are ready, let them move gently over the whole surface of your face. Movements may include circular motion with fingertips, pulling the skin in different directions, kneading, slapping, following the contours of the face with finger pressure. Be sure to breathe calmly and deeply while you are doing this.

3. Move your fingertips up onto your skull; run them through your hair. Try tapping vigorously with fingertips, scratching lightly with the fingernails, grasping hair by the roots, and firmly moving the skin of the scalp in different directions. Smoothly and gently move hands over hair, ears, face, neck. Talk to yourself as you do it. Tell yourself positive and loving things. Enjoy. Allow yourself to be creative.

4. Use fingertips to massage your gums by feeling them through the cheeks. This is a rare treat. Some people love it.

5. Finish by holding your hands over your face and resting.

Music to Create Calmness

The kinds of music we play in the environment greatly influence our emotional and physical responses. Steven Halpern discusses in depth the powerful influence of sound and music on our state of stress or calmness.

Children, like adults, respond quickly, even though often unconsciously, to environmental sounds. We encourage parents to select background music in their home that can assist in creating an antifrantic atmosphere.

The following are recommendations for music to use for various levels of stress in your environment.

When you and/or your child (children) are highly stressed (a high-stress state requires music with faster movements and more variation in order to engage the mind and body. Sounds of nature can be especially renewing—rain, running water, wind, ocean, birds, and so on):

Ron Dexter. *Golden Voyage*, vols. 1-3 (Awakening Productions, 4132 Tuller Ave., Culver City, CA 90230; $7.98 each. This is very captivating, with slow and moderate music with sounds of birds, bells, crickets.

Steven Halpern (Halpern Sounds, 620 Taylor Way, Belmont, CA 94002). *Ancient Echoes*, with Georgia Kelly (HS 783; $7.98). Harp, keyboard, flute, some low chanting sounds. *The Rain Meditation*, with Sunil K. Bose (HS 722; $6.98); Chanting, keyboard, tabla, tambora—a blend of Eastern and Western, blues with Indian raga and jazz.

Georgia Kelly (Heru Records, P.O. Box 954, Topanga, CA 90290. *Rainbow Butterfly*, with Emmett Miller (cassette tape, $6.98). Experiential poetry and music for meditation.

When you and/or your child (children) are moderately stressed (this state requires some variation in musical style, but the speed can be slower):

Steven Halpern (Halpern Sounds). *Spectrum Suite* (HS 770; $7.98). Solo electric piano showing the relation between the seven tones of the musical octave and the seven colors of the visual octave to the seven etheric energy centers (chakra) in our bodies. *Starborn Suite* (HS 780, $7.98). Strings, occasional choir, keyboard. Like "crystal petals tinkling in the solar wind." *Eastern Pace* (cassette tape, HS 782, $7.98). Electronic keyboard, tambora, bamboo flute. *Zodiac Suite* (HS 771, $7.98). Bamboo flute, electric violin, wind chimes interwoven with keyboard. Relates the twelve chromatic tones of the musical octave and the twelve signs of the zodiac.

Georgia Kelly (Heru Records) *Seapeace* ($6.98). Harp; flowing, watery motions. *Tarashanti* ($6.98). Harp and flute; measured beats and up/down flowing rhythms.

Marcus Allen and John Bernoff. *Breathe* (Whatever Publishing, 158 E. Blithedale, Suite 4, Mill Valley, CA 94941; $7.98). Keyboard and vibes—soothing, gentle, has an almost underwater feel.

Tony Scott. *Music for Zen Meditation*, with Shinichi Yuize on koto and Hozan Yamamoto and shakuhachi (Verve V8634; $6.98). Slow, light, varied Eastern sounds.

Iasos. *Inter-dimensional Music through Iasos* (Unity Records, P. O. Box 12, Corte Madera, CA 94925; $8.98). Sunrise, sunset, waves, graceful play of nature spirits. Active, flowing, deep resonating music, many instruments. Electronic sounds.

When you and/or your child (children) are low stress (the following assists in maintaining the calmness):

Gordon de La Sierra. *Gynosphere: Song of the Rose* (Unity Records, $7.98). Music for gymnastics, developmental pastimes. Slow and meditative piano beats.

Larkin-Stentz. *Wind Sung Songs* (Wind Sung Sounds, P. O. Box 7227, Stanford, CA 94305; $6.98). Flute–slow, meditative rhythms.

Environments. *Meditational Environments* (Syntonic Research, 175 Fifth Ave., New York, NY 10010; $5.98). Very slow, ultimate heartbeat and wind in the trees.

The above musical selections are available through most music stores. For a complete catalog of calming, relaxation music, the reader may write to:

Backroads Distributing Company
4008 Idaho
Evans, CO 80620

Relaxing to Music

To assist children in relaxing to music, the following is helpful:

Lie on your backs, close your eyes, pretend your hands are beautiful butterflies and let them dance to the music. When they get tired, let them rest on your tummies . . . feeling the air coming in and out. When they are rested, let them take off again.

Lie on your backs; close your eyes. See lots of colors in your mind. Pretend you're holding magic paintbrushes in both hands. Let them splash beautiful colors in the sky. . . . let's make big round circles. . . . let's make tall mountains . . . etc.

Lie on your backs and close your eyes. . . . now feel in what part of your body you're holding your wiggles. Now wiggle that part. Wiggle up and wiggle down each part until you get all your wiggles out. . . . then let your body be calm and take some deep breaths.

Enhancing Calmness Through Color and Light

Just as an infant responds to a bright object placed before his or her vision, we respond in subtler fashion to color and light in our environment every day. The colors are the slower vibrational end of the spectrum; the reds, oranges, and yellows invite a loud and active response. Cooler colors make us feel slower, quieter. Green is the center, nature's choice for life, and is the most calming. The blues remind us of water; the purples bring harmony and balance.

In any environment with children, our tendency is to provide a variety of objects and colors for stimulation. Just as we are soothed by the simplicity of an oriental design, so children are soothed by the simplest environments—soft colors, indirect lighting, and simple decoration.

In well-documented studies by Dr. John Ott we find evidence that the high-frequency light waves emitted by fluorescent lights create a stage of agitation in children. Our children deserve the care we can provide by designing environments without such hidden sources of discomfort. Lights that emit a full spectrum vibrationally balance and enhance any environment with a more natural restful illumination.

Nature Reflections

Take children for a walk in a quiet place in the outdoors. Open their sensory awareness by really exploring and talking about what they see, hear, feel, and touch. Find a place to sit silently for a few minutes. Ask them to make their bodies calm, feel the breeze, hear the sounds, smell the smells, etc.

When you are back home you can ask the children to go back to this pleasant spot and to be there in their mind's eye and again feel the sensations and the peace of the place. This works well to create calmness once again.

Natural Sounds

Another form of this activity is to ask your child to sit quietly (you sit with them also) and close his or her eyes. Quietly listen to the sounds around you, and as you are ready (keeping the eyes closed), share with each other the new sounds as you hear them. Doing this for five minutes can assist in calming you both.

Family Quiet Time

Schedule a specific time each week—or even daily—for a family quiet time. This time is set aside for silence—no television, no radio or stereo, no talking, no noise interference of any kind, just quiet and calm for a period of time. We recommend at least thirty minutes to make a difference. An optimal time period is an hour. Children and parents can write in journals or keep a diary during this time or read. This can also be used as time that individuals would like to simply sit and contemplate; an activity most people give themselves little time for.

This hour of quiet on a regular basis can assist families in knowing what it is like to be creative and calm together.

Speak Positively

Speak in positive terms to your children (and everyone, for that matter). Instead of saying "Stop that," or "You're not going anywhere because you didn't make your bed," say, "When your bed is made, you may go outside." Rather than negative reprimands, ask your child to do a QR—"calm your body." Stress-related disorders such as ulcers, headaches, anxiety, acting out, and so on are manifestations of negative energy. Replace the negative with positive energy, and you help to alleviate stress.

Calming Resources

This is a collection of resources we have found useful for parents in creating calmness with their children.

Assagioli, R. *Psychosynthesis.* New York: Viking, 1965.

Canfield, J. and H. Wells. *100 Ways to Enhance Self-Concept in the Classroom.* New Jersey: Prentice-Hall, 1976.

Carr, R. *Be a Frog, a Bird, or a Tree.* Garden City, N.Y.: Doubleday, 1973.

Creative Therapeutics. *The Talking, Feeling, and Doing Game: A Psychotherapeutic Game for Children.* 155 County Road, Cresskill, N.J. 07626. 1973.

Diskin, E. *Yoga for Children.* New York: Warner Books, 1976.

Feldenkrais, M. *Awareness Through Movement.* New York: Harper & Row, 1972.

Fleugelman, A. *The New Games Book.* New York: Doubleday, 1976.

Franck, F. *The Zen of Seeing/Drawing as Meditation.* New York: Vintage Books, 1973.

Gross, B., and R. Gross, eds. *The Children's Rights Movement: Overcoming The Oppression of Young People.* Garden City, N.Y.: Anchor, 1977.

Gunther, B. *Sense Relaxation.* New York: Macmillan Collier Books, 1968.

Harmin, Merril and Saville Sax. *A Peaceable Classroom—Activities to Calm and Free Student Energies.* Minneapolis: Winston Press, 1980.

Hartle, D., et al. *Secrets of Breathing for Children with Asthma and Their Parents.* Salt Lake City, Utah Lung Association, 1980.

Hendricks, Gay, and Thomas B. Roberts. *The Second Centering Book.* Englewood Cliffs, New Jersey: Prentice-Hall, 1977.

Hendricks, Gay, and Russel Wills. *The Centering Book.* Englewood Cliffs, New Jersey: Prentice-Hall, 1975.

Huang, A. *Embrace Tiger, Return to Mountain.* Moab, Utah: Real People Press, 1973.

Jampolsky, Gerald. *Love is Letting Go of Fear.* California: Celestial Arts, 1979.

Jencks, B. *Respiration for Relaxation, Invigoration, and Special Accomplishment.* Manual. Salt Lake City: Jencks, 1974.

Jencks, B. "Relaxation and recondition of the autonomic nervous system for children: The autogenic rag doll." Paper presented at the 18th Annual Scientific Meeting, ASCH, Seattle, WA, 1975. Printed by Jencks, 1977.

Kraft, A. *Are You Listening to Your Child?* New York: Walker, 1973.

Luce, G. G. *Body Time.* New York: Pantheon, 1971.

Miller, Lani, and Diane Rodgers. *We Love Your Body.* Washington: Morse Press, Inc., 1979.

Naranjo, C. and R. Ornstein. *On the Psychology of Meditation.* New York: Viking, 1971.

Nelson, E. *Movement Games for Children of All Ages.* New York: Sterling, 1975.

Neuman, Diane. *How to Get the Dragons out of Your Temple.* California: Celestial Arts, 1976.

Oaklander, Violet. *Windows to Our Children.* Utah: Real People Press, 1978.

Ott, J. *Health and Light.* New York, N.Y.: Cornerstone, 1976.

Peirce, J. D. *The Magical Child.* New York: Simon and Schuster, 1977.

Polland, Barbara K. *The Sensible Book, A Celebration Of Your Five Senses.* California: Celestial Arts, 1976.

Rozman, Deborah. *Meditation for Children.* California: Celestial Arts, 1976.

Rozman, Deborah. *Meditating With Children.* California: Univesity of the Trees Press, 1975.

Samuels, M. and H. Bennett. *The Well Body Book.* New York: Random House, 1973.

Seattle Public School District No. 1. *Rainbow Activities.* South El Monte, CA: Creative Teaching Press, 1977.

Singer, J. *Daydreaming.* New York: Random House, 1966.

Shah, Indress. *Caravan of Dreams.* London: Octagon Press, 1968.

Shah, Indress. *The Pleasantries of the Incredible Mulla Nasrudin.* London: Jonathan Cape, 1968.

Shou, J. E. *Go See The Movie In Your Head.* New York: Popular Library, 1977.

Stevens, J. Moav. *Awareness: Exploring, Experimenting, Experiencing.* Utah: Real People Press, 1971.

Thomas, M. *Free to Be . . . You and Me.* New York: McGraw-Hill, 1974.

Bibliography

Allers, Robert. "Helping Children Understand Divorce." *Today's Education.* November-December 1980, pp. 24-27.

Anderson, Hilary. "Children of Divorce." *Journal of Clinical Child Psychology.* Summer 1977, pp. 41-44.

Atkinson, Trudie L. "Teacher Intervention with Elementary School Children in Death-Related Situations." *Death Education.* 1980, pp. 149-163.

Bailis, Lawrence A. "Death in Children's Literature: A Conceptual Analysis." *Omega.* 1977-78, pp. 295-303.

Balkin, Ester; Epstein, Carole; and Bush, David. "Attitudes Toward Classroom Discussions of Death and Dying Among Urban and Suburban Children." *Omega.* 1976, pp. 183-189.

Barker, Hazel and Wills, Ursula. "School Phobia: Classification and Treatment." *British Journal of Psychiatry.* 1978, pp. 492-499.

Barnhill, Laurence R. and Longo, Dianne. "Fixation and Regression in Family Life Cycle." *Family Process.* December 1978, pp. 469-477.

Benedek, Elissa P. and Benedek, Richard S. "Joint Custody: Solution or Illusion?" *American Journal of Psychiatry.* December 1979, pp. 1540-1544.

Bennett, A. N. "Children Under Stress." *Journal of the Royal Naval Medical Service.* Spring-Summer 1974, pp. 83-87.

Berndt, T. J. "Developmental Changes in Conformity to Peers and Parents." *Developmental Psychology. 15*(6). 1979, pp. 608-610.

Bernstein, Joanne E. "Literature for Young People: Nonfiction Books About Death." *Death Education.* 1977, pp. 111-119.

Best, Connie and Best, Winfield. "Kids Afraid to Grow." *Parents.* October 1977, pp. 58, 59, 64, 84.

Bibace, Roger and Walsh, Mary E. "Development of Children's Concepts of Illness." *Pediatrics.* December 1980, pp. 912-917.

Bigelow, B. J. "Children's Friendship Expectations: A Cognitive Developmental Study." *Child Development. 48.* 1977, pp. 246-251.

Boulding, Elise. "Children's Rights." *Human Rights.* November-December 1977, pp. 39-43.

Brazelton, Berry T. "Helping Your Child Get Along with the Doctor." *Redbook.* March 1976, pp. 93, 194.

Brazelton, Berry T. "When a Child Is Sad." *Redbook.* March 1980, pp. 42, 44.

Brazelton, Berry T. "When Your Child Is Sick: Help for Mothers Who Feel Helpless." *Redbook.* July 1978, pp. 24-25.

Brent, Sandor B. "Puns, Metaphors, and Misunderstandings in a Two-Year-Old's Conception of Death." *Omega.* 1977-78, pp. 285-293.

Browning, Diane H. and Boatman, Bonny. "Incest: Children at Risk." *American Journal of Psychiatry.* January 1977, pp. 69-72.

Bruner, Joseph. "Schooling Children in a Nasty Climate." *Psychology Today.* January 1982, pp. 57-63.

Bruns, Bill and Tutko, Tom. "Dealing with the Emotions of Childhood Sports." *ARENA.* Winter 1978, pp. 3-13.

Buchanan, Denton C.; LaBarbera, Carolyn J.; Roelofs, Robert; and Olson, William. "Reactions of Families to Children with Duchenne Muscular Dystrophy." *General Hospital Psychiatry.* 1979, pp. 262-268.

Burgess-Kohn, Jane. "A Death in the Family." *Parents.* October 1978, pp. 72-74, 110.

Business Week. "How to Relate to Your Children." December 12, 1977, pp. 117-119, 122, 127.

Campbell, Judith L. and Dave, Mahesh R. "Childhood Depression." *The Journal of the Indiana State Medical Association.* October 1980, pp. 669-673.

Cantor, Dorthea W. "Divorce: A View from the Children." *Journal of Divorce.* Summer 1979, pp. 357-361.

Carlyle-Gordge, Peter. "Saving Sick Kids from Sick TV." *Macleans.* July 21, 1980, p. 45.

Carro, Geraldine. "Children and Divorce." *Ladies Home Journal.* September 1980, pp. 80-82.

Carro, Geraldine. "Mothering." *Ladies Home Journal.* June 1977, p. 54.

Carro, Geraldine. "What Worries Kids Most?" *Ladies Home Journal.* June 1980, p. 126.

Cater, John I. "Separation and Other Stress in Child Abuse." *The Lancet.* May 3, 1980, pp. 972-973.

Chambers, R.B. "Orthopaedic Injuries in Athletes (Ages 6-17)." *American Journal of Sports Medicine.* 7(3). 1979, pp. 195-197.

Changing Times. "Kids and Money. What They Need to Know When They Need to Know It." June 1981, pp. 17-20.

Chapman, Jennifer A. and Godall, Janet. "Helping a Child to Live Whilst Dying." *The Lancet.* April 1980, pp. 753-756.

Check, William A. "How One Hospital Allays Children's Fears of Surgery." *Jama.* December 1979, p. 2526.

Chess, Stella and Thomas, Alexander. "Defence Mechanisms in Middle Childhood." *Canadian Psychiatric Association Journal.* December 1976, pp. 519-525.

Costello, Joan. "When Your Child Goes to the Hospital." *Parents.* July 1980, p. 83.

Crase, Dixie R. and Crase, Darrell. "Attitudes Toward Death Education for Young Children." *Death Education.* 1979, pp. 31-40.

Cremin, Lawrence A. *The Transformation of Schools.* New York: Random House, 1964.

Cretekos, Constantine J.C. "Some Techniques in Rehabilitating the School Phobic Adolescent." *Adolescence.* Summer 1977, pp. 237-246.

Davis, Jane. "Explaining Death to Children." *British Medical Journal.* March 1981, pp. 1069-1070.

Delisle, Robert G. and McNamee, Abigail S. Woods. "Children's Perceptions of Death: A Look at the Appropriateness of Picture Books." *Death Education.* 1981, pp. 1-13.

Dickman, David and Steinhauer, Paul D. "Role of the Families Physician in the Management of Psychologic Crisis in Children and Their Families." *CMA Journal.* June 1981, pp. 1566-1569.

Doan, Mary. "Visiting Hours Are Over." *Parents.* January 1976, pp. 24-26.

Donady, Bonnie and Tobias, Sheila. "Math Anxiety." *The Education Digest.* December 1977, pp. 49-52.

Dubois, P. "Competition in Youth Sports: Process or Product?" *Research Quarterly. 49*(1). March 1980, pp. 151-154.

Dunn, Judy; Kendrick, Carol; and Macnamee, Rosanne. "The Reaction of First-Born Children to the Birth of a Sibling: Mother's Report." *Journal of Child Psychology.* February 1980, p. 1.

Eisen, Peter. "Children Under Stress." *Australian and New Zealand Journal of Psychiatry.* 1979, pp. 193-207.

Eisenberg, Leon. "Failures in Learning and Failures in Teaching." *Pediatrics.* February 1980, pp. 361-377.

Elkind, David. *Hurried Children: Stressed Children.* Addison Wesley: Menlo Park, California, 1981.

Everly, Kathleen. "New Directions in Divorce Research." *Journal of Clinical Child Psychology.* Summer 1977, pp. 7-9.

Francke, L.B.; Sherman, D.S.; Simons, P.F.; Abramson, P. Zabarsky, M.; Huck, J.; and Whitman, C. "The Children of Divorce." *Newsweek.* February 11, 1980, pp. 58-63.

Fine, Stuart. "Children in Divorce, Custody and Access Situations: The Contribution of the Mental Health Professional." *Journal of Child Psychology and Psychiatry.* 1980, pp. 353-361.

Friske, Edward B. "Found! A Cure for Math Anxiety." *Parents.* February 1980, pp. 64, 66, 67.

Foster, Susan. "Explaining Death to Children." *British Medical Journal.* February 1981, pp. 540-542.

Fox, Mervyn. "Psychological Problems of Physically Handicapped Children." *British Journal of Hospital Medicine.* May 1977, pp. 479-490.

Frank, John L. "A Weekly Group Meeting for Children on a Pediatric Ward: Therapeutic and Practical Functions." *International Journal of Psychiatry in Medicine.* 1977-1978, pp. 267-283.

Freeman, Jayne. "Death and Dying in Three Days." *Phi Delta Kappan.* October 1978, p. 118.

Fredlund, Delphie J. "Children and Death from the School Setting Viewpoint." *Journal of School Health.* November 1977, pp. 533-537.

Gardner, Richard. "Children of Divorce—Some Legal and Psychological Considerations." *Journal of Clinical Child Psychology.* Summer 1977, pp. 3-6.

Gardner, Richard A. "Ten of Advice from a Psychiatrist to Help Parents Avoid Some Common "Tender Traps" of Child-Raising." *Parents.* January 1975, pp. 44, 45, 68, 69, 70.

Gershenson, Charles P. "Child Maltreatment, Family Stress and Ecological Insult." *ASPH.* July 1977, pp. 602-604.

Gerson, R. "Redesigning Athletic Competition for Children." *Motor Skills.* 2(1). 1977, pp. 3-14.

Gillman, Andrew. "Taking the Bite Out of Dental Visits." *Family Health.* January 1980, pp. 22-23.

Gilmartin, David."The Case Against Spanking." *Human Behavior.* February 1979, pp. 18-23.

Ginott, Haim. "Driving Children Sane." *Today's Education.* November/December 1973, pp. 20, 22, 23, 24, 25.

Goddard, G.F. "Who Needs to See a Psychiatrist?" *British Medical Journal.* January 1980, pp. 21-22.

Goldberg, B. et al. "Childhood Sports Injuries: Are They Avoidable?" *Physician and Sports Medicine.* September 1979, pp. 96-101.

Goslin, Evelyn Roberts. "Hospitalization as a Life Crisis for the Preschool Child: A Critical Review." *Journal of Community Health.* Summer 1978, pp. 321-333.

Gottman, J.; Gonso, J.; and Rasmussen, B. "Social Interaction, Social Competence, and Friendship in Children." *Child Development. 46.* 1975, pp. 709-718.

Greendoefer, S. and Lewko, J. "Role of Family Members in Sport Socialization of Children." *Research Quarterly.* May 1978, pp. 146-152.

Grollman, Earl A. and Grollman, Sharon H. "How to Tell Children About Divorce." *Journal of Clinical Child Psychology.* Summer 1977, pp. 35-37.

Grollman, Earl A. "Explaining Death to Children." *The Journal of School Health.* June 1977, pp. 336-339.

Guerney, Louise and Jordon, Lucy. "Children of Divorce—a Community Support Group." *Journal of Divorce.* Spring 1979, pp. 283-291.

Hain, William R. "Children in Hospital." *Anaesthesia.* 1980, pp. 949-951.

Hammond, Janice M. "Children of Divorce: A Study of Self-Concept, Academic Achievement and Attitudes." *The Elementary School Journal.* November 1979, pp. 55-62.

Hawkes, Thomas H. and Furst, Norman F. Research notes: race, socio-economic situation, achievement, IQ, and teacher ratings of student's behavior as factors relating to anxiety in upper elementary school children. *Sociology of Education.* Summer 1971, pp. 333-350.

Heller, Brian P. and Schneider, Carl D. "Interpersonal Methods for Coping with Stress: Helping Families of Dying Children." *Omega.* 1977-78, pp. 319-331.

Henning, James S. and Oldham, Thomas J. "Children of Divorce: Legal and Psychological Crisis." *Journal of Clinical Child Psychology.* Summer 1977, pp. 55-58.

Hetherington, Mavis E. "Divorce—a Child's Perspective." *American Psychologist.* October 1979, pp. 851-858.

Holmes, Kay. "My Child Is in the Hospital." *Parents.* September 1980, pp. 42, 44, 46, 48, 50.

Holroyd, Jean and Guthrie, Donald. "Stress in Families of Children with Neuromuscular Disease." *Journal of Clinical Psychology.* October 1979, pp. 734-739.

Horn, Jack. "The Vulnerable Age. When Moving Brings Special Problems." *Psychology Today.* March 1977, pp. 28, 30.

Intellect. "Problems of Raising Children in a Changing Society." November 1977, pp. 177-179.

Jacobs, Joseph. "The Child at Risk." *CMA Journal.* June 1981, pp. 1449, 1450.

Jacobson, Doris S. "The Impact of Marital Separation/Divorce on Children: Interparent Hostility and Child Adjustment." *Journal of Divorce.* Fall 1978, pp. 2-19.

Kalnins, Ilze V.; Churchill, Pamela M.; and Terry, Grace E. "Concurrent Stresses in Families with a Leukemic Child." *Journal of Pediatric Psychology*. 1980, pp. 81-93.

Kanigher, Steve. "Incest Intolerable Abuse, Audience Told." *Greeley Daily Journal*. January 29, 1982, p. A-3.

Kaplan, Bert L. "Anxiety—a Classroom Close-up." *The Elementary School Journal*. November 1970, pp. 70-77.

Katz, Lilian G. "Lies and Half-truths We Tell Our Children." *Parents*. December 1977, p. 78.

Katz, Lilian G. "Teach Your Child to Cope with Problems." *Parents*. August 1977, p. 80.

Kelly, Joan B. and Wallerstein, Judith. "Part-time Parent, Part-time Child—Visiting After Divorce." *Journal of Clinical Child Psychology*. Summer 1977, pp. 51-54.

Kelly, Joan B. and Berg, Berthold. "Measuring Children's Reactions to Divorce." *Journal of Clinical Psychology*. January 1978, pp. 215-221.

Kempe, Henry and Kempe, Ruth S. *Child Abuse*. Cambridge, Mass.: Harvard University Press, 1978.

Keniston, Kenneth. "More Rights for Children—What an Expert Says." *U.S. News and World Report*. 1977, p. 33.

Klagsbrun, Micheline and Davis, Donald. "Substance Abuse and Family Interaction." *Family Process*. June 1977, pp. 149-173.

Kohn, J. B. "A Death in the Family." *Parents*. October 1978, pp. 72-74.

Krell, Robert and Rabkin, Leslie. "The Effects of Sibling Death on the Surviving Child: A Family Perspective." *Family Process*. December 1979, pp. 471-477.

Lamb, Michael E. "The Effects of Divorce on Children's Personality Development." *Journal of Divorce*. Winter 1971, pp. 163-173.

Langway, Lyyn; Abramson, Pamela; and Foote, Donna. "The Latchkey." *Newsweek*. February 1981, pp. 96-97.

Leder, Gilah. "Bright Girls, Mathematics, and Fear of Success." *Educational Studies in Mathematics*. 1980, pp. 411-422.

Leo, John. "Single Parent, Double Trouble." *Time*. January 1982, p. 81.

Lewis, Nancy. "The Needle Is Like an Animal—How Children View Injections." *Child Today*. January 1978, pp. 18-21.

Lieberman, James E. "Why Marriages Turn Sour—and How to Get Help." *U.S. News & World Report Inc.* 1975, pp. 44-46.

Long, Clive and Moore, John. "Parental Expectations for their Epileptic Children." *Journal of Child Psychology and Psychiatry*. January 1979, pp. 299-312.

Light, K. "Activity for Activity's Sake. *JOPER*. March 1978, p. 38.

Lobsenz, Norman. "How Big Should Your Child's Allowance Be?" *Family Weekly*. September 1981, p. 6.

Laurie, Reginald S. and Schwarzbeck, Charles III. "When Children Feel Helpless in the Face of Stress." *Childhood Education*. January 1979, pp. 134-140.

Lund, Doris H. "Helping Children Cope with Sorrow." *Parents*. February 1975, pp. 42, 66, 67, 72.

Magill, R.D. "Youth Sports: An Interdisciplinary View of Readiness and Effects." *JOPER*. January 1977, pp. 56-57.

Magrab, Phyllis. "For the Sake of the Children: A Review of Psychological Effects of Divorce." *Journal of Divorce*. Spring 1978, pp. 233-245.

Marks, J. "Some Practical and Sensible Advice for Breaking the Bickering Habit." *Seventeen*. November 1977, pp. 136-137.

Martin, A.W. "Is High School Really Worth It?" *Orbit*. April 1979, pp. 14-15.

Masthoff, Sheila. Children's Booklet on hospitals focuses on fears, fantasies. *Hospital Progress*. November 1979, p. 30.

Mason, Edward A. "Hospital and Family Cooperation to Reduce Psychological Trauma." *Community Mental Health Journal*. 1978, pp. 153-159.

Matthews, Jill T. "Beyond Divorce: The Impact of Remarriage." *Journal of Clinical Child Psychology*. Summer 1977, pp. 59-61.

McCleave, Jill; Madsen, Barbara; Flemings, Thomas; and Haapala, David. "Homebuilders: Keeping Families Together." *Journal of Consulting and Clinical Psychology*. 1977, pp. 667-673.

McGuigar, R.A. "Children Under Pressure: Four Doctors' Views." *Today's Health*. September 1967, pp. 62-65.

McLendon, Gloria Houston. "One Teacher's Experience with Death: Education for Adolescents." *Death Education*. 1979, pp. 57-65.

Medalic, Jack H. "The Changing American Family and Society: Implications for Family Physicians." *Journal of Family Practice*. 1981. pp. 15-16.

Meehl, J. "Youth Sports for Fun—and Whose Benefit?" *JOPER*. March 1978, p. 85.

Mendez, Lois; Yeaworth, Rosalee C.; York, Janet; and Goodwin, Michael. "Factors Influencing Adolescents' Perceptions of Life Change Events." *Nursing Research*. November/December 1980. 384-388.

Menig-Petersen, Carole and McCabe, Allyssa. "Children Talk About Death." *Omega*. 1977-78, pp. 305-317.

Milofsky, David. "What Makes a Good Family?" *Redbook*. August 1981, pp. 58, 60, 62.

Moore, Bridget. "When I Was Nine . . ." *Readers Digest*. January 1981, pp. 143-144, 146.

Mueller, James M. "I Taught About Death and Dying." *Phi Delta Kappan*. October 1978, p. 117.

Nelson, Richard C. and Petersen, William D. "Changing the Last Great Taboo: Death." *The School Counselor*. May 1977, pp. 353-358.

O'Brien, Charles R.; Johnson, Josephine; and Schmink, Paul. "Death Education: What Students Want and Need." *Adolescence*. Winter 1978, pp. 729-734.

Ogilvie, Bruce. "The Child Athlete: Psychological Implications of Participation in Sports." *American Academy of Political and Social Sciences*. 1979, pp. 47-58.

Olson, Kate. "Anxious? Try Fantasy." *Psychology Today*. January 1981, p. 32.

Orbach, Israel and Claubman, Hananyah. "Children's Perception of Death as a Defensive Process." *Journal of Abnormal Psychology*. 1979, pp. 671-674.

Orbach, Israel and Claubman, Hananyah. "Suicidal, Aggressive and Normal Children's Perception of Personal and Impersonal Death." *Journal of Clinical Psychology*. October 1978, pp. 850-857.

Ordal, Carol. "Treatment of Death in Selected Child Care Books." *Death Education*. 1979, pp. 121-130.

Ordal, Carol. "Death as Seen in Books for Young Children." *Death Education.* 1980, pp. 223-236.

O'Roark, Mary Ann. "How Children Feel About Their Working Mothers." *McCalls.* September 1978, pp. 89-91.

Parkhouse, B. "To Win What Do You Have to Lose?" *JOPER.* June 1979, pp. 15-18.

Peterson, Lizette and Ridley-Johnson, Robyn. "Pediatric Hospital Responses to Surgery on Prehospital Preparation for Children." *Journal of Pediatric Psychology.* 1980, pp. 1-7.

Pines, M. "Psychological Hardiness." *Psychology Today.* December 1980, pp. 3-14.

Poichuk, N. Buckley and Fraser, C. "I.V. Therapy for Children: Reducing Parental and Patient Fears." *Dimensions in Health Services.* August 1980, p. 32.

Pomarico, Carole; Marsh, Kathleen; and Doubrava, Patricia. "Hospital Orientation for Children. *AORN Journal.* April 1979, pp. 864-875.

Popper, Adrienne. "Superkid." *Parents.* May 1981, pp. 58-60.

Pope, A.J. "Children's Attitudes Toward Death." *Health Education.* May/June 1979, pp. 27-29.

Reisman, T.M. and Shorr, S.I. "Friendship Claims and Expectations Among Children and Adults." *Child Development.* 1978, pp. 913-916.

Remer, R. "Athletes: Counseling the Overprivileged Minority." *Personal Guidance Journal.* June 1978, pp. 626-629.

Renshaw, Domeena. "The Dying Child" Proceedings. Institute of Medicine of Chicago. April/June 1980, pp. 59-61.

Richman, Naomi. "Behaviour Problems in Pre-School Children: Family Social Factors." *British Journal of Psychiatry.* 1977, pp. 523-527.

Robbins, Stacia. "The American Family—How Is It Changing?" *Senior Scholastic.* February 1981, pp. 14-17.

Roberts, Francis. "When Trying Leads to Failure." *Parents.* April 1981, p. 96.

Rodgers, Nilah. "It Won't Hurt, 'Cause You're My Brother." *Readers Digest.* March 1979, pp. 116-120.

Rohrlich, John A.; Ranier, Ruth; Berg-Cross, Linda; and Berg-Cross, Gary. "The Effects of Divorce: A Research Review with a Developmental Perspective." *Journal of Clinical Child Psychology.* Summer 1977, pp. 15-20.

Rosenblum, Constance. "Dying Children: Candor About Certain Death." *Human Behavior.* March 1979, pp. 49-50.

Rothstein, Peter. "Psychological Stress in Families of Children in a Pediatric Intensive Care Unit." *Pediatric Clinics of North America.* August 1980, pp. 613-620.

Rowe, Mary P. "Offices Are for Children Too." *Parents.* August 1978, p. 26.

Rubin, K.H. "Egocentrism in Childhood: A Unitary Construct?" *Child Development.* 1973, pp. 102-110.

Rubin, Lisa and Price, James. "Divorce and Its Effects on Children." *The Journal of School Health.* December 1979, pp. 552-556.

Rutter, Michael. "Protective Factors in Children's Responses to Stress and Disadvantage." *Annals Academy of Medicine.* July 1979, pp. 324-338.

Ryan, A. "The Sick but Victorious Athlete." *Physician and Sports Medicine.* May 1979, p. 35.

Salk, Lee. "When Your Child Must Be Hospitalized." *McCalls.* November 1978, p. 132.

Sage, George. "American Values and Sport: Formation of a Bureaucratic Personality." *Journal of Physical Education and Recreation.* October 1978, pp. 10-12.

Sandler, Irwin N. "Social Support Resources, Stress, and Maladjustment of Poor Children." *American Journal of Community Psychology.* 1980, pp. 41-52.

Sandler, Irwin N. and Block, Maxine. "Life Stress and Maladaptation of Children." *American Journal of Community Psychology.* 1979, pp. 423-440.

Sandler, Irwin N. and Ramsay, Thomas B. "Dimensional Analysis of Children's Stressful Life Events." *American Journal of Community Psychology.* 1980, pp. 285-302.

Science News. "U.S. Children Give Families High Marks." April 2, 1977, pp. 214-215.

Segal, Julius and Yahraes, Herbert. "Five Ground Rules for Fighting Around the Kids." *Family Health.* April 1980, pp. 28-30.

Selye, Hans. "How to Master Stress." *Parents.* November 1977, pp. 25, 34-35.

Sheridan, Mary S. and Kline, Karen. "Psychosomatic Illness in Children." *Social Casework.* April 1978, pp. 227-232.

Silverstein, B. "Injuries in Youth League Football." *Physician and Sports Medicine.* September 1979, pp. 105-108.

Simon, S.B., Howe, L.H., and Kirschenbaum, H. *Values Clarification.* New York: Hart Publishing Co., 1978.

Smoklin, Shelley. "Fear of Figuring." *Working Woman.* January 1979, pp. 54-55, 65.

Smoll, F.L.; Smith, R.E.; and Curtis, B. "Behavioral Guidelines for Youth Sport Coaches." *JOPER.* March 1978, pp. 46-47.

Smoll, F.L.; and Lefebure, L.M. "Psychology of Children in Sport." *Int. Journal of Sport Psychology.* 1979, pp. 173-177.

Spanier, Graham B. "The Changing Profile of the American Family." *Journal of Family Practice.* 1981, pp. 61-69.

Stillman, Diane. "Help for Hospitalized Kids." *McCalls.* March 1980, p. 48.

Stoddard, Alexandra. "A Child's Place." *Harper's Bazaar.* July 1975, pp. 57, 83, 86.

Strickland, Donna. "Friendship Patterns and Altruistic Behavior in Pre-adolescent Males and Females." *Nursing Research.* July-August 1981, pp. 222, 228, 235.

Stutz, Sara D. "Taking the Score out of Childhood Surgery." *Parents.* January 1974, pp. 48-49, 56, 70.

Sussman, Marvin B. "The Family Today: Is It an Endangered Species?" *Children Today.* March-April 1978, pp. 32-37, 45.

Tobias, Sheila. "Managing Math Anxiety: A New Look at an Old Problem." *Children Today.* September-October 1978, pp. 7-9, 36.

Tobia, Sheila. "Math Anxiety: What Can You Do About It?" *Today's Education.* September-October 1980, pp. 27GE-29GE.

Trunzo, Candace E. "Mixing Children and Jobs." *Money.* November 1980, pp. 80-81, 84, 86.

Tyler, Nancy B. and Kogan, Kate L. "Reduction of Stress Between Mothers and Their Handicapped Children." *American Journal of Occupational Therapy.* March 1977, pp. 151-155.

USA Today. "Stress in School." August 1978, pp. 9-10.

USA Today. "Children and Surgery." April 1980, pp. 13-14.

US News and World Report. "As Parents' Influence Fades—Who's Raising the Children?" October 1975, pp. 41-43.

Van Horne, Harriet. "Working Parents: Wonderful Kids." *Parents.* April 1978, pp. 55, 83-84.

Venham, L. L. et al. "Child-rearing Variables Affecting the Preschool Child's Response to Dental Stress." *Journal of Dental Research.* November 1979, pp. 2042-2045.

Viorst, Judith. "The Hospital that Has Patience for Its Patients. A Look at Children's Hospitals, in Washington, D.C." *Redbook.* February 1977, pp. 48-49, 52, 54.

Visintainer, Madelon A. and Wolfer, John A. "Psychological Preparation for Surgical Pediatric Patients: The Effect on Children's and Parent's Stress Responses and Adjustment." *Pediatrics.* August 1975, pp. 187-202.

Wallerstein, Judith S. and Kelly, Joan B. "Effects of Divorce on the Visiting Father-Child Relationship." *American Journal of Psychiatry.* December 1980, pp. 1534-1538.

Wallerstein, Judith S. and Kelly, Joan B. "California's Children of Divorce." *Psychology Today.* January 1980, pp. 67-78.

Wang, Julie. "The Trauma of Separation: School, Divorce, Hospital, Death." *Harper's Bazaar.* July 1977, pp. 88, 105-106.

Wass, Hannelore, et al. "United States and Brazilian Children's Concepts of Death." *Death Education.* 1979, pp. 41-55.

Wass, Hannelore and Shaak, Judith. "Helping Children Understand Death Through Literature." *Childhood Education.* November-December 1976, pp. 80-85.

Weininger, O. "Young Children's Concepts of Dying and Dead." *Psychological Reports.* 1979, pp. 395-407.

Weiss, Joan Solomon. "And Baby Makes Four: How to Prepare Your First-born for Your Second." *Redbook.* July 1981, pp. 27-29, 129-131.

Weissbourd, Bernice. "Sleep Problems and the Working Mother." *Parents*. December 1980, p. 82.

Wellborn, Stanley N. "Nurses . . . Bring Your Kids to Work." *US News and World Report*. September 14, 1981, pp. 42-47.

Wessel, Morris A. "When a Child Faces Surgery." *Parents*. November 1979, p. 26.

Wessel, Morris A. "Coping with Death." *Parents*. January 1981, p. 34.

Whelan, W. Michael and Warren, William M. "A Death Awareness Workshop: Theory, Application and Results." *Omega*. 1980-1981, pp. 61-71.

Whitehead, Linette. "Sex Differences in Children's Responses to Family Stress: A Re-Evaluation." *Journal of Child Psychology and Psychiatry*. 1979, pp. 247-254.

Whiteside, Marily. "The School Phobic Child." *Today's Education*. January 1974, pp. 29-33.

Wilkinson, Joseph F. "The Special Hazards of Childhood Obesity." *Parents*. August 1975, pp. 34-35, 60, 62.

Williams, Phoebe D. "Preparation of School-age Children for Surgery: A Program in Preventive Pediatrics—Philippines." *International Journal of Nursing Studies*. 1980, pp. 107-119.

Wilson, Clare and Orford, Jim. "Children of Alcoholics: Report of a Preliminary Study and Comments on the Literature." *International Journal of Rehabilitation Research*. 1980, pp. 94-96.

Wolff, G. "Cardiologic Assessment in Participants of Pop Warner Junior League Football." *American Journal of Sports Medicine*. 1980, pp. 200-201.

Zager, Ruth P. "The Pediatrician and Preventive Child Psychiatry." *Clinical Pediatrics*. December 1975, pp. 1161-1167.

Zager, Ruth P. "Emotional Needs of Children in Hospitals." *Delaware Medical Journal*. May 1980, pp. 265-270.

Zimbardo, P. "The Social Disease Called Shyness." *Psychology Today*. May 1975, pp. 69-72.

Index